HENRY BELK

'SON OF SWEET UNION'

Moses Rountree

MOORE PUBLISHING COMPANY
Durham, North Carolina

About the Author

Goldsboro writer Moses Rountree knew Henry Belk from the time he came to Goldsboro in 1926 to work for the Goldsboro News (later combined with the Goldsboro Argus) until his death in 1972.

Rountree is the author of *Hookworm Doctor*, a biography of Dr. Charles F. Strosnider of Goldsboro, and *Strangers In the Land*, the story of the Weil family of Goldsboro. He has been a newspaper correspondent, feature writer and columnist.

"Man ought to learn from nature. He, too, must go into the quiet places to replenish his energies, his faith. Man must quit his full rush and revive his spirits periodically. For man, like the earth, is eroded by the beatings of time, circumstance and existence."

— Henry Belk

Introduction

Henry Belk liked to refer to himself as "this poor country editor."

The description fitted him. He accumulated very little worldly goods and, for all his knocking about in high places, he never strayed far from his 'Sweet Union' beginnings. The "red clay banks of Pleasant Grove," the "bowers and forests of Goose Creek," were in his blood and in his writings.

It was "the mirror of life" that illumined his writings--"the reflection of little things which man gives himself to, his bornings and his dyings, his babies, his church, his clubs, his comings and goings, his great loneliness and his need always of assurance. Of such is news."

"He interested himself in the small vignettes of life," said the Greensboro Daily News, which ran a weekly column of Henry's embodying the best of his writings in the News-Argus.

"The small things that give meaning to living have not escaped him," said the Raleigh News and Observer.

The larger things were equally important to Henry--education, culture, agriculture, industry, everything that promoted progress and a better life for his people. His favorite people were his own, but his influential voice was not tainted with provincialism.

"He was a significant force in the advancement of North Carolina in many ways," said former Governor Terry Sanford. "His devotion to public causes made him one of the most valuable North Carolinians of his generation."

The real story of Henry Belk lay in the magnificent manner in which he overcame the handicap of blindness. Bolstering his courage, guiding his steps, was his devoted wife, Lucile, who, as one editor said, "pushed him outward into the world to contribute brightness out of darkness."

This might in truth be called the story of Henry and Lucile Belk.

Goldsboro, N.C.   —Moses Rountree

Governor Thomas Walter Bickett, a native son, gave Union County its nickname of 'Sweet Union'. Another native son, Editor Henry Belk, gave the title of endearment to the world.

"His frequent references to his native 'Sweet Union' County have projected the good image of the homeland far and wide," said the Monroe Journal, on which Henry got his newspaper start.

Henry wrote of 'Sweet Union' from the fond light of memory. Bittersweet would have been the impression of his boyhood days.

The little things he described so intimately, in retrospect, were seen largely with his mind's eye. Born with congenital cataracts in both eyes, he could not even distinguish a bird in flight until he was a grown man.

"I cannot remember," he once said, "when my eyes were not a source of pain, of trouble, of distress. Yes, and of fear, if you must. I kept placing that fear out of my mind. There was nothing else to do, you know."

It was his strong-willed mother who inspired him with determination to overcome his handicap. She taught him at home until he was able to enter school, at the age of nine, in the third grade. She recognized his capacity and was determined for him to get an education.

Henry was born May 8, 1898, in Monroe. He was the second child of Robert Lee Belk and Lou Rape Belk. His father was a native of Lancaster County, South Carolina, the birthplace of William Henry Belk, founder of the mercantile chain. Henry was named for the merchant, a distant relative, but the only value the connection was worth to him, he said, was a shiny dollar the merchant gave him upon learning Henry was his namesake.

Henry's grandfather, Lafayette Belk, farmed in Lancaster County. He served in the Mexican and Civil wars and was awarded a medal by the State of South Carolina for his service in the Mexican War.

Robert Lee Belk was farming in Sapps Corner, just inside the North Carolina line, on land left to him by his father, when he married Lou Rape of Prospect, a small community in Union County. Not liking farming, he sold his farm and moved to Florida, but stayed there only a short time. Coming back to North Carolina, he went to work as a carpenter for the Shute brothers in Monroe. The brothers — Jim, Raymond and Henry — owned a variety of enterprises, including a general store, cotton gin and lumber mill. The store boasted of selling "everything under the sun, from a pinhook to a Gatling gun."

Monroe was an agricultural marketing center with a population of 1,500, about one-tenth its present size. Cotton was the principal crop grown on the small outlying farms. Long lines of wagons filled with cotton were a common sight on the town's streets.

After working for the Shutes for a number of years, Robert Lee Belk took a foreman's job with a Monroe construction firm. He superintended the construction of a number of business buildings in Monroe and border towns, as well as a building at Cherry Hospital in Goldsboro. He was putting a roof on a house at the age of 83, after retiring. He died in 1956, three years later.

Henry came by his great height naturally. His father was six feet four inches and his mother five feet nine — above average for a woman. All four of their children were tall, Henry's brothers, George and Hazel, being well over six feet.

George, the oldest child, died in 1960 at the age of 65. He was manager of the Railway Express Agency in Monroe, a position later held by Hazel, who is now retired.

The youngest child, Ware, a girl, was named for Dr. W. R. Ware, a Methodist minister who served two terms as pastor of Central Methodist Church in Monroe. He had 75 children named for him, attesting to the esteem in which he was held.

Ware married Clarence Dent, a watchmaker, and together they ran a jewelry store in Monroe for a number of years. The couple still lives in Monroe, as does Hazel Belk.

Henry was the only one of the children to go to college.

Henry's parents were good Methodists and made their children attend church regularly.

"On Saturday night we would take a bath in a tin tub, then lay out our clothes so we would be ready for Sunday School the next morning," Hazel recalled. "We had to attend worship services morning and evening."

Henry, who later joined the Baptist Church, was not "overly" religious, but "had religion", Hazel said.

The parents were firm, but not "overly" strict.

"We had to behave, but they would let us make up our minds about things."

Mrs. Dent said her mother kept a stack of switches which she used on Hazel and herself "when we were mischievous. She never had to correct Henry. 'Each of you is different,' she said."

The Belks never had a home of their own, living about in several rented houses.

"Times were tough when we were children," Henry once said.

Unable to play like other boys, Henry spent his time reading and hanging around the kitchen.

"I liked to help Mama cook," he said.

Because of the cataracts, Henry had only a "glimmer" of vision, but had a book stuck under his nose all the time, according to Hazel.

Henry explained in one of his columns how he was able to read.

I was able to read by assuming a most awkward position. I covered the left eye with my left hand, leaving a small slit between the thumb and the index finger. Through this slit I was able to peer, holding the book or paper with my right hand almost against my face, and to read.

Some of the school boys would mimic Henry when he passed by, by holding a hand over one eye, according to Mrs. Vann Secrest of Monroe, who was in Henry's grade at school.

"He probably didn't see them do it. If he did, he ignored them. He had a sweet disposition. He would help students with their home work. He was the smartest boy in school, quiet and reserved. He was always neat. He was tall and very thin."

"I had to drink muddy water to make a shadow," Henry told his wife, Lucile.

Henry had no interest in girls and only a few close boy friends.

"When he went to parties, he would sit alone," Mrs. Secrest said.

Mrs. Velma Marsh, who also was in Henry's grade, said he was a "brilliant" boy and a "loner."

"He sat in the back of the room and was well behaved. He showed no interest in the female members of the class, perhaps because they all looked alike to him. After we graduated from high school, I didn't see him again until he had finished college. By then he could see a little, as the result of an operation. He told me, 'I never knew what you looked like until now. All I could distinguish you by was your voice.' I had never realized he was that blind."

Surgeons were unable to do anything about Henry's cataracts when he was a boy. He didn't wear glasses, which would have been of no benefit.

Despite his "glimmer" of vision, Henry had his boyhood pleasures. Such as 'Making a Fish Net'.

The pull of big water must be planted in man's soul by millions of years of living near or on the water.

Landlocked as we were, as a boy in Union County, the water pulled and strove with us. And the biggest water there was Richardson's Creek.

Every summer we boys made us a homemade boat. We shaped it and fashioned it from pictures of rowboats. Robinson Crusoe had better tools than we had and our boat showed this. We calked her — let's say it that way because boats carry a feminine gender — with putty, and where the cracks were too big, we filled in with cotton. I don't remember that any of the boats carried us more than across Lee's Mill Lake two or three times, but it was a joy to make them.

And every summer we made several seines. Our landlubberness was shown, in that we called them seines, not fish nets. We would take a ginny sack, unravel the closed sides and end, and fasten sticks to the sides. I am not sure but I think we had corks from large bottles attached to the ends. The idea was to keep the ends a bit higher than the middle, so the fish wouldn't escape when we hauled them up. Once we caught a minnow three inches long. No modern boy gets such a thrill.

In another of his "Recollections of Boyhood", Henry wrote about 'Frog Songs'.

It's funny how little things stick in your mind. For days I have been recollecting some frog choruses I have heard at night.

First was the symphony set up by hundreds of frogs who lived in a low spot on my paper route when I was a boy in Monroe. It was on the southeast edge of town and lonely. I got to that point usually after dusk had come and the world had taken on a misty mysteriousness.

Houses were few and far between and lamps had not been lit. It was before electricity had become general. The houses were small and squatted close to the earth, and there was no sound of human stirring, no traffic, only the chant of the frogs. Up and down, up and down, up and down. The rhythmic pulsation seemed to vary with the strength of the wind across the little swamp. I listened as I hurried to my next subscriber, and I wondered.

It was some years later. Some of us Monroe boys were making an excursion to Wilmington to see the ocean for the first time. There was a snarl in the train traffic, or a wreck, or something, and our hot, dirty, smothery-feeling car was sidetracked in a swamp near Acme.

This was a man-sized swamp. Growth was tangled and dense, and the night was dark, so dark we boys trained our eyes and ears to penetrate the dark forest and feel out what was there. Bears, deers, snakes — plenty of snakes, no doubt — and some alligators. And we were tense with the strangeness of the swamp around us.

From everywhere rose the song of the frogs. Where there were millions on my paper route in Monroe, here were billions. And their voices were stronger, more strident. But they had that same rhythm, that same bubbling note that spoke of warm nights and spring and nature's automatic begetting of life. Their sound rose above the tops of the tall trees, interlaced by vines that we could make out against the dark sky through the window. Their song filled the stuffy, dirty car with something strange and alive.

These sounds of frogs in boyhood had not come back to me in years. And then, as spring fought to break through, I spent an afternoon at Ski Lake south of Goldsboro. Faint and far away the frogs were singing, just as they had been in Sweet Union.

Henry's brother, George, paid his way to the beach to see the ocean for the first time. It must have been a memorable occasion for Henry, who developed a great love for the ocean.

Monroe High School, which Henry attended, was the former county home. Doubtless it had been converted into a school because it didn't require much remodeling and had aesthetic appeal. It was a pretty wooden building sitting on a slight hill behind a grove of elms and white oaks. The building had eight downstairs rooms that ran across the front and two upstairs in the middle. The rooms were heated with potbellied, wood-burning stoves. There was outside drinking water.

The Walter Bickett High School, now used for an elementary school, was built on its site.

Henry graduated from high school in 1917, at the age of 19. There were 18 in his class — 6 boys and 12 girls. Henry won all three medals given and a two-year college scholarship given by B.D. Heath, a prominent Union County businessman.

The high school annual, the Mohisco, said of Henry:
He is a prodigy.
He thinks he's a dummy.
He wants to be a writer.
He probably will be a literary light.

Henry towers far above the level of the ordinary. This is true, taken both literally and figuratively. Physically, he tips the notch at 6 ft. 2 in. (Henry leveled off at 6-6.) Mentally he reaches the high watermark of 97. An insatiable desire for reading, a keen appreciation, an original brain, a clever pen, and a humorous turn — make the consensus that his future career in the literary world has limitless possibilities. Moreover, he is a staunch believer in Ben Franklin's philosophy.

"May the world of Literature be good to him,
And the Muses of Literature be kind to him,
When into their world he goes."

Henry was voted the best all-around student and the senior "genius".

The class prophecy envisioned his literary future.

Henry Belk was last seen in Chicago writing histories of the present war. He had written several novels and, at the request of the public, sometimes wrote poetry. His works are being read enthusiastically throughout the world.

Henry's "Senior Class Poem" did not stamp him as any potential Keats or Tennyson.

> Spring returns with its blooming flowers,
> And our stay at the High is numbered by hours.
> Unnumbered are the times we've paused to sigh,
> When we've thought how near the end draws nigh;
> But we are cheered by the thought that it's not in vain,
> For the good accomplished o'erbalances the pain.
>
> All life is just one great school;
> Each day we learn or miss some rule.
> And death is but a graduation day
> Which starts us on a better way.
> If we've lived right before that time,
> We only move to a better clime.
>
> If life's like school, school's like life,
> Preparing us for the future strife.
> The studies that give us pain and woe
> Will help us our future row to hoe,
> And the ones we think useless as a counterfeit dime
> Will grade the road in life's hilly climb.
>
> Later, when life's tide we're breasting,
> And after a hard day's work we're resting,
> Before our mind there will appear
> The old High School we love so dear,
> And each face with joy will gleam,
> When we think of past joys in the Class of Seventeen.

The opus was signed "Henry Clay Belk".

Henry adopted the middle name for himself when he was in high school. There is no evidence that he used it later.

8

The Class History reflected the contemporary call to arms in World War I.

History is generally termed as a record of man and his deeds — mostly in wars — but this, the history of the Class of 1917, is not one of war. Nevertheless, there has been a struggle, and we are victorious. We are now landed safely on the shores of Seniorhood.

The world today is calling for men, men, men, only to be used as machine-gun food. They are answering this call daily by the thousands. Why is the call of opportunity neglected as it is? Of course a warring nation needs men, but the world needs more influential men — the ones who will answer opportunity's call.

Turn to the class roll if you would see some of our future presidents, congressmen and congresswomen.

There were no statesmen in the class, but the members did all right. Henry became an influential editor. His best friend, George Presson, practiced law in Florida. Earl Hinson was a professor at the University of North Carolina. Andrew Monroe held a high position with Carolina Power and Light Company. Furman Maness was an official with Frederickson Motor Lines in Charlotte.

And one of the girls in the class, Mary Douglass (Mrs. Vann Secrest) was Miss North Carolina 1925.

"Henry was what he always wanted to be — a newspaper man," said Mrs. Dent.

During high school Henry submitted feature articles to several daily newspapers. When the Charlotte Observer published one he had written on "Uncle Commodore Funderburke," a Negro who fattened 'possums for sale, and gave him a by-line, his career was decided, Henry said.

It was two years after finishing high school, however, that Henry saw his way, financially, to enter college. During the time he worked as a reporter, at $3.50 a week, for the Monroe Journal and also corresponded for the Greensboro Daily News. He had a column in the Journal titled "Under the Courthouse Dome".

Union County had a stately, historic courthouse, which had been built in 1886. Henry had a sentimental attachment for the old courthouse and in 1965, when there was talk of tearing it down, he voiced strong opposition to the idea.

My sister, Ware, and I are in a running argument.

We got into the predicament in discussing the much discussed proposal in Monroe that Union County's old red brick courthouse be razed. The air in Sweet Union is supercharged with arguments for and against the proposal.

Ware wants to tear down the good, solid structure and make way for progress.

"I'm for change and advance and progress," she declares.

Actually it seems to me that what she desires is to replace the clock-crowned building hard by the Confederate monument with more parking space.

I grant that Union and Monroe have grown so big and rich and busy that the stately old courthouse is not large enough for county government purposes. For that matter it was outgrown a quarter of a century ago, and offices once quartered in the building, where I covered my first court, were taken care of in new and separate buildings erected off the main business district.

That's what I hope Union will do in meeting its new space demands, go out from the square and put up an office building especially planned and built for the special purposes of the departments to be housed.

The old courthouse is peopled with memories for me. There I was fascinated by such pleaders and presenters as Judge John J. Parker, "Bunk" Lemmond, W.B. Love, J.C.M. Vann, Judge A.M. Stack and others. The Union bar was a bar of splendid minds and an ornament to the great profession.

Second door to the left, as you enter the courthouse from the door opposite Monroe Hardware, I covered my first recorders court with Judge Stevens, father of Frank Stevens of Winston-Salem, a big wheel in the Belk store chain, presiding.

I still recall with a shock the pitiable narcotic who was brought into the court one day. Drugs had reduced him to sub-human condition.

When he could get powders to sniff, he sniffed. When he could get a shot, he took it in his arm and both arms were pock-marked with needlings.

Judge Stevens was a quiet man, but you could feel his sympathy going out to the poor devil before him. He sent the man to the county jail until he could get some control of himself.

The sheriff's office was across the hall from recorder's court and Cliff Fowler was the sheriff. Cliff was more the well dressed man of style than he was the gun-toting image now associated with sheriffs. He was medium height and had not an excess pound on his wiry frame. But when he had to, he could bring in the most obstreperous.

Cliff was a past master at keeping himself elected. His charm was that he sincerely liked people and smiled and back-slapped them because he liked them. They returned the compliment by returning him to office.

Deep in the vaults of the old courthouse are the archives records. They lie where they have been since they became records.

And that clock sticks in my mind. The proud boast of Monroe used to be that it was the most accurate town clock between Washington and Atlanta. By night it was, in its illuminated tower, a beacon light that could be seen for long distances.

I don't think it would be the thing to do to pull down the sturdy old building. Our American fetish for change so often leads us to waste a lot of money and sacrifice a lot of history.

I cannot go along with razing the Union courthouse, not even for my favorite sister, Ware.

Evidently there were many of Henry's persuasion. The old courthouse was not razed. It still stands, empty and unused, while citizens ponder what to do with it. And the clock in the tower, now electrically operated, continues to give accurate time.

A block away is a $4.5 million courthouse built in 1971 through a bond issue approved by taxpayers.

But taxpayers are content to let the old courthouse be.

"It won't be torn down in my generation," said Mrs. Dent.

She sounded as much attached to it as Henry.

Henry entered Trinity College in Durham in the fall of 1919. A group of Monroe men, including a judge, went on his note to get necessary funds.

His parents didn't have the money, but after he was in college his mother would enclose a dollar or two in her letters to help him along.

She knew Henry was destined to be somebody.

When she died in 1950, at the age of 81, Henry had become editor of the Goldsboro News-Argus.

2

Henry was 21 when he matriculated at Trinity College. He must have looked out of place among the other freshmen, several years his junior; certainly conspicuous, with his great height. He always stood out in any crowd.

Henry had his scholarship, which paid for his tuition, and he found a way to earn his board by representing a boarding house near the campus. The money he had borrowed was enough for his other expenses.

Like most freshmen, Henry was too busy getting acclimated to take part in many activities his first year. He did join the Columbian Literary Society, a debating union, serving as corresponding secretary and on the executive committee.

"Henry and I were members of the Society together and were good friends," said Kelly L. Elmore of Sheffield, Alabama. "I admired his character, good mind and ability to organize his material for a Society debate. He and I used to take walks along the streets near the campus at night. He was a warm companion and an excellent conversationalist. I saw him in 1967 and was surprised to learn he was blind. He still had a keen interest in the University and in its former student."

In his sophomore year Henry was on the Student Life Committee and a reporter for the Chronicle, the college's weekly newspaper. With the editor-in-chief, Robert Dwight Ware, he also organized a local reportorial service.

"It was a rather interesting team-up," said Dr. Ware, a retired Methodist minister, now living in Asheville. "We reported sermons, book club meetings, receptions, etc., for any group desiring to have it in the Durham Sun. We had entry with the Sun editors and they readily used what we gave them. Our charge for the service was $3 a meeting. Our business grew and when we were unable to attend a meeting, we turned it over to one of the Chronicle reporters, paying them $2 and keeping $1 for ourselves. When I graduated in

1922, I sold my interest in the enterprise to Jim Secrest for $25. I understood he and Henry continued to make a go of it."

Henry had a part in naming Trinity's football teams the 'Blue Devils', a suggestion that had originated with Ware.

"After overcoming strong conservative forces which had outlawed football for many years, it was reinstated in 1920 on an intramural basis. In 1921 we began playing intercollegiate football. We had a strong schedule, featured by a game with New York University in New York City. It resulted in a 7-7 tie, as I recall.

"Much had been made that fall of a visit to New York by French Generalissimo Ferdinand Foch. I read the New York newspapers. In one of them there was an article about the famous Blue Devil legions of France, with a picture showing them going over the top.

"We held a pep meeting in the Trinity chapel to discuss giving our football team a name. I suggested 'Blue Devils', but Dr. Hersey Spence, professor of Bible at Trinity, killed my suggestion. He reminded us of the fight to get football reinstated and said many church people would criticize Trinity College if it adopted such an 'irreverent' name as 'Devils'. His opinion prevailed and the team went unnamed that year. The next fall, I was told, 'Blue Devils' was arbitrarily adopted by Henry Belk, who had become college publicity director, and Bill Lander, who had succeeded me as editor of the Chronicle."

Henry was Trinity's first paid publicity director. His pay was $35 a month.

Henry was assistant editor of the Chronicle his junior year, and assistant editor of the Chanticleer, the college yearbook, his sophomore and junior years. He was on the Lecture Committee his junior year, as well as being secretary of the Y.M.C.A. and secretary-treasurer of the Union County Club, which he served as president his senior year.

Henry belonged to Chi Tau, a social fraternity founded at Trinity in 1921, and to Sigma Upsilon, a national literary honorary fraternity. He was a member of Tombs, a secret honorary society, and of the Folklore Society.

Henry began contributing to the Trinity Archive, the college's monthly literary magazine, in his freshman year. His first contribution was a poem. It showed improvement over his high school efforts.

To My Mess-Hall Card

In other times, 'mid other scenes,
I've drunk with kings and dined with queens;
Then ten-course dinners were my style,
Topped off by waiter's obsequious smile.
You see it was my business luck
To play reporter on the sheet;
The nabobs must be written up,
And so I had their friends to meet.
But now, dear ugly mess-hall card,
Thou art my hungry lease on life;
To me thy tattered countenance means
Cold coffee, wieners, prunes and beans;
For which I now do honor thee,
My dear old ugly mess-hall card.

In December, 1921, Henry had an imaginative article on browsing through Trinity College Historical Museum. It was titled 'Time Turned Backward'.

Cobwebs festooned the room. The dust of years covered the exhibits and obscured the pictures of the celebrities who gazed with unconcern on the scene around them. A smell of rotting papers — dank, dark, sepulchre-like — rose to their nostrils. Still the celebrities gazed in condescension at the conglomeration of things. Too long had they looked from the walls to be affected.

The glimpse of the home life among the pioneers was old to them. The Indian relics brought no mind picture of the Red Man slipping through the forest, probably to tomahawk the frontiersman. They saw none of the mystery, the lure of the Far East, in the decayed wooden head intended to represent a cow, before which probably thousands of Orientals had bowed in supplication. The souvenirs from Spain, France and Belgium brought to them no actuality of those countries. For those pictures on the walls of the Trinity College Historical Museum looked at the specimens in the same manner that Trinity students have looked for generations — as so much wood, so much stone, or so much paper, and nothing more. They could not see the romance of adventure, of home life, of war, or religion, and of travel, which the museum reflected.

But let us wander through the museum, looking for these things.

Here are a couple of spinning wheels. How old? No one knows. Here is a loom with the tread still in place on the shuttle. Here is an old grandfather clock.

"Nothing but junk?" did you say.

But use your imagination. Here is a complete cycle. Night after night some mother of the days when America was young sat before this wheel and twirled it in monotonous repetition. Her children played at her side. The old clock ticked off the time as the string came off the revolving wheel. Enough string, and the mother changes her occupation. The loom is set going. Can't you hear its cumbersome clank as the shuttle went through and was returned? But that was life and joy for that woman, for she worked for her loved ones.

Here is a pair of Indian moccasins. There is an arrowhead. Maybe these shoes were worn by the Indian as he slipped through the woods to surprise the home of the woman who works the loom. Move on a little farther. Maybe the man of the house used that old musket there in thwarting a massacre. You can't tell, but don't you begin to see the romance in the objects?

Take a moment at these exhibits from China.

"A support for meditation. This stick was used by the priests of a famous Buddhist temple near Warsaw to lean their heads upon when in deep meditation."

That is the inscription attached to a forked stick about two feet long and worn smooth by the handling of the priests. The object was given by Rev. S.A. Stewart, a Trinity man now preaching the gospel in China. For hundreds of years, no doubt, this stick has rested the heads of followers of Buddha. No telling what plans have been thought through, as the head of the Oriental lay between the forks. Is it not possible that the last priest who bowed on the stick was contrasting the Christian religion with that of Buddha, and deciding for the first named, left the old temple, carrying the stick with him, and gave it to Rev. Mr. Stewart?

Very near this meditation support lies an ordinary looking piece of wood labeled "Ancestral tablet used by Rev. T. Kugimyas' father for hundreds of years." Think of that for a moment. For centuries the forefathers of Rev. Mr. Kugimyas had used this tablet in performing their religious duties to their ancestors. Daily they placed upon it a little bowl of rice that the spirits of the dead might have sustenance. The tablet to them was sacred. It was an outlet for the most pronounced desire of man — a source of omnipotence to which he can turn in time of trouble. But T. Kugimyas found another source and broke the precedent of centuries. As millions of Chinese see it, he committed sacrilege. He not only abandoned the worship of his ancestors, but sent his ancestral tablet to be marveled at, at a heathen college.

Lining up with the tablet is a Chinese parchment. The note, written by Rev. Mr. Stewart, who gave it, says it is the history of an old Chinese temple. What marvelous adventures may it not relate? Of course there must be descriptions of soft-footed Chinese shuffling to the shrines to do their homage. They may have come thousands of miles from farthest China to perform their vows. The old parchment almost talks, despite the characters in which it is written.

And here is the idol head. Originally it was properly meant as that of a cow. Set up at some crossroads in the Far Eastern country, hundreds of human beings stopped daily to bump their heads in abject submission before the piece of wood. But missionaries ventured into the country, Trinity men in the number. The Christian religion taught the folly of such homage to idols. Probably the missing nose of the cow is explained by the fact that a newly converted Chinaman, in his zeal, wielded the ax on the idol.

The exhibits, however, are not all Eastern. Carefully concealed under layers of dust and files of old newspapers are found a series of little boxes. Look at this one. "A twig from a tree planted by Robert Burns at his home in Mossingill, Scotland." When you look at it, do you not feel closer to the nature poet, who would have been better off if he had had the benefits of prohibition. Other boxes of the collection give glimpses into historic spots of France, England, Switzerland and Italy.

Now dip further back into the centuries. See Columbus with his three little sail boats bravely headed into the unknown. All this can be done in the specimen labeled "A piece of flag carried by Columbus when he landed in America."

But the collections are far too numerous to be treated in their entirety. Go over to the library some day and take a stroll through the museum, looking at the objects with the idea of seeing not so much junk, but the life which is behind the junk.

In April, 1922, Henry had a short story in the Archive titled 'A Dark Deed'. All but the last four paragraphs was consumed in background atmosphere preparing the reader for "one of the darkest deeds in history." The deed? Well, let Henry describe it.

Having thus summarily disposed of his victim (with a feather brought down over his head), the villain, who by the gentleness of his attack has revealed himself as none other than Gyp, the Grape Juice, gets busy. Working hastily, yet surely, he opens three receptacles in rotation. No, that is an error. Subsequent investigation has revealed that he opened four receptacles in rotation, one after another. From the first he took an object shaped like a miniature torpedo. From the second he took an object shaped like a stick of dynamite. The object that he had taken from the second receptacle, having previously broken open the object. From the third receptacle, opened in rotation, he took a quantity of brownish liquid resembling T.N.T. and poured it over the object which he had previously created from the objects taken from the first two receptacles opened in rotation. Now, still in rotation, he opens a fourth receptacle and takes from it a number of shiny bits of something strangely looking like silver. These bits he adds to the objects which he has created by opening the first three receptacles in rotation.

He places the object thus created by opening the four receptacles in rotation to his mouth. He eats. The terrible gleam leaves his eyes.

"A very good weenie," he mutters to himself.

Thus softened, he goes toward the wide-awake sleeper and feels the bump raised by the blow from the feather. Satisfied that it is not serious, he turns out the lights and leaves.

Always a gourmet, Henry apparently had become enamored of the tasty 'hot dog', introduced in World War I, and thought nothing could be more vicious than stealing one.

According to Dr. Ware, Henry was "never really a campus personality in the usual sense. He was a serious student who worked conscientiously and well. His was a retiring, studious nature which sought neither campus leadership nor personal office. There was a quiet, infrequently used humor about him."

Henry Sprinkle of Mocksville, secretary of Associates for Philosophy of Religion Inc., was at Trinity College with Henry.

I knew him well during the period of four or five years we were together on the campus at Durham. Only infrequently have our paths crossed in the years since then, but the splendid record he has made, the contributions of his genius to the educational, literary, and political life of the State and region are not surprising to me. All the fine qualities that have found expression in his many and notable services to the institutions and the broadening outlook of the people in this part of the country were present in the youth who entered Trinity College in the fall of 1919.

Henry stood tall among his classmates. Everyone looked up to him. Just as his lanky six-foot-six towered over the rest of us, there was a maturity, a calm superiority, a wider vision that won the appreciation and respect of his contemporaries no less than his teachers. His reputation as a wit, an intellectual, a writer, a critic, and a man of parts and ability was well established before his senior year. And it was no great surprise that he soon wooed and wed perhaps the most influential and brilliant young lady on the campus in those days when coeds were a rather select and special group.

Down the hall from the office where Henry held forth as college publicity director was the office of Trinity President William F. Few. His secretary was Lucile Bullard, a 1916 graduate of Trinity College and valedictorian of her class. While in college she had taken a business course and worked in the office to help pay her college expenses. Following her graduation, President Few offered her a job as his permanent secretary. She had signed a contract to teach, but accepted his offer on condition that he would get her released from her teaching contract, which he did.

Miss Bullard was a native of Autryville, in Sampson County. Her father, Platte Bullard, was agent for the Seaboard Railroad. He died when Lucile and her sister, Ruth, now Mrs. W.S. Williams of Middlesex, were very young. To support them, his widow, Mrs. Marie Louise Royall Bullard, went to work teaching school, a profession she followed for many years. She got her master's degree in botany from Peabody College when she was past fifty and taught at several sessions of summer school at Duke. When her daughters were growing up, she had taught in Durham, where she thought they would have better educational opportunities. Lucile enrolled at Trinity College after graduating from East Durham High School.

Henry's future 'General Manager' had noticed a tall boy working in the office down the hall. They began exchanging conversation (there was no formal introduction) and soon were chummy enough to split the cost of a subscription to the News and Observer. Lucile read it in the morning, while Henry was on class, and turned it over to him in the afternoon.

"He was very shy; we didn't date until the spring of his senior year. We went to a movie on our first date."

To celebrate his graduation, Henry bought a second-hand car for his courting. He was able to drive a car because of eye operations he had had in the summers of his sophomore and junior for removal of the congenital cataracts. The operations were performed by Dr. Ben Wit Key, a noted New York eye specialist, to whom Henry had been referred by a Trinity professor who was a brother-in-law of the doctor.

"To that time," Henry wrote, "I had graduated from high school, worked as a reporter for two years, and had finished two years of college. All the sight I had was a little glimmer."

Henry's sister, Mrs. Dent, said that following the operations, Henry wrote her jubilantly, "I have seen a bird."

Henry received a B.A. degree from Trinity College in June, 1923. The yearbook, the Chanticleer, said of him:

This elongated son of Union has more backbone than any other man in college. He is sure to make a cub reporter of class. O Henry, O Moon-fixer, thy Cupid-like figure, thy tortoise-rimmed specs, thy sarcastic wit and the click of thy typewriter will be missed when thou art gone.

Below was a limerick which read:

Now here's a tall gink from Monroe,
Six-six from his head to his toe;
    If they fall for sarcasm
    Belk certainly has 'em —
He's the sarcasticest person we know.

Henry was trained for newspaper work, but decided to try his hand at teaching after being offered a job as instructor in freshman English and journalism at Wake Forest College by President William Louis Poteat. It seemed a good billet for a man taking a wife.

Henry and Lucile were married October 7, 1923, at the home of her uncle, Letus T. Royall, in Smithfield, where her mother was teaching at the time.

Henry described the wedding on the occasion of their 32nd wedding anniversary.

Lucile and I were married in the antique parlor of her uncle, L.T. Royall, superintendent of Johnston County Schools, in Smithfield.

I have never been more frightened in my whole life, not even the day when as a child a barn in which I was playing collapsed about me, pinning me by my neck.

I had come down from Wake Forest College, where I was teaching, the Saturday afternoon before and checked in at the upstairs brick hotel. I don't know why but I still remember that on Sunday morning at breakfast, my last day as a bachelor, I had sausage and scrambled eggs.

Only the immediate family was present for the wedding. I met people right and left, but I was in an unconscious daze and my acknowledgments of introductions came mechanically. Except for Uncle Letus and his wife, I can't remember a person who was there.

Then shortly before the piano, Lallah Rook Stevenson playing, struck up with "A Wild Rose," Lucile disappeared. I thought I would fall through the floor. I had such a gone feeling. Dear, kind, calm Mr. D.H. Tuttle, Methodist minister who once served Saint Paul in Goldsboro, pronounced the vows. But that service is a blank in my mind.

The newlyweds spent their wedding night at the Yarborough Hotel in Raleigh and proceeded to Wake Forest the next morning.

What attracted Lucile Bullard to the "tall gink from Monroe"?

"He was a nice young man, intelligent, high-principled, and with a delightful sense of humor. I guess it was a mutuality of interests that drew us together."

3

The Belks "loved" Wake Forest.

"It was a quiet, peaceful village with lovely old homes and an atmosphere of gracious living," said Lucile. "Its people were warm and friendly."

The reposeful campus was dotted with magnolias that lent a fragrant enchantment to the scene. They were part of a beautification program that had been started by President Charles E. Taylor (1882-1905) with the loving assistance of 'Dr.' Tom Jeffries, the college janitor for over half a century.

'Dr.' Tom was so beloved that when he died, six Doctors of Philosophy from the faculty spoke at his funeral, held in the college chapel.

"When I fus' came here," 'Dr.' Tom was quoted as saying in the 1925 college yearbook, the 'Howler', "the place won't nothin' more than a stock pasture. Dr. Taylor and me decided to beautify it by settin' out trees and shrubs. I useter go out in the woods and git trees."

'Dr.' Tom and President Taylor also built a low stone wall around the campus.

The tree-planting became a community project, according to Mrs. Margaret Gill Hawkins of Goldsboro, a Wake Forest native.

"People would donate trees, especially magnolias. Plaques with the name of the donor were attached to the trees."

At the east entrance to the campus was a granite arch, donated by the Class of 1909, with the college motto on it: Pro Humanitate (for the benefit of mankind).

The Baptist institution was not as large as Carolina or Duke (in 1925 its enrollment was about 600) but it excelled in academic standing and in sports. Its law school, headed by Dean Needham Y. Gulley and Professors E.W. Timberlake and Robert Bruce White, was one of the best in the South. It had a good two-year medical school headed by Dean Thurman D. Kitchin, later Wake Forest president.

The faculty boasted respected names: President William Louis Poteat, who taught biology; his son, Dr. Hubert McNeil Poteat, professor of Latin Language and Literature; Dr. George W. Paschall, professor of Latin and Greek; Dr. William B. Royall, professor of Greek Language and Literature; Dr. Benjamin F. Sledd, professor of English Language and Literature; Dr. William R. Cullom, professor of Bible. The physics department was headed by Professor James L. Lake, father of State Supreme Court Justice I. Beverly Lake, a 1925 graduate of Wake Forest College.

The college turned out strong debating teams and had an excellent glee club, directed by Professor Hubert Poteat.

Baseball was the major sport, but Wake Forest was also a threat in football, winning the state championship in 1925, under the direction of Coach Henry ("Hank") Garrity.

One thing the college was short on was Greek fraternities. In 1925 it had ten fraternities, but Kappa Alpha was the only national one and most were of recent origin. There were no fraternity houses on the campus, or off the campus, the fraternities using rented quarters in town. At one time students had been expelled for belonging to secret fraternities.

Henry helped organize a chapter of Chi Tau at Wake Forest in 1923. He had belonged to the fraternity at Trinity. One of the other faculty members was Dr. Daniel B. Bryan, professor of education. He and Henry were good friends and years later Henry brought him to Goldsboro to speak at Madison Avenue Baptist Church.

Dancing was prohibited on the campus, but frat men would sponsor dances in Louisburg, Raleigh and other nearby towns.

Wake Forest was strictly a boys' school, but on Society Day the boys could invite their sweethearts for a day of social functions, debates and oratorical contests, and athletic events.

Society Day was sponsored by the Philomathezian and Euzelian Literary Societies. The two debating unions held forth in separate wings of the library building. Members were domiciled in separate dormitories flanking the administration building. Phi's came from the eastern part of the state and E-U's from the western part.

There was no snobbery on the campus. Students traditionally spoke when they passed each other, and as traditionally tipped their hats to professors.

One of the favorite diversions of students was to meet the 1 p.m. Seaboard train, then hang around the town's little post office to see if it had brought them any mail.

The Belks lived in a cottage owned by President Poteat and sitting in his side yard. It had a porch, living room, bedroom, kitchen and bath. The Belks ate in the kitchen but when entertaining guests used a gate-leg table in the living room.

President Poteat and his wife had the Belks for meals and the Belks would return the favor. Mrs. Belk was Poteat's secretary and the families were close.

Henry was a great admirer of "Dr. Billy", who was a man of independent thought. His teaching of evolution in his biology course made him a controversial figure for years, but he was loved by his students and by the townspeople.

The theory of evolution was considered heresy by a lot of Bible-believing people, in particular Baptists, and factions in the Baptist State Convention had tried unsuccessfully for years to have him deposed. Poteat received many nasty letters, which Mrs. Belk would answer.

"He didn't let them bother him. He would dictate replies to me in which he patiently explained his stand and suggested books on evolution for the writer to read."

One of the critical letters was recalled by E.L. Roberts of Wayne County, who was a lab assistant to Poteat.

"He came in the lab one day and said he had a letter he wanted to read to us. It started off with: I'd like to call you Brother Poteat, but I can't claim Christian kinship with somebody holding your views. And I can't call you 'Doctor', because that assumes superior knowledge. So I will have to call you Mr. Poteat.'

" 'I know that man; he's a good man,' Dr. Billy said. 'But he doesn't think he can be a Christian and believe scientific facts.' "

Roberts, who formerly pastored a rural church in Wayne

County, said Poteat's teaching of evolution "strengthened my faith."

The Belks stayed busy. Mrs. Belk took dictation from Poteat from 9 to 1 ("He would write out what he wanted me to say in a five-cent notebook") and, in addition to his teaching, Henry was the college publicity director, with an office on the campus.

"He would bring home theme papers for me to read and grade," said Lucile, who had been an assistant in the English Department at Trinity.

There was not much social life except exchanging visits with members of the faculty. Dr. Daniel Bryan, who in addition to teaching education was the college dean, and his wife had the Belks for dinner, and vice versa. The Belks also visited Professors Royall and Sledd, both of whom were blind. Henry never discussed his own visual handicap with them, Lucile said. He could see then.

For recreation, the Belks took afternoon walks.

"We walked out in the woods or sat on campus benches under the magnolia trees."

At 25, Henry had matured and bore little resemblance to the touseled-haired youth in his high school annual. His hair was neatly combed and his eyes looked out confidently from behind thick-rimmed glasses. He looked the part of a young college professor.

And he was a good teacher, according to two Goldsboro men who had English under him.

"He knew his subject and was well accepted by the students," said realtor Charles S. Norwood, who took a course in business English. "He had a sense of humor and liked to kid members of the class."

City Attorney Edwin C. Ipock got along well under Henry, but on one occasion came in for some of his proverbial sarcasm. "Your idea of college seems to be that it is a good winter resort," Henry wrote on one of his themes.

Ipock took Henry's journalism course and reported some of the football games.

Henry didn't think he communicated with his students.

"I found out later I was wrong," he said.

The Belks' only child, Marie, was born October 1, 1924, while they were at Wake Forest. She was delivered by Dr. Thurmond Kitchin, dean of the medical school, assisted by a trained nurse from Raleigh. The delivery took place at the Belks' cottage. Time of birth was 12:05 a.m.

"Henry walked me up and down till the pains got too bad," Lucile recalled. "He wasn't too excited, but he was a proud father."

The Belks didn't send out any birth announcements, but an old friend of theirs, Dean S.F. Mordecai of the Trinity Law School, heard about the event and sent Marie a sterling silver spoon. An accompanying note said: "Dear Belks: Now that you have started raising Baptists, I am sending Marie a spoon; not a baby spoon but a tablespoon, because if she takes after her father, a baby spoon would be too small and it would probably be thrown out in the dish water, anyway."

Mrs. Belk was a Baptist. Henry was still a Methodist, but had been exposed to Baptist doctrine since coming to Wake Forest. A Baptist Church was the town's only place of worship.

Dean Mordecai had given Lucile the title of 'General Manager' because of the efficient manner in which she had run the president's office at Trinity. Henry later began using it in his editorials and fellow editors took up the habit.

Henry took graduate work in journalism at Columbia University in the summer of 1924 and got a leave of absence from Wake Forest to continue his studies there in 1925-26. He lectured in journalism one day a week at New Rochelle College, New Rochelle, N.Y. Mrs. Belk was secretary to a professor at Teachers College, at Columbia.

While attending the summer school at Columbia in 1924, Henry wrote an article for the Trinity Alumni Register titled 'Trinity Faces Among the Six Million.' It told of meeting up with people he had known at Trinity.

Lucile and I were walking along Riverside Drive on a pleasant Sunday afternoon. Suddenly there was a rift in the milling crowd, a familiar face appeared, a hand was outstretched and we were greeting Byrd I. Satterfield, '22 of Roxboro. During the bus ride to the Pennsylvania Hotel, where we went to visit the North Carolina headquarters of the Democratic National Convention, in swapping news, we learned that two years of success as principal of a high school in Person County have cast Satterfield's lot permanently in the field of education.

On the seventh floor of the Pennsylvania, Satterfield stopped to speak to a small man that I could not remember having seen before, "This is Dr. Knight," Satterfield said and instantly he was known to me. Dr. Edgar W. Knight, '09, of the faculty of the University of North Carolina. At the present time Dr. Knight is a figure of national note in the field of Southern education, his book on this subject having won wide attention. He is teaching in the summer school at Columbia and his courses are mentioned as being in great demand.

I was in my hotel room when the telephone rang and the black impudence who runs it and the elevator said, "A gentleman is calling. Can he come up?" Show him up," I replied and started toward the door, trying to guess who it could be. I found K.W. (Ken) Litaker, '23, of Concord. Members of the Class of '23 will recall him as the fellow with the easy pen, in fact an artist of merit.

We made an engagement to see "The Show-Off" — rated by critics as second best among the plays of the past season — on Saturday. It seemed like old times and Trinity was very close to us as we sat together at the show and reviewed our first year out of college. To Prof. Holland Holton's education he ascribed credit for the easy time he had had as principal of a five-teacher high school in Anson County.

On Broadway, one night at dusk, we came upon Jay L. Jackson, '23, of South Bend, Ind. At the last minute last fall, Jackson made up his mind to enter the law school at Columbia. He will continue his work this year.

"What is Leo Brady, our classmate, doing now?" I asked Jackson. "I haven't heard a word from him since graduation."

"Leo went to Paris in a responsible connection with the Chicago Tribune," Jackson replied.

Jackson also related that Bill (W.H.) Lander, A.B., '23, M.A., '24, is now living at the Sigma Chi house at Columbia and working for an advertising agency in the city.

"Hen-ne-rry Bell-le-ke!" The words, pronounced with a Japanese twist, just as I had heard them frequently during my senior year at Trinity, came to me as I started to cross Amsterdam Avenue near 117th Street. Sure enough, there was Richard Shiokawa, the Japanese boy sent to Trinity in 1922 by Rev. N.S. Ogburn, a Trinity graduate now serving as a missionary in Korea. Shiokawa had just landed in New York after attending the first summer session at Trinity and was as lonesome as they get to be. He was overjoyed to see somebody he knew and even more so when I gave him the addresses of several Trinity men.

Henry always maintained strong ties with his alma mater, as did his wife, who served as president of the Duke Alumnae Association in 1940-41. Henry served a term as president of the Wayne County Duke Alumni Association. The couple were a familiar sight at alumni reunions and, in later years, at meetings of the Half Century Club.

"Henry's contributions to Duke cannot be measured in specifics," said Duke President Terry Sanford. "He was the kind of loyal alumnus who is the backbone of a great university."

Henry was teaching at a Wake Forest summer school for teachers in Craven County, in 1926, when he made the decision to give up teaching. Teaching journalism was not like practicing it and he had always wanted to be in newspaper work.

W.W. Minton, business manager of the Goldsboro News, called Henry and offered him the position of editor. Henry accepted the offer. He had been a reporter on the Goldsboro paper in the summer of his junior year at Trinity College. His old boss, Roland F. Beasley, editor of the Monroe Journal, had gotten him the job.

Beasley had been one of the organizers of the News, Goldsboro's first morning newspaper, in 1922. He was made editor. Others among the organizers were Beasley's nephew, John Beasley, who became secretary-treasurer; Col. John D. Langston, who was president; Matt H. Allen, who was vice president; Minton, who first served as advertising manager; and R.E. "Red" Powell, a friend of the Beasleys, who had started the ball to rolling for the organization. Powell, who became a well-known newspaperman, stayed with the News only a short time.

John Beasley went to High Point in 1923 and Roland F.

Beasley had gone back to Monroe when Henry came to Goldsboro. Minton severed his connection with the paper in 1928. Col. John D. Langston was chief stockholder when the News merged with the Goldsboro Argus in 1929.

Henry reported for duty on July 1, 1926. He would remain editor of the News for three years, then later edit the News-Argus for the rest of his newspaper career.

28

4

At least one Goldsboro resident would have remembered Henry
from four years before, when he was reporting for the News.

The second morning after he went to work, Henry was catching
some shut-eye when an irate citizen burst into his room at the
home of Ben Campen, brandishing a copy of that morning's paper
listing him as having been tried in Mayor's Court for driving drunk.

The citizen was shouting threats at the drowsy reporter when
Henry got out of bed, yawned, stretched himself to his full six
feet, six inches, and asked the intruder what he had in mind doing
about it.

The man took one look at Henry, gulped, "Nothing," and
backed out of the room.

It was probably the only time that Henry was threatened with
physical violence. Like any editor, he got tongue lashings, but no
one wanted to tangle with his 234 pounds of bone and muscle.

The Belks lived at the Isler Apartments, across from the
courthouse, the first month they were in Goldsboro, then took an
apartment at the home of Miss Rebecca Slocumb at 700 E. Walnut
Street, about eight blocks from the News office. Henry walked the
distance for a while, then bought a car.

The Belks moved to the Slocumb home upon recommendation
of T. Frank Jones, a friend of Henry's, who with his wife occupied
an upstairs apartment. The Belks had a downstairs apartment
taking up one side of the house.

Miss Slocumb recalled an incident, involving Henry, when Mrs.
Jones was "desperately" ill with pneumonia.

"We were sitting on the front porch, expecting her to die,
when, unknown to her nurse, who had stepped out of the room,
she got out of bed, in a stupefied condition, and came downstairs.
Henry heard the nurse scream and rushed inside. He picked up
Mrs. Jones, as if she were a baby, and took her back upstairs,
putting her back to bed."

The Joneses later lived across the street from the Belks.

While staying at Miss Slocumb's, Henry was told the story of Mary and Ezekiel Slocumb, of Revolutionary fame. Ezekiel was Miss Slocumb's great-great-great grandfather.

The story told of Mary's nocturnal horseback ride to be at the side of her husband, who, she dreamed, had been mortally wounded at Moore's Creek Bridge. Henry referred to the incident frequently in his writings.

The Belks stayed at Miss Slocumb's nine months ("Henry said it was a pleasure staying at my house") then moved to a house at 1409 E. Walnut Street, which they had bought on credit. It became their permanent home. It was a frame house which was later brick-veneered as result of a contest, sponsored by Borden Brick and Tile Company, which Henry won. He submitted a 25-word entry on how to use brick.

The month after becoming editor of the Goldsboro News, Henry wrote an editorial paying tribute to his old friend, Dr. William Louis Poteat, who had announced that he was retiring from the presidency of Wake Forest College on account of his age, after withstanding numerous attempts to force his ouster.

The year before, Poteat and President Harry W. Chase of the University of North Carolina had been responsible for the defeat of legislation, sponsored by Governor Cameron Morrison and religious fundamentalists, that would have outlawed the teaching of evolution in any state-supported school.

Henry's tribute to his old mentor was a moving piece of writing.

Bloody but unbowed, Dr. W. L. Poteat will next June retire from the presidency of Wake Forest College "on the sole condition of my age and none other."

Thus it is that "Dr. Billy", as his boys affectionately call him, wins his 26-year-old fight for enlightened thinking, for truth. Almost single-handedly he has fought a fight against the forces of narrowness and prejudice. And when he steps back from the front to a quieter spot, he will step back the outstanding educator of the South and the man who is responsible for, as Walter Lippmann said, "making the name of Wake Forest nationally known.

Dr. Billy will be past seventy when he retires, but he has raised up a valiant army of young disciplines who will carry on his fight with thrilling joy.

The defeat of the Poole bill, the collapse of the movement started by the Committee of One Hundred, the failure of Dr. Marby and his followers — all this may be directly attributed to the years of heroic fighting by President Poteat.

"You have fought our battles long enough," said President Chase of the University of North Carolina, when the Poole bill was up, "and now we are going to do some fighting." And right there, we believe, is where the tide turned toward enlightenment in North Carolina.

Time after time certain forces in the Baptist denomination have thought that they had President Poteat where they wanted him, that they were going to put him and Wake Forest College to looking through a tiny gimlet hole of intelligence, that they were going to force him to adopt creeds and dogmas, to sign his soul away or step down from his position. And each time, great soul that he is, he has been able to evade their snares and to put himself and his college more firmly on the mountain of truth.

The spectacle of this man meeting his tormentors with a declaration that left the least intelligent of them realizing that they were in the presence of a divine inspiration — the spectacle of the Winston-Salem convention of several years ago, is one which men will tell to their children for generations.

President Poteat has been an imposing figure when compared with some penurious-souled leaders who rush to the innermost rooms and hide for fear that they will be called on to make some open declaration. When compared with some of these leaders who first find out what the Brothers and Sisters of Zion's Crossroads are going to say about the matter. When compared with some of the leaders who leap agilely from one side of the fence to the other or balance perfectly on its top.

How he has been able to preserve that beautiful equanimity of character in the face of some of the blackguard tactics which have been employed against him, is a mystery which we have never been able to understand. We have seen him receive the most scurrilous letters, damning him to hell and condemning him in all manner of bitter terms, and we have seen him straightway send the gentlest answer and one in which he would attempt to explain the facts as he saw them.

Yes, Doctor Billy, you win, God bless you.

Henry later had an editorial chiding the author of the Poole Bill.

We hope that D. Scott Poole, Hoke, has read what Dr. E.Y. Mullins, president of the Southern Baptist Theological Seminary in Louisville, had to say before Baptist educators about anti-evolution laws. We wish that Dr. Poole was given the address of the Louisville preacher-educator, shut up in a quiet, comfortable room with it, and required to read and meditate on it for a whole day. Here is what Dr. Mullins said.

"I think it is a blunder and foreign to the New Testament faith to lay hold on legislatures and the civil powers to compel certain interpretations of the Bible. It is a reversal of our Christian position. Christ's religion calls for spiritual weapons of defense, not laws and penalties, courts and juries.

"Christian education must give a square deal to the growing mind of a boy or girl. They will meet the theory of Organic Evolution at every turn in later reading. You had better prepare them for a true and sane attitude, if religion is to make its contribution to the world.

Henry's early editorials reflected some of the matters he would be occupied with in coming years — education, industrial development, responsible government.

On his second day as editor, he had an editorial on the progress of Wayne County schools.

A survey just made through the research department of the University of North Carolina shows Wayne County stands 35th on the list of North Carolina counties in the matter of money spent in 1924 and 1925 in educating our rural children.

Wayne County, it is shown, spent $23.07 on each child attending the rural schools in the county. While it does not compare with the $40.42 which was spent by Durham County, it is a fact that cannot be denied that Wayne made a splendid showing and far eclipsed many other counties along this line, some of them being larger and much richer counties.

A month later Henry took note of the growing poultry industry in Wayne.

We hope that the effort at securing a full-time poultry expert for Wayne County will meet with success. If it does, it will mean many dollars in the pockets of farmers in Wayne and adjoining counties.

With $94,000 a year already being paid Wayne farmers for poultry produce, with a 63,000-egg incubator being built to serve the trade with young chicks, with a receiving point for one of the largest metropolitan poultry dealers established here, the foundation has been laid for an industry which can be made to rank with the most important in the county. It can be made to mean as much as the cotton and tobacco crops now mean to the farmers of Wayne.

In the same issue was an editorial on 'The Favored East', which contained Henry's first reference to his native 'Sweet Union' County, a subject of many of his later writings.

Farmers of Eastern North Carolina have no conception of the ease of the life they lead, the facility with which they can make a crop, as compared with the life of the farmer of the Piedmont section of the state, in particular 'Sweet Union' County.

O.A. Hamilton, superintendent of the Goldsboro city schools, has just had this fact impressed upon him on a trip to Union County — the red hills of Goose Creek Township, to be more specific — where he visited friends among boyhood scenes.

"I declare they have to work up there," said Hamilton. "The farmer down this way doesn't know what it is to plow and drudge among the rocks. No, our folks don't realize how kindly nature has smiled on them."

On a cultural note, Henry called attention to an upcoming band concert.

Music hath charms to soothe the savage breast.

And it can sometimes lift common, ordinary mortals like you and me to the heights of divine inspiration. The greatest thrill I ever had was in listening to a blind violinist — at one time a member of the New York Symphony Orchestra — play before students of Duke University. There was soul in that music and that soul became tuned with my soul.

Other folks felt as I did, for staid, solemn, methodical Dr. W. P. Few wore Dean Wannamaker's hat away from the occasion and didn't know the difference.

Now Goldsboro has the opportunity of hearing a great band on Sunday afternoon. A band made up of 40 men to whom music is a love, a connection with higher things.

If you love good music, you cannot afford to miss the concert. Five thousand persons should greet the musicians.

Displeased with secret goings-on at city hall, Henry wanted to know "What Is It All About?"

The administration of municipal business is a public business. Is it, therefore, any of the public's business when our municipal government undergoes kaleidoscopic changes in executive session and the executive session adjourns leaving the wherefores and why still in executive session?

The News is of the opinion that executive sessions have no place in municipal administration. If matters are progressing properly, the public is entitled to know. If they do not progress properly, the public is entitled to know where the failures and deficiencies lie.

The municipal fathers are entitled at all times to the benefit of public opinion in all important matters. The public is entitled at all times to know the reactions of each official to the serious problems confronting him. The public is even entitled to the benefit of public opinion and counsel in the selection of other officials. It is not sufficient answer to this viewpoint that selections made otherwise are fully capable or possess to the fullest extent the confidence of the public. They should be weighed in the scales of public opinion and at least opportunity be given to the public to voice objection or approval.

When a municipality declines to assume the responsibility of opening streets without an expression from the public, it is rather a shock to the same public to find that important matters of accepting the resignation of a city manager and mayor, and the appointment of new ones, is none of their business.

So much for the duty owed the public by its officials.

As to the two officials who have been selected to fill the important offices of mayor and city manager, the News believes they are qualified by character and ability to serve the public well in their respective capacities, and that they will measure up to the responsibilities that now rest upon them.

The board's action involved the appointment of Mayor Zeno Hollowell as city manager to succeed C.M. Grantham, who was

---

Page 34

entering private business, and the naming of Griff Porter to succeed Hollowell.

Henry was beginning to make himself heard. In October, three months after coming to Goldsboro, he was invited to join the Goldsboro Rotary Club. The invitation was extended through merchant A. A. Joseph. Not long afterwards, Henry joined the Goldsboro Masonic Lodge. Several years before his death he became a member of the Goldsboro Elks Lodge.

Henry began 1927 by calling attention to conditions at the Wayne County jail.

The grand jury leaves the matter of remedying jail conditions to the "sound discretion" of the County Board of Commissioners. The jury finds, however, that there is insufficient space for the number of prisoners kept and that there is no space available in which to segregate the prisoners.

As soon as public demand becomes insistent enough, the commissioners will see their way to take action in the matter and not before. Commissioners are going to do what they believe their constituents want, and right now they believe the people of Wayne County had rather see the black hole of Calcutta jail of ours continued than to see some of the county's money spent on an addition.

On January 27, Henry had a piece of 'Old Ocean Calls'.

The winds which blew loud-voiced out of the east a few days ago brought to us from a hundred miles away the call of the old ocean as he throws himself in ceaseless fury on the shore of Core Bank in Carteret County, retires and throws himself again.

Tingling with poetic pleasure, we slipped into bed at 2 o'clock in the morning. Into the bed but not to sleep. Instead, we walked again under the great stars along Core Bank, while the wind rushed by, shouting in its power, and the great waves burst with a roar a few feet to our right.

As we walked in memory, wandering sand dunes lifted themselves against the dark horizon, dropped away as we passed. We lived again the night, the stars, the sand dunes, Old Ocean, and again we were filled with a sense of the majesty and power of it all, that brought a catch to our throat.

Inside, the wind died away, ceased to shake threateningly at the doors and windows, and Old Ocean's call to us from his home in Carteret wore off. We slept.

Henry had gone to Core Sound the summer before, when he was teaching at the Wake Forest summer school in Craven County. It had been his first explorative visit to the North Carolina coast and the region would be in his blood from then on.

From dreaming about the ocean, Henry turned his thoughts to Goldsboro's economic development: establishment of a broadcasting station to "bring the city directly to the front in progressive moves in Eastern North Carolina"; promotion of Goldsboro as a distribution center.

Goldsboro's greatest future lies in her capitalizing her position as the gateway to Eastern North Carolina. The city is ideally located for a distribution center. Shipments from Goldsboro can reach destination in 46 of the counties of North Carolina quicker than they could if shipped from any other city in the state.

Come April, Henry hailed the advent of spring.

Spring, most beautiful of the seasons, is just around the corner. Soon the air will be scented with the redolent fragrance of flowers. The birds will be returning from their Southern home, filled with new life and new energies and preparing for their summer sojourn. Their songs of greetings will be heard from every side. The trees will be bursting into bloom for the glorious months to come.

Spring is the time when all nature is busy and it is a time in every person's life when he rejoices to be alive. Human beings soon will be breathing in the very vernal spirit of the season radiated by all the animal and plant life around them.

Everything looked rosy to Henry, rounding out his first year as an editor.

Henry continued to be occupied with local matters in 1928, but before the year was out, he became embroiled in a burning national issue — politics.

On January 1, he announced "The News Program for Goldsboro During 1928."

The boxed program appeared at the top of the editorial column the entire year. It included a town clock, a summer playground program, a new bus station, the paving of Center Street, a municipal airport, additional housing facilities, promotion of Goldsboro as a distributing center, adequate support of the Chamber of Commerce, and closer cooperation between the city and rural sections.

Two of the most pressing needs — a new bus station and the improvement of Center Street — were met during the year. Others followed, in the course of time, but the city never got around to installing a town clock — something inspired, no doubt, by Henry's fond recollection of the town clock in Monroe.

On January 20, Henry paid tribute to Rabbi J. L. Mayerberg, who had died after serving Goldsboro's Jewish congregation for over 35 years.

To serve a people in God's ministry in the same section for more than a quarter of a century is a record of usefulness attained by few.

Rabbi J.L. Mayerberg served his synagogue in Goldsboro actively for 35 years and as Rabbi Emeritus for three years before his death. Such service denoted a capacity to love the people among whom he moved and ministered, and the worthiness of the affection of those he loved and lifted.

And not only was he held in affection and veneration by those of his own, his generous impulses, his paternal concern for those in sorrow, his charity in judgment, his friendly spirit, his sage counsels, captured the hearts and minds of the entire community in which he lived, and held them captive even unto his passing.

It is not to be wondered that such a servant has given to the world a remarkable family, three doctors, one rabbi, and a daughter whose record of service as a teacher is so well known to our community. Only a man who seeks the best in life, and having sought and found it, who gives back to life his richest treasures, is entitled to the unreserved tribute of his people. Measured by this scale of service, Rabbi J.L. Mayerberg passes while his people grieve.

Spring went by uneventfully, with Henry addressing himself to such matters as the urgent need of a bus station, commendation for the city fathers for not increasing the tax rate, and the need of "a highly developed public opinion condemning the violation of the prohibition law."

Then came the nomination of Alfred E. Smith to be the Democratic Presidential standard bearer, which plunged Henry into the hottest political fight of his career.

A life-long Democrat, himself, he had no patience with anti-Smith party deserters, as expressed in "Where Will You Go, Wanderer?"

Those Democrats who, in their disappointment over the nomination of Governor Smith, talk of staying at home on election day, or voting the Republican ticket, will do well to weigh their duties as citizens before taking a step they might regret.

If you are a conscientious believer in the principles and practices of prohibition, will your lot be improved by aid and comfort to the Republican Party, which has been tried for seven years and miserably failed and refused, under the influence of the Secretary of the Treasury, whose fortunes have built up by the liquor traffic, to enforce the prohibition laws? Is a party that has been tried and that has refused to enforce the Constitution and the laws relating to the liquor traffic, to be trusted in preference to one that has not been tried, even if its leader holds wet views? Better to experiment with the untried, where its leader has the reputation at least of political honesty, than the party that has been tried and has been found wanting.

If you are a believer in honesty in government, are you willing to retain in office a dishonest government simply to carry your point about one issue out of many fundamental issues?

If you have the interest of the farmer at heart; if you want him again to have a fair chance at prosperity, are you willing to retain in office the party that repudiates him at every session of Congress? Are you willing to let him continually suffer in order that you may carry your point about one issue, upon which, to say the least, the Republican Party has no advantage?

If you sincerely believe the ordinary citizen has not had equality of opportunity under Republican administration, are you willing to let your views about the one issue of Prohibition blind you to every other issue in the campaign? Does the language of Smith, who openly speaks his mind, but promises to support the law, cause greater apprehension in your mind than the seven years record of non-enforcement of the Republican Party, and the straddling language of Hoover, who has thought too little of the interests of the Commonwealth to even vote when other citizens voted?

If there are no questions under the sun except the prohibition question, then we agree with the view of some that there should be a separate party with prohibition as its sole platform. There is no question that prohibition is an important question. Yet we are prepared to run the risk of being charged with frank heresy by voicing the opinion that honesty in government is a greater issue; that insurance of a fair deal for labor and agriculture approaches it in importance; that the protection of the public domain from the grand larceny of the dominant party is an issue not to be frivolously treated; that the reinstatement of the United States in a place of dignity and influence among civilized nations is an issue of serious consideration.

Yes, there are numbers of fundamental issues requiring the adherence of good citizens to the Democratic Party, because it is the party that holds out the only hope of relief on those issues. One issue can never build a nation, even if the issue is prohibition.

On August 3, Henry took time off from politics to talk baseball. There was an upcoming double-header between Goldsboro and Wilmington of the Eastern Carolina League. It was a critical series, with Wilmington trying to overtake Goldsboro for the lead. Yet, Goldsboro fans, as hosts, had the duty to extend proper courtesies to the visitors.

We must all go out and help win those old ball games this afternoon and tonight, as they used to argue so earnestly in the good old college days. We must win them because we are bucking up against Wilmington, the team we displaced a month ago and the team which is closest to Goldsboro in the very close and highly exciting pennant race.

We must win those games, but we must not forget that Goldsboro is the host town. There will be hundreds of Wilmington fans here for the games and we have an opportunity of doing a job in neighborliness and good fellowship that will put the visitors wondering. Let's do it. The Eastern Carolina League can do no better job than to make us better acquainted with the cities who are our close neighbors, can do no better job than teaching us self-control, proper regard for the other fellow. Such a challenge faces us today.

Let's make it a special point to give the Wilmington team and the Wilmington fans an especially fine greeting. Let's cheer them to the echo as the team comes to bat, and then let's recognize a good play whenever it is made. Now, we don't mean let's pay all attention to the Pirates and not enough to the Manufacturers. Far from that. But let us not forget to be courteous and considerate of Mr. Weafer and his club and the Wilmington fans.

Wilmington took the afternoon game, but Goldsboro came back to win the nightcap and remain four full games in the lead.

On August 16, Henry returned to the political wars with 'Underhand Attack'.

The right of free speech certainly has the limitation that what is spoken and written should be the truth.

There is being circulated upon the streets of Goldsboro a newspaper entitled "The Woman Voter," which to the square inch contains more misrepresentation, fraud and untruth than could be charged against Tammany Hall, with all of its iniquities. Under the caption of "Smith and Negro Equality," this paper states that "it is an open secret that Governor Smith believes in equality among the blacks and whites." What the paper intends to suggest is that Smith believes in social equality between the races. Not a particle of evidence is offered to support this untruth. The paper further refers to Smith as "a man who would try to force upon the people of the South Negro equality, as Governor Smith has indicated he would do on more than one occasion." Not a particle of evidence was offered in support of this untruth."

These statements are so vicious as to invite a reaction on the part of those who, but for such false and thoroughly vicious and irresponsible statements, might otherwise be inclined to look with disfavor on Smith.

This paper, "The Woman Voter", is evidently being circulated by hand. Those who are responsible for its circulation would do well to remember that it is just as wrong to circulate a lie as to originate it.

The next day Henry ran an editorial titled 'Frankness or Subterfuge — Which?'

"Two characteristics of Governor Alfred E. Smith are outstanding in conferences on the porch of the executive mansion at Albany, where the Democratic nominee and his political visitors discuss issues upon which the Presidential election will pivot.

"We speak frankly," said the Governor.

"We find an atmosphere of old-time Southern hospitality," said the departing guests.

The above quotations appeared in a story in the News and Observer the other morning. Both of these characteristics are commendable, but we believe that the outstanding one is frankness. And Al Smith is frank. There is no doubting that, even by the opposing party. Every detail of his political actions and statements since the Houston convention have shown that frankness. Smith may not agree with the policies and views of every Democrat in the country, and he admits it, but he has accepted the platform adopted by his party which he has chosen to lead, and he will stand squarely on that platform.

Isn't this frankness better than subterfuge, camouflage and other "hide and seek" methods that have been employed by leaders of the Republican party during the past eight years?

Henry supported Josephus Daniels for National Committeeman from North Carolina.

Josephus Daniels and not Cameron Morrison should be named National Committeeman for North Carolina to succeed Sen. F. M. Simmons.

It is not that we love Morrison less or that we love Daniels more. It is that the Democracy of the state is faced with a crisis that requires delicate treatment. Morrison is a man of remarkable ability, a great campaigner, and is fired with zeal for his party as great as that of any of its leaders. He is bold, he is courageous.

These, however, are not the particular qualities essential to the job of the present hour. Morrison can enthuse the Saints. But the Saints are already enthused. It is the wavering ones that now demand the attention of the party. Morrison simply can't appeal to those elements. He plunged too far and too fast for those elements to catch up. The man who can appeal to the wavering elements is the man who, in pre-convention days, thought in the same language as the wavering ones and who had great difficulty of readjustment. Such a man can constitute an appeal to those who have a traditional yearning for the party, but whose spirits are being tried by conviction on moral questions that they at present think insurmountable.

Daniels had always been the driest of the drys. He exudes honesty. He is a ramrod where convictions are concerned. Everybody recognizes these facts. Yet he sees the necessity of electing Smith president. The psychology of the crisis is that the wavering ones will be led to follow the type that is similar to themselves in thought upon moral issues and in the difficulties had in the acceptance of the party's program, but will be driven further away by resentment against leadership of those who have not been thinking in their language.

On September 5, Henry reported that a building permit had been issued to W.A. Royall, Goldsboro businessman, for the erection of a bus station at the corner of Walnut and George streets.

The next day he delivered a broadside at snipers undercutting the Democratic candidate because of his Catholicism.

Of all the mean, rotten, un-Christian things that can be imagined in a supposedly civilized age, the meanest, rottenest and most un-Christian is the vicious, sneaking, cowardly attacks made upon men because of their religious convictions by means of whispering campaigns and the circulation of scurrilous, irreponsible newspapers.

We say this when the assault is made upon the Catholic.

We would say it if made upon any religion that teaches Christ, or, for that matter, any religion.

Those who indulge in it have not the slightest conception of the love of Christ. They are neither good churchmen nor good citizens.

They are not better in principle or conduct than those who were charged with the cruelties of the Spanish Inquisition.

At heart they may be compared with those who shared in the massacre on St. Bartholomew's Day.

It is simply a case of different religious claims, and a veneer of civilization very thin at that.

Quit it!

On September 15, Henry was in an ebullient mood over Goldsboro's winning the pennant, following a play-off with Wilmington.

It's a grand and glorious feeling, this here one of being proud possessor of the pennant for the first season of the Eastern Carolina Baseball League. It's a grand and glorious feeling to contemplate how we came by it, from whom we captured it, and how we captured it.

This is the first time in the history of Goldsboro that she has found herself owning a pennant, and twice valued it is, accordingly.

With the winning of the pennant, closes the first season of organized baseball for the city, a season which has truly vindicated the pioneer spirits who sacrificed in the beginning to make the team possible.

On November 4, two days before the election, Henry issued 'A Word of Caution'.

We are at the fag end of as bitter a campaign as North Carolina and the nation have ever known. Tuesday is election day and it behooves all men to look well to their self-control on that day. Under the stress and strain of the last minute drive, some of our partisan feelings may get the best of our cool, more collected selves. If we do not guard against it, we may find ourselves in an argument, and that may bring on more talk or worse.

Already, in North Carolina one life has been offered up on the political altar. Tuesday there is bound to come, somewhere in the state, a fight with whatever it may bring forth.

But here in Goldsboro and Wayne County let's keep our heads. The other fellow has his opinion and is entitled to it. Let's remember this and avoid any scene which would disgrace the sacred duty of voting, which we shall on Tuesday exercise.

'What Will You Do. Democrats?', Henry editorialized on Election Day morning.

Democrats, this is an appeal to you. The party for which your fathers and forefathers stood is threatened with disaster in this, the Southland, its stronghold for more than half a century. For months now you have been assailed by headlines of the opposition, villifying your candidate, bearing false witness against him, appealing not to your reason, but to your passion and prejudices. Those forces have called themselves the true Democratic Party, but be not deceived. When they tell you how to vote, they tell you to vote for the Republican Party, the party that so nearly ruined your state a quarter of a century ago. They ask you to go to the polls, along with the Negroes, to cast

your ballot for a candidate who stands for everything that you, as white men
and women of the South, have fought for 63 years.

But, in order that you may not consider these the words of an alarmist, let
us consider some of the issues involved.

On the one hand you have a man pledged to continue the policies of the
Republican Party during its last seven years of rule, policies that have involved
this nation of ours in one of the most gigantic scandals in its history; policies
that provide special privileges for those fattened barons of wealth at the expense
of the farmer, the small business man, the professional man and the laborer;
policies for which the Republican Party was paid in cold cash, that it might win
the elections of 1920 and 1924.

On the other hand you have a man pledged to carry out a forward looking
program of constructive work that provides for the retention of our great
natural resources placed here by an All-Seeing Power for the common good of
men; a program that assures the farmer, that much abused economic unit of
this country, of his equal opportunity for success, along with the Mellons, the
Sinclairs and the Donhenys; a program of constructive tariff reform which
gives equal protection to the small business man and farmer, as well as to
those bloated big business interests of the East who are the special pets of the
Republican Party.

What are you going to do about it?

What they did was to elect Herbert Hoover by a vote
unprecedented in U.S. history, breaking the hitherto solid South.

"For the first time in over 25 years, Wayne County voters
turned their backs on the Democratic nominee for President," the
Goldsboro News reported.

Henry noted the results in an epigrammatic bit of sarcasm.

Returns indicate that our people have been saved from the Pope. Now they
can go calmly to their bedchambers, leave the windows unfastened, their
doors unlocked, with full assurance that the Pope will not appear suddenly
from the outer darkness and gobble them up.

Passion and prejudice seem to have triumphed in North Carolina.

God save the State!

Thus did Editor Belk emerge loser in his first political fight.

After licking his wounds for three weeks, he found something
pleasant to write about — 'Backbones and Spareribs'.

Backbones and spareribs. What a wealth of memory is bound up in that phrase. What pictures of country dinners in country homes — than which there is no sich.

And talking about backbones and spareribs, D. M. Talton of Buck Swamp has hung up a record for the rest of the crowd to shoot at.

Hanging in his smokehouse this morning is something that is about the size of a mule. But it is not a mule. Much more rounded and plump than a mule. It is 775 pounds of dressed, rather than undressed hog. His Majesty of the Sty was only 30 months old.

Anybody around here beat that record?

6

Henry had a slightly revised program for Goldsboro for 1929. In place of the bus station and Center Street improvements, which had been taken care of, he added a new fire station, promotion of the Goldsboro tobacco market, construction of hard-surfaced road to Seven Springs and points east, and efforts to make ·Goldsboro "the city beautiful". A town clock was still on the list.

Henry could not foresee that the merger of the Goldsboro News with the Goldsboro Argus would leave him without an editorial voice before the year was out. Nor did he anticipate the stock market crash in October, which would negate projects involving financial expenditures.

On January 25, Henry took a swipe at prophets of hard times in 'Hard Times, Shucks!'

This is a knock at knockers, a show-up of pessimists as pests, and the setting forth of a few concrete facts to demonstrate that these are not hard times but good times; the insatiability of the day for too many luxuries that creates the idea that money is not as plentiful as it should be, with especial reference to Goldsboro and vicinity.

Any number of the live, wide-awake firms in various lines in this city will tell you that the year 1928 proved a successful one and showed a substantial increase in business over previous years. And January sales held in several stores, backed by well organized advertising, were well attended and much money was put in circulation.

If you see or hear a man complaining of hard times, put him down as non-aggressive, a debt-ridden-by-luxury-loving person, whether he be merchant, professional man, farmer, mechanic or laborer. There's as much and more of the world's goods in circulation as ever. It's just up to the individual to "git up and git."

As we have said before, never before in the history of the world has the poor man been tempted into the liking for the good things in life as at present, never before have they been easier to procure. This movement started within the last half-generation.

Certainly it will take more than that time for us to accommodate our aroused and cultivated taste for luxury to the size of our purse.

Elsewhere, Henry called attention to the death rate from diphtheria, which still claimed a heavy toll.

During the 5-year period ending January 3, 1927, cases reported to the State Department of Health totaled 18,435, with 1,499 deaths. The department emphasizes that diphtheria is preventable and that deaths are due to neglect.

In succeeding weeks, Henry had editorials on Goldsboro's low showing as a tobacco market; the repeal of an ordinance prohibiting cows in the city; commendation for Governor Gardner for appointing Captain Nathan O'Berry, Goldsboro industrialist, as State Treasurer; and cracking down on traffic violators.

We are glad to note that the city police are beginning a campaign to stop speeding in the city. This is a matter that should be pushed to the utmost until conditions are corrected.

Something having to do with the operation of automobiles in the city came to our attention yesterday. "Sickness, Drive Slowly" signs have been placed on a certain block on East Walnut Street. We were amazed and shocked to note that numbers of automobile drivers paid not the slightest heed to the signs. Some of them raced by at 25 to 30 miles an hour. Sometimes they blew their horns. Mere thoughtlessness, perhaps. No driver, we think, would knowingly give more pain to one who is ill.

On July 11, Henry had a piece on an upcoming Negro concert.

A treat awaits us in the sacred concert which 100 leading Negro singers will give at Mason Theatre Sunday afternoon. These trained singers will sing the songs of their people, the spirituals with which their forefathers were wont to ease their hearts as they toiled as slaves before the Civil War.

It is 20 years since I went, as a boy, to hear the Negroes sing at their camp meeting at a country church in Union County. But still I can hear the songs which they sang. There was a quality of plaintiveness, of strange appeal, almost of eeriness, that made one shiver along his spine as he listened. As for rhythm, harmony, time, it was perfect.

Since that trip to the Union County church 20 years ago, I have discovered that these qualities of song are not peculiar to the Negroes of Sweet Union. They are qualities of their race.

I shall not miss the opportunity of hearing the Wayne Negroes in their concert Sunday afternoon.

It would be Henry's last reference to 'Sweet Union' in some time. Machinery had already been set in motion that would interrupt his editorial career.

In May, Talbot Patrick, a native of Chicago, and two associates had purchased control of the Goldsboro Daily Argus from Colonel Joseph E. Robinson, its founder, who was in failing health. The Argus was a beloved institution that had mirrored the life of the community since 1885, but Goldsboro had outgrown its peculiarly personal type of journalism.

Patrick was an experienced newspaperman who had worked on The Chicago Evening Post and two English-language dailies in Shanghai, China. Before coming to Goldsboro he was in the advertising department of the New York News.

Seeing an advertisment in *Time* magazine relating to the economic opportunities of Piedmont Carolina, Patrick made inquiries which led to an exchange of letters with Bill Arp Lowrance, Charlotte newspaperman and a former field secretary of the North Carolina Press Association. Lowrance had gotten a promise from Colonel Robinson that he would have first chance at purchase of the Argus when it was up for sale. That time had arrived.

Lowrance was looking for someone with newspaper experience — and apparently capital — to join him in taking over the Goldsboro paper. Patrick fitted the bill. Upshot was that a purchase was worked out giving Patrick 50 percent interest and 25 percent interest each to Lowrance and A. W. Huckle, publisher of the Evening Herald in Rock Hill, South Carolina. Patrick did not meet Huckle, whom he would later succeed as owner of the Rock Hill paper, until after Lowrance had set up the arrangements.

"After taking over the Argus from Colonel Robinson, we improved the paper rapidly," Patrick recalled. "Henry Belk was acting general manager of the News and realized that the afternoon field was a better field for a paper in Goldsboro than the morning field. Colonel John D. Langston, the majority stockholder of the News, became convinced of the desirability of selling his interest before the Argus got so much stronger that the News would be continually losing money and eventually be forced to suspend."

While negotiations with Langston were underway, Henry gave attention to one of his civic projects for 1929 — promotion of the Goldsboro tobacco market. On August 24, the News got out a 'Tobacco Supplement' ahead of the market's opening on September 3.

An editorial setting forth advantages of selling locally said George C. Royall was the "father" of the Goldsboro market, which had opened in 1895.

Three warehouses run by local men interested in building a market not for a season but for the future — that is what the tobacco farmer will find on the Goldsboro market this season. This is the first time in a number of years that the warehouses have been manned entirely by Goldsboro and Wayne County residents, and it is bound to be reflected in the poundage transferred from the raiser to the manufacturer on the warehouse floors. Experts expect the market to double its sales from last year. "I am sure we will sell at least 14 million pounds," one warehouseman said.

Three tobacco plants operate here. They could handle 60 million pounds of the weed each year.

The News later reported that in the first two days, the market had sold 484,000 pounds for an average of 12 cents. "W. G. Howell took high price honors. He sold one pile for 50 cents a pound."

In September, "through a combination of cash and notes," Patrick and his associates completed a deal with Colonel Langston for the purchase of his majority block of stock. At the same time, they assumed responsibility for small stock holdings of three News employees, including Henry Belk, that were being paid for over a period of years.

The first issue of the Goldsboro News-Argus came out on September 23. It was stated that "the name News-Argus was selected as the title for the merged afternoon paper because it was considered easier to say than Argus-News."

Getting out the first issue on Monday was something of a chore, Patrick noted editorially in 'Yes, We Did It'.

When we announced that we planned to move much of the equipment, including the linotype machines, from the Goldsboro Daily Argus plant to the newly enlarged quarters where the Goldsboro News used to be, we omitted to mention that Sunday was the equinox.

Sailors look for equinoctial storms on or about September 22. We got one. Moving a linotype machine in the rain would be about as wise as opening a watch and carrying it down the street with the works open to wet weather. A mist would be almost as bad.

So today's News-Argus was produced by machinery and a staff divided between two places. If it is half as good as we hoped the first issue would be, it is thanks to the utmost efforts of all who have a hand in the making of a newspaper. This issue is proof of their loyalty to the paper and to the cause of getting it out for you.

There was one bright omen — flowers and good wishes from Mrs. Henry Weil, whose husband had been a member of the firm that had been a mainstay of the Argus in its struggling years.

A beautiful vase of asters was delivered to the News-Argus office on James Street this morning. Accompanying the flowers was the card of Mrs. Henry Weil and the following note:

"Ave, News-Argus! May it grow and prosper and be valued by generations to come."

Patrick had big plans for the new daily.

Unless we are mistaken, every other city in North Carolina in which a seven-days-a-week newspaper is published is larger than Goldsboro. Yet we have great hopes of success in publishing the News-Argus every day of the week, of giving our readers both home news and outside news every day of the year except a couple of special holidays.

One great reason why the News-Argus will succeed, we believe, is that it will serve a community far larger than Goldsboro, a community composed of the people of Wayne, Duplin, Greene, Johnston, Lenoir and other counties of this section where so many people are bound together by the ties of kinship and friendship. It is the hope of the News-Argus, with its growing number of correspondents, to publish the news of this section and its people.

As we have announced, we have ordered the high-speed automatic printer service which is the same one supplied by the Associated Press to the largest papers in the state. And we expect to publish pictures of startling and important news events just as soon and many times sooner than the best known newspapers of North Carolina.

Your News-Argus will be a home paper, full of news of the home folks. And it will also provide the finest service available from outside, so that your home paper may be one you can be proud to show anywhere.

Below "The Goldsboro News-Argus," at the top of the front page, was "The Paper of the People in the Heart of Eastern North Carolina."

Patrick was listed as editor and general manager, and Henry as managing editor. Lucile Belk remained woman's editor, a position she held on the News.

The masthead carried the fabled motto of the Argus:

> This Argus o'er the people's rights
> Doth an eternal vigil keep;
> No soothing strains of Maia's son
> Can lull its hundred eyes to sleep.

The New Bern Sun-Journal made note of the fact that the motto had been carried on the front page of the Argus.

It must have been a severe blow to that prince of fellows, Col. Joseph E. Robinson, to see his fighting slogan disappear from its accustomed place. But it is not out of sight and will not be out of mind. It is safely tucked away atop the masthead on the editorial page. We are sure this was done as a compromise with the irrepressible Robinson who has preserved the sparkling verse for so many years.

Robinson was a lover of the classics, but the poetic motto had been the inspiration of his sister, Mary, who was a student of Greek mythology.

The Sun-Journal said the News-Argus "should step out and become one of North Carolina's outstanding afternoon newspapers. Henry Belk has developed into a very capable newspaper man. Mr. Patrick, a newcomer in the field, has the earmarks of a level-headed man and no doubt will add strength to this new project."

The leased-wire service that Patrick had promised failed to become a reality. Less than a month after the News-Argus started publication, came the stock market crash, which resulted in cancellation of the order for the automatic printer machine, and in further retrenchments as the depression deepened.

Patrick took a realistic view of the stock market crash. On October 29, after the market had begun to stabilize, following two days of tumbling prices, he had an editorial on 'Whose Stock Crash?'

The people who have lost money on the stock market, or those who are trying to make capital of some sort for themselves out of the tumbling paper values set on stocks, have many of them already set up a cry of blame on "Wall Street."

Somehow that cry seems a few years behind these times, when most of us know more about stocks than we used to, and when we have seen paper values set on other things go suddenly a-tumble.

When Florida land, bought and sold on margin almost like stocks by those who bought to sell rather than to hold, suddenly lost its inflated price tags, what street was blamed?

When stocks started going, who tried to keep the drop from being so low and fast as to kill off everybody but those who owned stocks outright, to prevent a wide panic and depression? The banking leaders of New York, who are generally meant by that term "Wall Street."

The people who boomed land in Florida were people from every Main Street in the U.S.A. The same Main Streeters bid up stocks without careful consideration of how much dividends the individual stocks actually paid, or any of the other things which would be considered by a man or woman putting out money so as to receive an income from it over a period of years. Main Street first over-expanded the stock market and then exploded it. Wall Street tried to save the fragments.

The fact that Wall Street saved the fragments for itself merely indicates that most Wall Streeters have more sense and knowledge about stocks than most Main Streeters. That is the truth that hurts.

On December 24, the News-Argus announced that it was "abandoning the experiment of publishing seven days a week" and was dropping the Sunday morning issue.

"Merchants had discovered they were getting more return on their advertising in the Wednesday and Thursday daily issues than they got from the Sunday issue," Patrick recalled. "We had rather anticipated that they would find this to be the case. In fact, we had really hoped this would be the case, because the Sunday issue was the most expensive one for us to produce."

The announcement of the change said the step was taken only because it was forced and that in taking the step, the News-Argus fell in line with "the other newspapers of North Carolina and neighboring states published in towns of similar size."

News-Argus personnel welcomed the announcement.

It is the biggest Christmas present that could have been given to members of the News-Argus staff, from the managing editor to the young chap in charge of mailing. The seven-days-a-week grind was wearing them all down and out. We believe a staff committed to putting out a good paper six days a week will be able to effect more of a real benefit than one on the seven-days-a-week treadmill.

As Goldsboro grows and its business increases, the paper may in time grow, either by beginning anew the Sunday edition or by putting out papers six mornings as well as six evenings.·

It was announced that the Sunday comic section would continue as part of the paper.

Henry Belk had started out 1929 by taking a swipe at prophets of hard times.

Talbot Patrick started out 1930 with a blast at preachers of 'Terrible Times'.

The scareheads, the worriers, the exaggerators, and the make-it-worse-at-any-cost boys, are trying to make out that these are terrible times.

That is bunk.

Nobody will deny that things could not be in far better state than they are. But any man or woman who was of age in 1900 will tell you that the first 30 years of the present century have contained some a lot worse than the year 1930 looks to be.

And most of the automobiles in this county, so far as we can make out, continue to run on gasoline that is paid for.

Patrick attributed the prevailing pessimism to an 'Emotional Pendulum'.

In crop country, such as this, the emotions are apt to be caught in a sort of seasonal pendulum swing.

Spring starts with hopes of good crops and high prices.

Summer may continue these hopes and raise them still higher. Or rain may damp them, as it takes weight off the tobacco and threatens rot in the boll for cotton,

Fall comes with high tension for the emotions, as prices vary from day to day and hopes for a good year seem one day to be little more than breaking even, and the next day to carry promise of a new model automobile.

But just before the Christmas rush begins, and before it has gathered much strength, pessimism takes a chance to swing the pendulum way down.

"There won't be a thing after Christmas" − "It will be a long pull to the fall" − even "Nobody will get much for Christmas this year" − if the crops have not been so good.

The first few days after Christmas are usually dull enough to dull many a hope.

But then comes the upswing of the pendulum. Business picks up. There is

54

little more money in circulation than anybody said there would be. Times aren't so bad, after all. And this year's crops may be the goods!

Up we go.

Let's go!

7

The News-Argus rode out the "terrible times," but it was rough sailing.

"At one point I called a meeting of the staff and told them they knew just as well as I did how much business the paper was carrying," Patrick recalled. "I said there wasn't enough work for everybody and that I was going to leave it to them whether we would keep everybody on the payroll, sharing the money that came in and working shorter hours to do what work was necessary to get out the paper, or whether they wished the staff limited to the people who would be working full-time and sharing what income there was. Then I left the room for their decision to be made in my absence. It wasn't long until they called me back and I was happy to hear that their decision was for everybody to stick together and share the work and the income. Previously all of us had had cuts in salary or pay, the biggest cuts naturally falling on those who had been the higher paid people, and that meant bigger not only in dollars but also in percentage of original pay.

"Some of the times were so hard that even though the price per paper and the money made by carriers in delivering and selling copies of the paper was much lower than it is nowadays, I knew of one family in which two sons were carriers and they brought in the only money the family had for more than a year.

"I'm glad to be able to believe that our people will never see such hard times again."

By the summer of 1932, conditions had gotten so bad that Wayne County Commissioners found it necessary to drop the services of the county farm agent and the county home demonstration agent.

Commenting on the development, Patrick said editorially that "We must turn our hopes toward getting this work back into the county as soon as possible. In a county which depends almost entirely on agriculture, as Wayne does, anything which helps farmers is of far more help to the county than anything else we can mention."

On August 16, Patrick reported that " Times may be hard and money may be tight, but the number of News-Argus subscribers is increasing. Forty-two new subscribers were added to the paper's family last week. Most of these new subscribers live in rural Wayne County. And they were added without any special efforts to obtain new business. Most of them accepted an invitation to subscribe as extended by solicitors working regularly now in rural sections. Others came by the office to give their subscriptions."

Two days later a foreign news item took one's attention off the hard times. From Edolo, Italy, came an announcement that Professor Auguste Piccard, the Swiss physicist, had brought his balloon down from a record ascent into the stratosphere of almost 10 miles.

Patrick was philosophical about the depression.

How much we miss things taken for granted, so long as we had them, has been forced home to every one of us during the last couple of years of the depression.

We never thought much about banks until the closing of a number of institutions limited banking facilities and, in addition, forced the remaining institutions to adopt policies of very limited loans.

We are learning to do without many material things, at least for a while. While we do, we might gain by turning our thoughts to the values in life which are less tangible, to ponder the sorrow which loss of them would cause, to show our friends and loved ones how deeply we realize the richness they put into our lives.

On September 10, the News-Argus sponsored a demonstration of hard times that received national attention. It was a "Hoovercart Rodeo."

Time magazine, in an illustrated story on the event, described what a Hoovercart was.

In Wayne County, N. C., a depressed farmer cut off the rear end of his disused automobile, fastened shafts to the axle, backed in a mule, went riding. Other farmers, unable to buy 23 cents gasoline with 7 cents cotton, or $5 tires with 11 cents tobacco, did the same. Soon the roads of eastern North Carolina were overrun with similar vehicles pulled by mules, horses, oxen, goats or a pair of husky boys. North Carolinians, many of whom had been Hoovercoats in 1928, transposed two letters of the term, called their conveyances Hoovercarts.

Eugene Roberts, a member of the News-Argus news staff, hit on the idea of having a Hoovercart Rodeo. He worked on the plans and Henry handled the promotion angle. So well was it publicized that it drew entries from eight counties.

"The biggest throng in Goldsboro since William Jennings Bryan's famous speech here in 1896," the News-Argus reported. "We are proud of the spirit of the farmers of Eastern North Carolina who invented Hoovercarts, or whatever you choose to call them. It is the American spirit that makes the most of what one has to get along with, in hard times as well as good."

With the Presidential election less than two months away, the event served to point up the dissatisfaction of farmers, in particular, with the Hoover administration.

A week later Hoover was quoted by the press as saying: "No man or child shall go hungry or unsheltered in the approaching winter."

The gesture came too late to stem the Democratic tide.

With Franklin D. Roosevelt at the helm, 1933 was a better year for business, including the News-Argus. That winter Patrick completed negotiations for the purchase of a brick building on North James Street, a block from the News-Argus, that had been occupied for some years by Goldsboro Grocery Company. It was remodeled to fit the needs of a newspaper plant, and was occupied by the News-Argus in May, 1934. Hundreds were on hand for the formal opening.

It was the first time in half a century that a daily newspaper in Goldsboro had had a home of its own.

A smart "Yankee" had come into the community and made the dream a reality.

World War II brought an end to Patrick's editorship of the News-Argus and the re-emergence of Henry Belk.

A second lieutenant in field artillery in World War I, Patrick had sought a commission as a reserve officer in Army Intelligence after the war ("I had done a bit of intelligence work for American officials when I was in the Pacific") but there were no openings.

"After World War II started, I was asked to come to Washington fairly early after the U.S. became involved in the war to set up a news service to small dailies and non-daily newspapers for the government. This was under Archibald MacLeish and was called the Office of Facts and Figures. Later that group was merged with a couple of others to form the Office of War Information.

"While I was at the Office of War Information I was asked by a Colonel in the Pentagon if I would accept a commission as a specialist in newspapers and news services for military government. I said I would and I was commissioned a Major. I came out as a Lieutenant Colonel."

Patrick was absent from Goldsboro from March, 1942 to February, 1946. During his absence he contributed occasional editorials to the News-Argus, but Henry Belk served as acting editor.

It was easy to detect the transition. The month after Patrick left there was an editorial that bore Henry's mark — 'Dried Fruit'.

One of the delights of visiting Grandmother on the old farm was to have a part in preparation of dried fruits.

Modern canning methods had not been invented then, but the taste for good pies was just as strong as it is now. Grandmother took care of the needs of the family during the fruit season by drying apples and peaches and storing them against the day when the fresh fruit would be gone.

Our recollection of the steps of the food-saving process is rather hazy. As we recall, however, the fruit was cut into small sections and placed on a white cloth in the hot sun to dry. After it was dried, it was stored in small quantities in, as we recall, flour sacks. The sacks were hung from rafters in the attic or storehouse in a number that assured plenty of air.

When winter came and pie was on the menu, or stewed fruit desired, Grandmother simply pulled down one of the sacks. It was easier than opening a can.

War regulations this year will curtail greatly the supply of cans for preserving foods. We expect that many a grandmother will be called on to re-instruct the children in the art of drying fruit.

On May 7, Henry had a piece on Corregidor, the island fortress in Manila Bay that had fallen to the Japanese after a heroic stand by General Jonathan Wainwright's men.

The mourning doves in the trees outside our window woke us at dawn. Over and over they repeated sadly, "Corregidor, Corregidor, Corregidor."

The wind in the tall pines caught up the refrain and whispered, "Corregidor, Corregidor."

Men of Bataan, men of Corregidor, you have lost a good fight. You have fought beyond all believing.

You have not fought in vain. You have steeled the great heart that is America to carry on in all hardship and in all sacrifice until you are vindicated.

Over and over the mourning doves called "Corregidor, Corregidor, Corregidor," and the tall pines whispered the word sadly.

On May 19, Henry voiced his opinion on gasoline hoarding.

Gasoline rationing or not, many Goldsboro filling stations may be out of gasoline by the end of the week. So the operator of one large station reports.

Reason? A flock of selfish, unpatriotic, thoughtless softies rushed to buy up gasoline and store it in tanks, cans, buckets, jars, before rationing went into effect.

These people rushed like a flock of scared sheep to buy and store gasoline secretly before they thought through their action.

If a group of us is not willing to cooperate with the desperate efforts of the government to conserve materials, if a great group of us is so reckless of the national good, in the face of our personal pleasure — if this be the case, the days that lie ahead are dark indeed.

On May 22, Henry had a word of admiration for 'Rugged Individualists.'

Z. M. L. Jeffreys, 85, Goldsboro business man, saw his first movie Wednesday night. He went because it was a private showing of a MGM feature in which his granddaughter, Ann Jeffreys, had a part.

Mr. Jeffreys is not alone in his distinction of not following the herd. There are probably a lot more men his age, or near it, around Goldsboro who have never seen a movie. Another we know of is a comparative youngster, Bill Whitted of LaGrange. At 65, he goes past a movie house nearly every day. He sometimes looks at the posters, but never goes in.

Ed Gurley of Pikeville, Rt. 2, is probably in his sixties, though we don't know his exact age. He owns several hundred acres of rich farmland out that way and has half a dozen sons settled around him, all married and doing well.

But Mr. Gurley doesn't raise cotton or tobacco. Why? Too much interference. Doesn't believe in money, anyway. He raises what he needs, principally food stuffs for man and beast.

He says the Agricultural Adjustment Administration has sent him checks at one time or another for soil improvement practices. At least, he supposes they were checks. He was told they were. But he didn't open the letters. Just threw them away. Doesn't believe in anybody telling him how to run his business. He's a good farmer, by golly, and if you don't believe it, go out and take a look at his rolling acres.

Well, we're all pretty well regimented, especially in these war days. But it is still possible for a man to be a rugged individualist. It takes more courage, of course. More bull-headedness sometimes.

But at least in this country anyone can truly say, "I am the master of my fate. I am the captain of my soul."

Henry was in the driver's seat again, but he had problems. There was a shortage of manpower on his staff, due to the war, and he had to settle for female help. Henry was not accustomed to having women around him all day, much less working a batch of them, and the experience was trying both for him and them.

"He cracked a mean whip over his women staffers," recalled Mary Medley of Wadesboro. "Somehow I stood up to him. I had endured a mean bunch of newsroom boys on the High Point Enterprise."

Miss Medley, who had the courthouse beat, was the only one of the distaff workers with newspaper experience and has since worked on a number of papers. She is also a poet of note and had served as treasurer of the North Carolina Poetry Society. She was represented in an anthology published by John F. Blair and is the author of *Dogwood Winter*, a book of verse edited by Richard Walser.

It was Henry who discovered Miss Medley's poetic talent.

"Somehow he heard I wrote poetry and demanded to see some of it. He affected a very disdainful attitude. 'Let me see it,' he said, almost jerking the manuscript from my hand. He closeted himself for a period of time. I quaked in my shoes as he came forth from his inner sanctum, fearing that I would be branded a presumptuous fool before the rest of the staff. He handed me a note which read, 'I have spent a thrilling hour reading your poetry and feel that you should seek a publisher.' His face was almost benign. He could have deep, dark days, then other days he would break out with smiles on his big, broad face that would give him an elfin and lovable quality."

Miss Medley left the News-Argus in 1946 because of deaths in her family.

"Henry thought well enough of me to call me back to help with two special editions."

The News-Argus' 75th Anniversary Edition, published in 1960 won a certificate of merit from the North Carolina Society of County and Local Historians.

Mrs. Roy J. Parker, Jr., nee Anna Mae Duke, who had the city hall beat, stood in awe of Henry at first.

"I was young and inexperienced. He said he would rather have someone without experience. He meant he could do the training, I suppose. He was hard to please and very critical, but in a constructive sort of way. When things didn't go to suit him, he would look over his glasses and yell at us. We were all in the same room and my desk was next to his. Once I was on the phone, trying to get a story, and he kept saying, 'Ask them this, ask them that.' I turned and said, 'Mr. Belk, if you will just be quiet a moment, I think I can get the story.' He laid off me after that.

"One thing he demanded was puntuality. If you were five minutes later, you would find his pocket watch lying on your typewriter to remind you of the fact. After allowing time for the lesson to sink in, he would pick up the watch without saying a word.

"Having a woman reporter at city hall was something new, but I made out all right. Chief H. T. Hines passed the word there was to be no funny business and there wasn't."

In addition to her reporting, Anna Mae acted as Henry's secretary.

"When I was turning over the job to my successor, Mr. Belk said, 'Anna, show her how to type a good letter.' "

The reason Anna quit was that she had gotten married and wanted to keep house. Henry suspected it was because of something else.

"After he had read my letter of resignation, which I laid on his desk, he asked me to come with him into an empty room where newsprint was stored. I thought, What is he up to? After we entered the room, he asked point-blank if I was pregnant. I had been married three months. 'No, sir,' I said, blushing. He then said if I would stay on, I could make my own terms. I thanked him but said I wanted to keep house.

"Mr. Belk was hard to get along with at times, but I grew to respect him."

Mary Lib Hart (Mrs. Greg Collins of Elkin) divided her time between city hall, courthouse and being Woman's Page editor, during her five years on the News-Argus. She was the youngest of the women.

"I have never felt Mr. Belk was prejudiced against women reporters. If he showed displeasure, or gave us a rough time, I am sure it was because he knew how a newspaper should be run and was forever seeking excellence. I came to think of him more as my teacher than as my employer."

One thing Mary Lib learned, in covering the city hall beat, was that Henry didn't tolerate favoritism in reporting arrests.

"Many times people came to him requesting that a certain name on the police roster be omitted from publication. Mr. Belk was always skillful enough to refuse the request and at the same time assuage the person's feelings to the point that they both walked to the door, shook hands, and separated on a friendly note. On one occasion I recognized the name of a friend of Mr. Belk's on the roster who had been arrested for driving under the influence. I asked him if he wanted me to leave the name off the publication list. He answered with an emphatic 'No!' and looked at me as if to say, 'I thought I had taught you better than that.' In spite of this, I knew it was a painful experience for him and that he suffered inwardly. Publishing the truth often brings criticism and hard feelings. Henry Belk knew this, but never, to my knowledge, did he compromise his integrity.

"In covering criminal sessions of Superior Court, I learned to separate the facts from hearsay and the manner in which court testimony is reported. If any reporter inserted his opinion as part of the news story, Mr. Belk would immediately strike it out, or would have it included in an article with a by-line, giving the reporter full responsibility for what was being said.

"Something else I learned from Mr. Belk was that if a newspaper is getting no controversy from the public, it is not a good newspaper, because people probably are not reading it. Every time we settled into a fairly quiet situation, Mr. Belk would start typing as fast as he could, only occasionally looking up over this thick-lense glasses. He was whipping up an editorial designed to bring in letters to the editor. It always worked; the editorial was criticized both pro and con, making us know the paper was being read."

Mary Lib took over the Woman's Page when Mrs. Belk became ill. Henry taught her not to say a wedding was "beautiful" unless she was there or that the dessert was "delicious" unless she had partaken of it.

"To me this made sense. Now, when I read such expressions in news columns I am immediately prejudiced against the newspaper. I know it is not honest, straightforward reporting, and that the article has not been properly edited."

While Mary Lib was Woman's Page editor, Henry asked her how she would like to go to Washington to cover the last inauguration of President Franklin D. Roosevelt.

"Even though I was young and inexperienced, I jumped at the opportunity. While on the train I received a wire from Mr. Belk saying that, because of the difficult times, the inauguration was to be a closed affair, with invitations going only to members of Congress, the White House staff and special friends. Naturally I was disappointed, but the next morning, after my arrival in Washington, something was slipped under the door of my hotel room which turned out to be an engraved invitation to the inaugural from Congressman Graham Barden. Mr. Belk had contacted him, telling of my situation. The inauguration that year was held on the back portico of the White House. I got a front page by-line story in the News-Argus giving my impressions of this rare and wonderful occasion. I keep it quietly in my memory as one of the proudest and most privileged experiences I ever had. And it was all because Mr. Belk had trust in me and was big enough to delegate the responsibility to one so young and inexperienced.

"In retrospect I have seen many times the unusual and admirable characteristics of this man. I never heard him complain about his poor health and near-blindness. He was like a fortress and in spite of his formidable demeanor he was compassionate and tolerant, always giving the other fellow a chance to express his opinion."

The News-Argus photographer and engraver during the emergency was Mickey Savage (Mrs. David Lingle) who had been trained for the job by chief photographer Bill Futrelle before he entered the service. Not being easily replaced, she came in for less of Henry's scolding than the other women, but that did not keep him from faulting her on occasion.

"He wanted perfection and that was impossible, with the equipment we had. We did the engraving by hand, which made it hard to get a good print. Mr. Belk didn't seem to understand this. I was scared of him at first. He would walk in where I was working and clear his throat to get my attention. I knew what it meant. A picture had turned out bad, or I was late making the deadline. He would grunt his displeasure and sometimes snap at me. It angered me until I discovered his bark was worse than his bite. I observed that, after jumping on the other girls, he would later find it convenient to compliment them about something. He did the same with me. After blaming me for a bad picture, he might come in the next day and say, 'You did a good job with this one.'

"He liked for you to stand up to him, but if you were wrong about anything, you had better admit it. If he was hard on you, it was usually because he liked you and thought you had possibilities. He was good at molding a person.

"He had deep compassion for his fellowman, but he didn't let it affect his sense of right and wrong. One morning a prominent citizen came in and asked him to keep it out of the paper about his son being in Mayor's Court. I didn't hear Mr. Belk's response, but after the man left he was furious. He said the request was degrading. 'I felt for him, but why should his son be given any more consideration than any other man's son?' he said."

Mrs. Lingle went to see Henry at a nursing home two weeks before his death.

"He had been up for a while and they were putting him back to bed. It distressed me to see how he had wasted away. He complained of his feet being cold. I massaged them for him until he said they felt warmer. He was very appreciative. I loved the man. He was a wonderful person."

On April 12, 1945, the News-Argus got out a special edition. Two words screamed across its front page: ROOSEVELT DIES!

The next day Henry editorialized on the shattering event.

Let not your hearts be troubled. God moves in a mysterious way His wonders to perform.

Our great leader, Franklin Delano Roosevelt, is gone.

Roosevelt was uncommon among men. He was born to the ways of the aristocrat, with a silver spoon in his mouth, as we are wont to say. Men born of such background too often know only the soft comforts of life, the easy way, the carousing way, the way of selfishness and personal consideration only.

Roosevelt was unique in that he departed completely from what we accept as the pattern.

As a beginner in politics, he exhibited unusual interest and sincerity in the little people.

Followed by a brilliant career, and in the mid-span of life he was crippled by infantile paralysis. A lesser heart would have broken and shriveled under the ordeal. Not so the great-souled Roosevelt. Out of that experience he won back health and a deeper realization of the need for better ways for the common man.

All of us recall, as if yesterday, the new hope he gave us when he became our leader in the depths of the depression, when all around us men were losing their nerve and the way seemed dark and dreary. Our only enemy was fear, he said, and smiled. We caught the glow, sang, "Happy Days Are Here Again," not because there was any great change immediately accomplished, but because he had banished fear and knew that man, in his own right, is the ruler of his destiny.

Came the New Deal honeymoon and then darkening confusion.

Grew the war clouds over Europe. The menace of Hitler. Nations overrun by the Nazis. Roosevelt here again proved the man and the time had met, as if to lead the world from the wilderness. He directed the mind of this nation in such a channel that we were partly ready when the blow came. After Pearl Harbor, the Commander in Chief organized such a group of men, backed by the nation, that the world gazed in astonishment at the miracles America performed.

The victory is near. A victory that Roosevelt, more than any other man, made possible. In a few days now, representatives of all nations of the Allies will meet in San Francisco to work toward a world peace structure. Roosevelt had planned to be there. He will be there in spirit, his marvelous soul — a soul which inspired the little people and the persecuted people to see the stars and hope.

We must close ranks around the memory of the Chief who is gone and hold up his dead hands to the end that his life may bring him a memorial of temporal peace.

Let not your hearts be troubled.

President Truman is undersold to the nation. He demonstrated qualities of greatness when he served as the head of the investigating committee. What he can do, without pomp or display, he showed under those trying times.

We are not afraid because of his experience. We know that, as well as any other man, except the one who is gone, he had a fine understanding of the issues at home and abroad.

We are not afraid. He is a modest man. He is a sincere man. He is our President.

We are the people. If America falls, it will be because the people fall. The death of Roosevelt has brought us together with a oneness not seen since Pearl Harbor.

Let not your hearts be troubled.

8

Talbot Patrick returned from Washington in February, 1946.

"Then the Patrick family bought out the Huckle family in Rock Hill and I took charge as editor of the Evening Herald on July 1, 1947. For about a year and a half I commuted between Goldsboro and Rock Hill. My family moved to Rock Hill about the beginning of 1948. My commuting was due to the fact that I had a man lined up to be general manager of the News-Argus, but at the last minute he went instead to Georgia to become publisher of a small paper there, and I was some time trying to find a satisfactory man to head up the business management side of the News-Argus."

Patrick turned over the editorship of the News-Argus to Henry Belk in 1949, while still the owner of the paper.

Henry continued on as editor when the paper changed hands on September 30, 1953. Patrick sold it to the Wayne Printing Company, Inc., headed by Hal H. Tanner, who became the publisher. Tanner came to Goldsboro from Spartanburg, S. C., where he had been business manager of the Herald-Journal newspapers.

Henry was made vice president of Wayne Printing Company.

In relinquishing control of the News-Argus, Patrick said:

For me, personally, this is a great wrench. For nearly 25 years, the News-Argus has meant much in my life. I believe that this change starts a new step forward by the News-Argus in its services to its readers and advertisers. Under the new ownership the paper will be free to progress without problems arising out of a divided ownership.

Henry was a stout defender of 'the people's rights', but he didn't stick his neck out often in connection with controversial local issues. An exception was his advocacy of Alcoholic Beverage Control stores for Wayne County in 1949, the year he became editor of the Goldsboro News-Argus.

Proponents of liquor stores had lost by less than 100 votes in an election held in 1937. Now, twelve years later, they had high hopes of victory. With the coming of Seymour Johnson Air Force Base, Goldsboro's population had increased substantially and it was generally expected that the bulk of the newcomers would vote wet. A big urban approval was needed to offset the dry rural vote.

Another thing that the proponents had going for them was the money being funneled out of Wayne by liquor stores in adjoining counties. Goldsboro imbibers practically kept up the store in LaGrange. Why should Wayne money go to support Lenoir County, a lot of voters asked.

Proponents didn't play up the money angle, however. Liquor money had an evil connotation. Instead, emphasis was placed on law-and-order benefits that would accrue from ABC stores. Scapegoat of the argument was the insidious blind tiger who plied his trade in dark alleys and was often the purveyor of poisonous whiskey. ABC stores would do away with the blind tiger, it was argued, or at least sharply curtail his activities.

It was this line of argument that Henry adopted in coming out for ABC stores. On May 13, about two weeks before the election, he ran an editorial titled 'Let's Give a Trial to ABC'.

Wayne County has never tried the ABC system to bring alcoholic sale under control by law.

While we are on the books as dry territory, we are far from being dry.

A man with tears in his eyes told us yesterday that he had been under the influence of liquor almost constantly for 10 months. He is making a valiant effort to stop drinking. He said that it was buying drinks at blind tiger places in and around Goldsboro that started him down. He said in one community in which there is a very splendid church there are nine bootleggers. He said that these bootleggers even sell to children.

Twenty-five North Carolina counties now have the ABC system.

Wilson, Greene and Lenoir counties, which touch Wayne, have the ABC system.

You know that Wayne people buy more liquor at LaGrange than Lenoir people buy. You know that this is true also for Black Creek in Wilson County.

We do not say that the ABC system will stop all bootlegging.

We do believe that the ABC system will bring marked improvement in conditions as they now exist.

We have tried what we now have for many years. It has failed completely.

Let's give the ABC system an honest try. The ABC system would provide money for county-wide enforcement of the liquor laws. We do not have this now.

If we give ABC an honest try and a majority agree, after that try, that it has not worked, we can call for another vote and do away with it.

Apparently Henry was not long discovering that he had gotten out on a limb. Three days later he had an editorial titled 'It Can Be a Lonely Job'.

Being an editor in a city the size of Goldsboro can at times be a very lonely job.

The job is so personal in a town where everybody knows everybody else.

The editor spots a group of friends chatting on the street. He is in no particular hurry. He stops to pass the time.

The friends look just a little embarrassed. They fall suddenly quiet. Or some brave sould makes an ineffectual effort to start a conversation about the weather, or what time it is.

The little knot breaks up.

The editor feels lonely.

Of course he knows that the folks were afraid to go on with what they were talking about. They were afraid it would be in the paper . . . They probably wanted it in the paper, but they didn't want to be a party to getting it in the paper.

Of course the editor might escape the alone feeling by aligning himself completely and fully with some certain group, block, faction or clique. With them he would be a fellow-well-met.

But if the editor does his job of trying honestly and fairly to present all sides with equal justice, he can't keep face and faith with himself by being entirely one-sided.

An editor concerned with his responsibilities had better be lonely with the crowd than lonely with himself.

Or the editor could just print material that would never offend anybody anytime, anywhere.

If he did that, he and the paper would lose respect and the editor would lose respect for himself.

It can be a lonely job.

If Henry had any supporters for his ABC stand, they were not very vocal. Almost all letters sent in to the editor expressed opposition to the ABC stores.

Predictably some of Henry's fellow Baptists were disappointed in him. Baptists formed the core of the opposition.

The election was lost before the vote came. Dries, who apparently had been caught off-guard in the 1937 election, made dure the close call wouldn't be repeated. Mass meetings were held all over the county and anti-liquor support was sought from old and young alike. A letter was published in the News-Argus signed by 78 students at Goldsboro High School. "We consider the ABC stores a menace and disgrace," it said.

On the Sunday before the election a city-wide mass meeting was held at First Baptist Church. Speakers included Bishop W. W. Peele, of the North Carolina Methodist Conference, and Judge Francis Clarkson of Charlotte, president of the Allied Church League.

On the eve of the election the bedraggled News-Argus editor commented editorially: "There is one point on which both sides are agreed. Humanity would be infinitely better off without liquor of any kind."

Wayne residents who couldn't afford to go to LaGrange or Black Creek would have to continue to get along with the bootleg kind. The issue was defeated by a vote of 4569 to 3505.

"Wayne voters said in no uncertain terms that they will have nothing to do with establishing ABC stores in the county," Henry noted editorially the day after the election.

Thus was the issue laid to rest, for the time being, anyway. Nobody much cared. A lot of good people preferred traveling to LaGrange to being seen entering a liquor store at home. What would their friends say?

Henry wasn't too put out. You couldn't win them all. Besides, he was becoming known outside Goldsboro. In 1947 he had become a trustee of East Carolina College. In 1944-45 he had been president of the Eastern North Carolina Press Association. In 1942 he had started his long role in state affairs by serving as secretary of the North Carolina Railroad.

The wets had lost twice, but they were far from giving up. Ten years later — in 1959 — they tried again. This time Henry stayed on the sideline, as far as taking a positive stand.

The wets had no trouble getting enough names to call an election. On April 10, they presented a petition carrying 2300 signatures — almost double the number required — to the Wayne Board of Elections. The number had risen to 2800 by April 14, when the Board ordered an election for June 2.

The dries went into action the day the petition was presented. The action was taken note of by the News-Argus the following day.

The powerful Wayne County Sunday School Association went on record last night opposing Alcoholic Beverage Control stores. In a standing vote, an overwhelming majority of the 215 members attending the spring meeting at St. Paul Methodist Church joined the past president, J. D. Hines, in a motion condemning the ABC system. The Rev. Waldo Early, pastor of Adamsville Baptist Church and speaker for the program, said it was one time he didn't mind having the bootleggers voting on his side.

On May 21, as the election drew near, a rally by anti-ABC forces was held at Madison Avenue Baptist Church. About 75 persons attended. Speakers included Captain James Hipps, of the Salvation Army, who described liquor as "a rattlesnake ready to strike."

The next day Editor Belk commended the lack of bitterness the campaign had generated.

We are pleased with the manner in which both sides are conducting themselves in the ABC campaign. Both sides are working steadily and fairly.

We have heard of no bitterness or undue pressure being used anywhere. We hope that this will be the case right up to the day of voting and to the counting of the last vote and beyond. Each side is working hard, that is sure, but the issues are not being made personal issues.

The campaign in its welcome lack of bitterness and personal attacks is different from that 10 years ago. All should be pleased by this.

We should have, and we believe we will have, a large vote. Every voter should study the question as best he can and decide on the basis of logic and reason how he shall vote. No voter should be persuaded by group action, or the personal insistence of any individual as to how he will vote.

No man, it seems to us, should use pressure or position of occupation, calling profession, activity or job to compel others to think as he does.

No man should be frightened away from the polls because he is afraid of what someone else may think or ask about his vote.

On May 27, the wet forces held a rally of their own, attended largely by Goldsboro businessmen. Speaker for the occasion was Chevs Kerr of Clinton, a member of the Sampson County ABC Board and described as a "church and school leader."

"A vote for the ABC system is an honest attempt to improve the intolerable situation of bootleg sales you have now," Kerr was quoted by the News-Argus as saying. "If you vote against legal control, you are casting your vote to continue bootlegging and all of its allied vices . . . If alcohol should be abolished by legislation, so that all alcoholics would be cured because they couldn't get it, most people who have dedicated their lives to serving the cause of good would vote to abolish it."

On June 1, the day before the election, the News-Argus presented the arguments of 'Pros' and 'Cons' side by side on the front page. The presentation seemed to be slanted in favor of the 'Pros'.

It must be conceded by the opposition that:

ABC stores surround Wayne County, making alcohol available here.
Adjoining counties are deriving huge profits from Wayne County citizens.
Within the county, bootleggers and moonshiners are enriching themselves.
Wayne County ranks 22nd in the production of moonshine liquor in North Carolina.

Since the issue was defeated in 1949, the liquor situation has grown steadily worse.

Elsewhere was an editorial titled 'Take It Easy, Please'.

The world will still be here after the ABC election tomorrow. We must still live with our friends. Let us not take the matter too seriously. Let's don't run up our blood pressure. Let's don't feed our ulcers.

The man who views it differently from you is just as sincere and honest as you are. Those whom the gods would destroy they first make mad. Your vote counts just as much when you cast it with happiness as when you cast it with bitter recrimination against the man who is voting differently from you. Take it easy.

No matter which way the ABC vote falls tomorrow, let us make a pledge. Each of us in his own way and in his own field will join in a sustained and organized and continuing effort to teach that alcohol is dangerous, damaging and destructive.

Dries lost a little from their showing in the 1949 election but were able to run up a vote of 4507 to 3857.

"Opponents of the A.B.C. system won a clear-cut victory," Editor Belk said the next day. "The people said firmly with the ballot, that great weapon of democracy, that they cannot approve the system for Wayne County. These facts stand out. The same precincts that voted for ABC 10 years ago voted for ABC Tuesday. The same precincts that voted against ABC 10 years ago voted against ABC Tuesday. Congratulations are in order to those who led the successful fight. They won because they represented the true feeling of the people."

Editor Belk had other things on his mind when still another ABC election was held in 1964. There was a $2.5 million bond election coming up for Construction of a new Wayne Memorial Hospital and, more immediately, Wayne County Commissioners, joined by Goldboro's industrial Committee of 100, had scheduled an Industry Appreciation Week.

The appreciation event is a good time to make a point which this paper has made over the years. We must turn to our own men, our own brains, and our own capital for a speedier progress toward industry than is possible by always expecting to bring in plants and factories from the outside.

We want more from the outside. We shall give them every cooperation and welcome, but we must do it ourselves if we are to take advantage of our resources and responsibilities. Our surplus labor, our rich assets of forest, field and stream, our tremendous agricultural output, our balance in agriculture — all these give us a base that few counties can equal.

But before we can realize on these opportunities, we must give more attention to industry. We must think industry, talk industry. We must depart from the time-worn routine of depending on tobacco, of putting our capital in tobacco farms. Tobacco as a money source is in danger. The next quarter of a century will see tobacco planting cut to a fraction of what it is today.

But we can lift ourselves if we put our minds to it. We can utilize our crops and products for processing, and we can on our own initiative and leadership move into fields that are opening up with this changing world.

But if we give only a token attention to applying our money and brains to expanding industry, we shall be left at the post. We must do the big job ourselves.

While Henry was skirting the ABC issue, dries were pouring out their feelings in letters to the News-Argus.

"The name Alcoholic Beverage Control is deceiving. Having the stores will only control where the liquor may be sold."

"How long can Christian people continue to support by their silence and their ballots the greatest form of slavery in America?"

"I am confident it is one of the worst things that could happen in Wayne County."

"Once we vote for ABC stores, they will never be voted out."

The News-Argus noted, on the eve of the election, that "an expected 10,000 Wayne County voters will go to the polls tomorrow to decide whether the county will adopt the alcoholic beverage control system. More than 22,000 are registered — 1300 since the issue was proposed. This year's campaign has gained momentum in the closing days. Both ABC and anti-ABC forces have stepped up their tempo."

Editorially speaking, Henry urged readers to 'Vote Your Conviction.'

You should search your heart and to the best of your knowledge vote your conviction in the referendum. None of us should be swayed by fear of what someone else may think.

All should be pleased with the calm and moderate manner in which this campaign has been conducted. On the surface, at least, no one got mad at anyone else.

Public apathy and lack of cooperation in law enforcement have allowed moonshining and distilling in Wayne to put our county near the top in these dangerous and illegal practices. The bootlegger and the moonshiner could not flower so fragrantly among us if we gave proper support to enforcement.

We shall vote for control. But we do not seek to tell any man how he should vote. Let your best judgment do that.

Saturday, April 3, was election day. Sunday's News-Argus trumpeted the results in big headlines on the front page.

WAYNE FAVORS ABC
CITIES SWING VOTE

Wayne County went wet yesterday with an unofficial vote of 5859 for and 5152 against. A total of 11,011 went to the polls.

Goldsboro, Mt. Olive and Fremont swung the election. Mt. Olive broke with tradition and voted for ABC 637-614. Goldsboro voted 3457-1989, and Fremont's vote was 274-118.

The urban wets had finally prevailed over the rural dries.

It was bad news to many good church people, especially the militant Baptists.

For Baptist Henry Belk, it must have brought a sense of relief. Now he could turn his editorial abilities to less divisive issues.

9

Henry walked hand in hand with adversity all his life.

"I have been a man of sorrow and acquainted with grief," he once wrote.

The great tragedy in his life was the death of his only child, Marie, who was killed in an automobile accident at the age of 25. Henry is buried beside her in Goldsboro's Willow Dale Cemetery.

The tragic event occurred on February 28, 1950. Marie and her husband of 12 months, Dr. Edgar L. Lipton, were leaving Chicago to come to Goldsboro on a visit. At Lansing, a suburb of Chicago, their car skidded on ice and struck an utility pole. A door flew open and Marie fell out, striking her head on the pavement. She suffered a fractured skull and died enroute to a hospital.

She had been living in Chicago since her marriage to Dr. Lipton the previous February. He was a resident in psychiatry at a Veterans Administration hospital. She had been employed as a caseworker for the Cathedral Shelter, an Episcopal welfare organization.

The couple had met in Winston-Salem, where Marie was working for the Winston-Salem Journal and Dr. Lipton was an intern at the Baptist Hospital. He was a graduate of the Bowman Gray School of Medicine at Wake Forest University.

Marie had been a feature writer for the Journal since her graduation from Woman's College of the University of North Carolina in Greensboro in 1945.

At Women's College she was a member of Phi Beta Kappa, and during her junior and senior years was listed in Who's Who Among Students in American Universities and Colleges. She was an associate editor of the college newspaper. She majored in sociology.

Marie had studied sociology at Goldsboro High School and was on the staff of the Hi-News. She participated in dramatics and was in the Junior Play. She was a beautiful brunette, long-legged and lynx-eyed like Lauren Bacall.

"I thought she looked like Veronica Lake, the way she let her hair come down over one eye," said a male admirer.

The graduation write-up referred to Marie's "glamorous hair."

There were also references to her "figure" and her "lovely wardrobe."

"She looked like a model," said a classmate, Mrs. Elizabeth Royall Sutton. "She had a knack for using clothes. I remember she took a bathing suit of her mother's and made it over, using a sash. I would say she was more mature in her thinking than the rest of us. She was liberal-minded and interested in what was going on in the world."

"She was the brainy one, but that didn't detract from her popularity," said another classmate, Mrs. Hilda Longest Smith.

Marie was popular with the boys and "a little flirtatious," but didn't have any heartthrobs over any of them. It was the other way around.

"I was madly in love with her, but she just laughed it off," said Graves Lewis, vice president of Smith Hardware Company. "She had a mischievous sense of humor. We dated, but often it was double-dating. Not many of us had cars. We had competition from the boys at Seymour Johnson Air Force Base, when it opened. The girls went for the airmen."

Apparently Marie didn't "go" for anybody until she met Dr. Lipton, who was a year older than she. He had grown up in New York City and was the sophisticated, intellectual type that would have appealed to one of her qualities.

Marie brought the doctor to Goldsboro on a weekend for her parents to meet him.

"He returned to Winston-Salem on Sunday afternoon," Mrs. Belk recalled. "After he left, Marie said to us, 'Would you accept Ed Lipton as a son-in-law?' I replied, 'We will accept and love whomever you accept and love.' "

The wedding was held at the Belk home in the presence of members of the two families. The Rev. A. J. Smith, pastor of First Baptist Church, performed the ceremony. Now, a year later, he would conduct Marie's funeral.

Marie hadn't been home since her marriage and the visit was eagerly awaited by her parents.

"Lucile told me on the phone that she was cooking up everything Marie liked," said Miss Rebecca Slocumb, at whose home the Belks had lived after they came to Goldsboro.

Goldsboro was stunned by Marie's tragic death and a great outpouring of sympathy went to her parents.

The News-Argus staff wrote their own editorial, which was carried in a box on the front page.

Words of sympathy and kindness have often been written in this column at the death of one who was known and loved by Goldsboro people.

Those of us in the News-Argus family who knew Marie through the years, and those of us who knew her only as the beloved daughter of the editor and Mrs. Henry Belk, can only hope that a Providential care will aid them at this time when sorrow is so deep.

Funeral services were held at the modest Belk home, which became almost a shrine during the years. A large crowd overflowed into the yard and upon the sidewalk.

The News-Argus account of the service was simple.

Her pastor, the Rev. A.J. Smith, used scriptural passages and lines of poetry in the service. A quartet of members of the choir of First Baptist Church, of which Mrs. Lipton was a member, sang. Hundreds of friends of the family from Goldsboro and out of town attended the services at the home and at the cemetery. Pallbearers were high school friends of Mrs. Lipton.

Henry went through the ordeal stoically.

"He was a tower of strength," said Mrs. A. J. Smith, wife of the pastor. "Before the service he told Lucile, 'I am depending on you to keep me from breaking down.' Actually, he was trying to bolster her strength."

Henry kept his anguish from the public eye. Exchange matter took over his editorial column for a few days, then he was back at his desk as usual.

The only revelation of his feelings was in a short piece on 'Bright Greetings from Little Child'.

She was just a little girl, three, we would say, clad in a gay yellow outfit with matching cap. As we passed, she smiled with vivid beauty and said "Hey!" And despite our personal gloom, the moment and the day were brighter.

For support, Henry turned to his pastor and friend, 'Al' Smith. There was a close personal relationship between them. Pastor Smith had "immersed" Henry when he joined First Baptist Church, after coming to Goldsboro, and the Belks were frequent guests of the Smiths at their summer cottage in Swansboro.

"After Marie's death, Henry got my husband to go on walks with him," Mrs. Smith recalled. "He said he couldn't sit still. Sometimes they would walk out in the country."

Perhaps it was one of the walks that Henry referred to, on March 18, in 'We Are Never Alone'.

In case you are optimistic, spring is not so far away. It won't be long until people are spending more and more time outdoors in the warm air, leaving behind the stoves and the fireplaces.

In a way we regret to see winter go. There's something about a clear cold day that does your blood good, and if you're wearing warm clothing, there's nothing better than a brisk walk under the trees and through the countryside.

Which brings us to a point.

We hate to see people out walking with heads cast forward and eyes on the ground. They are missing more then they realize. If they walk preoccupied in something or another that should have been left with their work, they aren't getting the full benefit of the day.

When you walk through the park or into a wooded area on a good winter day, you are far from alone. Little birds and animals are all around and they are frequently more friendly than you think. Squirrels we have a particular liking for. On a cold day they scamper around in the trees like high-flying acrobats, or form themselves into tiny balls of fir way up in the tree on a limb.

On April 25, Henry had a piece about 'Adventure On a Woods Walk'.

For a thrilling adventure, go walking with a four-year-old boy, a two-year-old girl, and their investigative cocker.

I tried it with Stevie, Diane and Rusty. Rusty is their dog. But there is nothing rusty about him.

We headed into the path to the north of the old Weil pecan grove. Charles Norwood had piled brick near the path for a couple of houses he is building in Woodford. Of course Stevie wanted to play Superman and fly on top of the bricks. Certainly Diane wouldn't let Stevie do anything that she couldn't. They were scampering about the brick pile before I hardly knew what was happening. Rusty wagged his stumpy tail in appreciation of their prehensile antics.

We plunged deeper into the overgrown path.

"Maybe we'll scare up a young rabbit," I remarked.

None of the three, not even Rusty, seemed interested. Rusty was busy poking his nose into every weed, bush, clump of grass or vine. He was hunting something, but it wasn't rabbits. Occasionally he gave a sniff that seemed to be an expression of disgust.

Birds hidden in the branches shook the leaves with a light rustling noise.

Stevie, Diane, Rusty and I turned bird watchers. None of us turned out to be a bird spotter.

We came to "Grandma's Path". It leads invitingly into a grove of stately pines. Stevie was all for going down its cool archway. Diane thought little of it. Rusty was too busy smelling to care.

You wouldn't think it could be so difficult to keep two small children and one dog under eye view.

We came to "Our Tree". A big limb has grown at right angles at a height of about four feet. On that limb the children of Edgewood play, have been doing it for years. Mounting it, they are a bucking bronco, if they are boys, and they ride away in great haste after the bad man, or they turn their eyes skyward and float off on some fleecy cloud, if they are girls, and are imaginative. The limb forks toward the end, affording a safe hold.

I lifted Stevie onto the perch, held him securely. He took hold of the fork and it was a bridle. He turned into Billy the Kid, pulled an imaginative six shooter from his holster, shot up the place, rode off with a thunder of hoof beats (That's the way the radio script reader should have it — "thunder of hoof beats").

Diane felt left out. There was Stevie, riding heel for leather, and she was left behind. So I boosted her to the perch. She fastened both arms around Stevie and rode off with him in great glee.

That kept up until there was a yelp from Rusty who had been making some surveys of his own. He had found a deep ditch with about 18 inches of water in the bottom. It was a chokingly hot day and Rusty wanted to cool off.

But with his short legs he couldn't jump to the bank. He was terrified. He could have gone either up or down the ditch a few feet and walked out safely. But having gone in at that spot, he knew he had to come out there.

Time after time he lunged for the top. Each time he barely missed and fell back into the water, clawing the soft bank with his feet as he slipped back. I tried to persuade him to go up the ditch where he could climb out. So did Stevie. So did Diane. Rusty would have none of it.

There was nothing to do but to take off my shoes, my socks, roll up the trousers legs, get into the stream and help him out.

So I did, picking up some ounces of good earth on the seat of my pants, on my hands, my legs. Stevie and Diane wanted to help and I trembled lest they roll in and get their lovely clothes soiled. I solved that by holding them off with my left hand while I reached for Rusty with the right.

We all laughed, including Rusty, when he was out of the ditch.

Tired and hot, we turned back along the path.

For an adventure, go walking in a woods with two lively youngsters and their livelier dog.

On one of the walks with Pastor Smith, Henry noticed that the minister appeared to be short of breath.

"Are you well, Al?" Henry asked.

"No, Henry, I'm not," the pastor replied.

Weeks later he was dead.

"Henry was remorseful, thinking he had contributed to my husband's death," Mrs. Smith said. "I assured him such was not the case, that Al had a history of heart trouble. He had gotten athlete's heart from playing football in college."

Smith died May 27, several days after undergoing a kidney operation. "Death was due to a heart condition aggravated by the strain of the operation," the News-Argus reported.

The article referred to Smith as "the loved and honored pastor of Goldsboro's First Baptist Church. An outstanding minister, teacher and layman, Mr. Smith came to North Carolina from Missouri, his native state."

Smith had observed his 24th anniversary as pastor of the Goldsboro church on May 6. Henry had heralded the occasion with an editorial titled 'Noting An Anniversary'.

The first Sunday in May, 1926, a young man preached his first sermon as pastor of the First Baptist Church in Goldsboro.

He was Rev. A. J. Smith. With his wife and three daughters, he had arrived a few days before from the mountain town of Franklin.

On Sunday, Rev. A. J. Smith will pass his 24th anniversary as pastor of the church. To Al Smith, Sunday will be just another day of serving his church and his people. But to members of the church and hundreds in the community, it will be a day of deep significance.

Mr. Smith has given broad, deep and devoted service to his own church people and to the community. He is a man of breadth and tolerance. Inside and outside his church he has touched thousands of people and always for the good.

The Baptist pastor is a buoyant and laughing spirit. To have converse with him is to feel a new courage and a new faith that God is in his heaven and all is right with the world. In his comforting of the sick, cheering the bereaved, and lending a helping and strengthening hand to the weak, Mr. Smith has truly shown others the untouched treasure of power that belongs to the man of faith.

And he has none of the pontificating holier-than-thou attitude that sometimes digs a ditch between the cloth and the man on the street.

Henry's anniversary tribute was read at the funeral service, which was "notable for its simple faith and assurance," The News-Argus said.

It seemed that the beloved pastor had prepared the service of worship himself. The body had lain in state at the church over the weekend. Long lines of saddened friends from all churches and all walks of life passed in silence before his bier. Services went on as usual at the church Sunday, as Mr. Smith would have wished. There was a feeling of emptiness as the worshipers missed their beloved pastor from the place he had filled for 24 years. Many wiped tears from their eyes as they silently took their places in the church.

Henry did not editorialize on the pastor's passing. He had said it all in the anniversary tribute and was too overcome to say more. Smith had been his source of strength in Marie's death. Now, three months later, he was dead.

The pastor had done more than build up Henry's religious faith. He had nurtured his faith in humanity.

At 'Wee Hame', the Smith cottage at Swansboro, Henry relaxed, pondered the imponderables, and fished from the bank of the White Oak River.

Actually, he did less fishing than writing about it.

Fishing is popular because fisher folk are so truthful. It is almost impossible to find a fisherman who exaggerates or tells fibs. Preacher A. J. Smith, bless his memory, comes to mind. He was, for a generation, the beloved pastor of First Baptist Church of Goldsboro. He loved his church, his Lord, his family, his fellowman and his fishing. And he always told the truth, regardless. He maintained a fishing lodge at Swansboro, not only for his own relaxation, but his friends were always welcome.

Once, so the story goes, he went to his lodge on a fishing trip; had no luck at all; did not catch a thing with scales. On his way back he stopped at Smith's store in Adamsville, bought four pounds of trout, had them dressed and neatly wrapped. He stepped back when the clerk offered the package to him. "Toss them to me," he said. "I want it to be the truth when I say I caught them."

Some weeks after Smith's death, Henry had a piece about a "sermon" the pastor had left behind in his will.

One of the finest sermons, and one which was indeed typical of his long ministry in Goldsboro, was left behind to be read after his death by Pastor Alfred Smith.

The beloved minister composed what was his last written sermon, in his will. It was five days before his death last May. The message, directed to his children and their children's children, is so fitting to the pastor's way of life that it brings to mind his happy work and faith.

His words could well be carved in stone, so that they might be regarded and cherished permanently.

Here is the way he put it:

"To my children, their children and children's children, I commend a living and explorative faith in God and His Eternal Goodness as revealed and exemplified in our Lord and Savior, Jesus Christ, of whom I testify that His Way is the way of meaningful life which makes death insignificant."

A Girl Scout campership was established in Marie's memory by her parents, assisted by Dr. Lipton. The Belks paid for sending one girl to camp each summer until income from the fund was self-sufficient. The Marie Belk Lipton Campership Fund has grown through the years until it now supports three or four girls at camp.

A warm relationship has remained between the Belks and their son-in-law. Dr. Lipton remarried and adopted two children, one of whom was named Rose Marie for his two wives. He married again after his second wife died and adopted another child. The Belks looked on all of them as their grandchildren.

10

Henry had been dealt a one-two punch, but had not been knocked out. He was no stranger to the buffetings of fate and this one he weathered with characteristic fortitude. Early in July, still bleeding from his wounds, he attended the annual convention of the North Carolina Press Association in Asheville, at which he was elected Association president for the coming year. The recognition must have been as a balm to his spirit.

The office gave Henry a state-wide forum for airing his views in matters that were important to him. In the president's column of the Association's monthly publication, "The North Carolina Press," he had something to say about the development of the state ports at Morehead City and Wilmington.

This should be a subject in which all newspaper people in the state should be interested. Development of adequate port facilities for North Carolina should help business in every part of the state. Sometimes we think of the ports program as being local to the ports themselves and to the eastern half of the state. This is not the case. Lack of adequate port facilities and the accompanying benefit of water transportation has long held back the growth of the state.

In another of his columns, Henry stressed the need of better news coverage for Negroes.

Did you editors ever have any twinges of conscience about the manner and scope of coverage you give Negro citizens of your community? I do.

For many years the News-Argus has followed the policy of giving due coverage to outstanding accomplishments of Negro citizens. When they stage their livestock shows, we picture the prize winners just as we do the white stock show winners. When a 4-H Negro boy or girl is selected as a district winner or as a state winner, we carry his or her picture with a story on the accomplishment. We regularly print the pictures of graduating classes of our local and county Negro schools. Lately we have begun a series of feature stories dealing with successful Negro citizens.

Nevertheless, we realize that we are not covering Negro news in the routine manner which it should have, with 40 percent of the population in our section being Negro.

We run a daily column titled "Negro News." It averages about 10 inches a day except on Saturday when it runs about 21 inches. We started the column about 25 years ago. Immediately a committee from a local order waited on us and told us we would have to discontinue the column. We tried to point out that the column gave news of an important segment of our population and that it was only fair to print it. We resisted the demand of the committee and by now the demand is forgotten except in our office. The column has approved standing with all of our people.

When the Jaycees in Goldsboro staged a talent contest, a Negro girl showed. She sang before the white audience. Their applause gave her first place in the contest. We used her picture on the front page.

However, we do not have a Negro reporter assigned to cover Negro news. So far as we know, the Winston-Salem papers are the only North Carolina papers of general circulation that have a Negro reporter on the staff. Some day, when the News-Argus can afford it, we want to see a Negro reporter covering the news of his race for our paper.

By and large, North Carolina papers are not adequately and systematically covering Negro news. We ought to do better.

Henry used the theme in his farewell address to the N. C. Press Association at Wrightsville Beach, when he stepped down as president in August, 1951. Associated Press carried a summary of remarks.

The North Carolina Press was challenged today to adopt a "sane and well-founded attitude on the new and pressing theme of race relations."

The challenge was made by Henry Belk, retiring president of the N. C. Press Association.

Regarding race relations, Belk said: "If our papers are sober, yet factual, in their approach, we can make a contribution here that can help solve with least friction a matter that must be solved.

"I think most of us need to recognize the news value of what our Negro subscribers are doing and to give adequate coverage in type and pictures to this news. Indeed, if a paper is published in a section that has a large percent of Negro population, it is not serving advertisers adequately unless this large percent is adequately represented in the news columns.

"I am not arguing that you rush hell-bent into something you have not attempted before. Too rapid a change might create friction which could well defeat the social gains of such a plan. But by slow degrees we can change our attitudes and policies. We will, in so doing, make our newspapers better sales mediums for the advertisers and more nearly do justice to a large group of our citizens now largely unnoticed in our press.

A decade later, blacks, as they preferred to be called, were demanding more than routine press coverage, and the time for change of attitudes and policies by slow degrees on the part of whites had run out. Blacks wanted equality of opportunity, not mere recognition of individual accomplishment, such as Henry's salute to a black Goldsboro educator in April, 1961.

H. V. Brown of Goldsboro has made a real contribution to history in his book on "Education of Negroes in North Carolina". The work represents research and study over many years. It represents most of the time since he retired as principal of Dillard High School in Goldsboro after 34 years.   .

The book will come from the press on May 15. It is a volume which should be on the shelves of libraries in all high schools and colleges in North Carolina.

It is of interest, we think, that the University of North Carolina Press took a very long look at the manuscript before returning it. Suggestion of the Press was that it needed a bit more of the professional touch of the trained historical writer.

We read much of the book in manuscript and found it well organized and detailed.

Dr. Hugh Lefler, in his address as president of the North Carolina Literary and Historical Association last December, cited the sad gap in historical research and publication in North Carolina. Professor Brown's book fills one gap and will be valuable to the history student who comes later.

In 1962, Henry took note of Negro industries that were springing up in Eastern North Carolina.

There is a large surplus of labor in Eastern North Carolina. A majority of the people in the labor surplus pool are Negroes. More power, then, to a new movement among Negroes in the agricultural East. Negroes, on their own initiative and purpose, are moving out to establish their own industries.

The organized groups to get into industry can look to the past for encouragement in their efforts. Durham leaders more than 50 years ago formed an insurance company which is now the largest of its kind in the world. Durham also has fine examples of successful establishment of banks and savings and loan associations with Negroes as the owners and operators.

Organization of Negro-owned companies and plants in no way mitigates against the extension of job opportunities in all businesses and crafts and professions. The new development, indeed, can be expected to be of help in furthering new attitudes and opportunities all around.

Lack of job opportunities was one of the main reasons for the black demonstrations that were moving across North Carolina.

In August, 1963, Henry had a column in which he sought to rationalize the demonstrations in terms of "Negro Psychology"

The generally held view that the Negro is a happy, contented, relaxed and little concerned individual has been exploded.

We have come to understand the contrary in talks we have had with Negroes and in reports from demonstrations in North Carolina.

Hidden deep inside, where it can frustrate and ulcerate, with many a Negro is a burning resentment, a feeling that he is regarded as a second-rate citizen. We have been close friends with Negroes of high and low and professional degree all our life. We now confess that we were completely blind to the cankering resentments and frustrations deep in the breasts of our friends.

Here are a couple of incidents which helped open our eyes.

General Capus Waynick, seeking to bring peace in Williamston, noticed a woman on the committee whose face was expressive of deep emotion. She said she would prefer that her children and grandchildren should die rather than they should exist under the cloud she had known.

General Waynick asked the woman how long she had had that terrible feeling. She replied since she was big enough to know and to realize.

A professional Negro took violent exception to an editorial we had written. His venomous misunderstanding took us aback. He had read into the editorial a meaning that was not there and was not intended or hinted. He, this highly educated professional man, of a good income, a good home, and a lovely wife and family, was violently emotional.

"All my life," he said, "I have been looked down on as a Negro. I have been brushed almost off sidewalks. I have had to step aside. I have not been able to live free and unafraid."

Floyd McKissick of Durham, CORE director, expressed it differently. A Negro, he said, seldom shows the white man truly what is within his mind. He cited the cook for a well known white family who told her employees she would have no truck with the NAACP. "Yet all the time that woman was giving $5 a week to NAACP," McKissick said.

These must be true and average instances. Otherwise the Negroes could not have pursued with such zeal and unswerving purpose the demonstrations they have set up across the nation from Los Angeles to Brooklyn.

All blacks were not bitter. In May, 1964, Henry had a "Cinderella Story" to tell, involving a Goldsboro girl.

It does one's heart good to see a sort of Cinderella story acted out in real life.

There are elements of the famous story of love and magic in the good fortune which has come to a senior at Dillard High School. Miss Gloria Jean Silver has been selected on the basis of scholarship to attend Emory University, Atlanta. If she measures up to required Emory standards, the scholarship is renewable for four years.

The Dillard principal, teachers and students have every confidence Gloria Jean will make good at Emory.

The Goldsboro girl is one from less than a dozen from Negro high schools selected to inaugurate a new program of the famous Atlanta university. A special fund was allocated to Emory to inaugurate the program.

Miss Silver is number one in scholarship in her class of more than 200 and has a record of leadership in school activities. She is editor of the Dillard Hi-News and president of the Dillard Honor Society.

What bout the Cinderella angle?

The award winner is the oldest child in a large family. She is the daughter of Mr. and Mrs. Joel Silver. Joel Silver for a number of years has been a member of the caretaker staff of the Goldsboro schools. He is a World War II veteran. He entered service before he finished Dillard but returned to graduate. Mrs. Silver is also a Dillard graduate.

Gloria Jean's family could not have financed an education for her at an institution such as Emory. The Cinderella story can still happen.

Gloria Jean, who majored in sociology, got her B.A. degree at Emory and her Master's at Atlanta University.

In September, 1964, Henry had a piece on "History is Made."

History was made in Goldsboro the other day. Goldsboro Rotary had as its speaker for the week's program a Negro attorney and member of the Board of Aldermen. He is Earl Whitted, Jr. He was the first member of his race ever to be invited to appear before the oldest civic organization in Goldsboro.

Formal notice had been given in the club bulletin that Whitted would give the program. There was a full attendance.

Whitted's topic was "Challenge of Today." As might have been expected, he was somewhat ill at ease as he began his talk; not at all the ease when he appears in the courtroom, where his standing with his fellow lawyers is excellent.

At the end of a formally prepared and read statement, he got long applause. There followed a question and answer period. The questions came thick and fast. Whitted in this exchange was ready with straight answers. All nervousness was gone. When the questioning was over, there was more applause. It was the most enthusiastic approval given a speaker in weeks.

If the same program had been given a year or two ago, it would have met with opposition. Some would have walked out. Most definitely there has been a marked advance in attitudes. There is recognition of the fact that the Negroes must be given the chance to be first-class citizens; and, as Whitted emphasized, they must prepare for and be qualified for their new acceptance.

Keeping communication channels open was the difficult task of bi-racial committees.

For several years, Dr. Andrew Best of Greenville has led a wide movement in Pitt County for improved health, education and citizenship. His program has won commendation from state and national officials.

Recently Greenville's Rotary Club had Dr. Best as speaker on a program on bettering relations among races. Dr. Best described the difficult task of members of race councils, or as they are called in some cities, bi-racial committees. He specifically applied his remarks to the Greenville committee, made up of 10 white members and 10 Negroes.

Negro members to serve must be brave. So many of the Negroes think of those from their race on the committee as Uncle Toms, who have let their own people down.

White members of the committee, Best went on, have an equally difficult task. So many whites look upon whites on the committee as illogical, idealistic do-gooders.

We have observed this attitude in Goldsboro. We have also observed, let us emphasize, that members of these committees, and of the Governor's Good Neighbor Council, have worked well. They have restored communication channels which had broken down between the races. The work of the groups has materially advanced full citizenship and opportunity for Negroes.

Every community owes a great deal of gratitude to every member of every committee who has, at a real sacrifice, worked in behalf of better cooperation and understanding.

Henry brought two Negroes to the writing staff of the News-Argus. In 1963, Henry Mitchell, a double amputee, was hired to edit "Community News," a new title for "Negro News." A year later, H. V. Brown, the retired school principal, was added to the columnists of the Sunday feature section. His "Browsings" combines discourse on the Bible with doings of "the Browser's children" whom he helped rear at Dillard High School.

Upon petition of blacks, Henry made one fund out of contributions to the Empty Stocking Fund, a projected started by Col. Joseph E. Robinson, founder of the Argus. Contributions previously had been listed separately for whites and blacks. Now they are divided equally between the races for purchase of gifts for underprivileged children at Christmas.

Henry took an active interest in "Operation Bootstrap," a self-help project founded in 1963 by Mrs. Geneva Hamilton, black civic leader of Goldsboro. The project drew national attention and recognition for Mrs. Hamilton, who was named to the N.C. Good Neighbor Council, serving under three governors. Columnist Drew Pearson, during a speaking appearance in Goldsboro, interviewed Mrs. Hamilton and published something about "Bootstrap", which had been copied by cities in the North. A London correspondent, writing something for his paper on racial attitudes in the South, interviewed Mrs. Hamilton, being escorted to her home by Henry and Lucile Belk.

Some years ago, Henry helped come to the rescue of Shaw University, black institution of Raleigh, which had gotten heavily in debt and was about to close down. Henry called school principal C. I. Bland and told him to bring one or two other black leaders to his office. Bland appeared with Rev. M. W. Morgan.

At Henry's suggestion, a fund-raising project was organized. A form letter was printed and mailed to possible donors suggested by Henry. Miss Gertrude Weil, Goldsboro philanthropist, responded with a check for $500. Some 40 donors contributed more than $5,000 which materially assisted in keeping Shaw alive.

94

11

1953 was a bad year for Henry, in his long fight against blindness. He underwent six operations on his "good" left eye at Duke Hospital. Four were for a detached retina — a condition that led to loss of sight in the eye.

His trouble began in January, when he had his first retina operation. It was preceded by an operation for a ruptured membrane and a decompression operation to relieve pressure in the eye.

Henry was away from his desk about eight weeks and guest editorialists took over for him during the interim. One of them was John D. Langston, Jr., assistant city editor (later editor) of The Durham Sun, who was invited to send in a contribution by Eugene Price, city editor of the News-Argus. He was an earlier protege of Henry's and responded readily.

To be invited to write anything, on any occasion, for anything Henry Belk is connected with, is an honor to me, although I would much prefer that the circumstances be different.

Henry will be back in Goldsboro before long. I am sure that the doctors at Duke will have him fixed up and that he will climb back in the saddle, the same old Henry that everybody in Wayne and surrounding counties knows and respects. Gene, I'm not an envious man, but it's pretty difficult not to turn a bit green when you think of a man who has the regard and respect of such a large segment of Eastern North Carolina.

Just between us, Gene, the guy's integrity and staunchness in line of duty has been a beacon to me. As you know, I grew up — in the newspaper sense — under the wings of Henry Belk, and he is the finest teacher that Tarheelia has produced in many a year.

Some time I want to come back to Goldsboro long enough to take a refresher course under him. Not just the simple rules of who, when, where and why. And not the simple mechanics of the "count" in a 24-point "chelt" or bodoni head. But in the philosophy that should be a part of every newspaper man's creed — that news is news just so long as it is not a mudball.

We learn something every day in the newspaper game. If one learns it under Henry Belk, he learns it.

On March 11, Henry ran a short editorial titled 'Thank You, Guest Editors'.

For about eight weeks some of your friends and neighbors in Goldsboro have served as guest editors in writing comment or report or observation to fill this column. They responded quickly when illness sent the editor to the hospital.

You have enjoyed their contributions on a variety of subjects.

Thank you, guest editors.

Henry had signified his return to harness on February 27, with one of his delightful essays on 'Cornmeal Mush'.

When B. G. Stowe and I meet up, he talks South Carolina and I talk Sweet Union.

"You probably don't remember cornmeal mush, or maybe they didn't have mush in Sweet Union," he said to me the other night.

"Down in Georgia, when I was a boy, it was a great dish, much prized. When company came — families with their troups of children — one always had a big pot of mush.

"Plates for the children were piled high with the mush and seasoned generously with red-eye gravy. There was chicken and ham piled on the table, but the children always got a plate of mush first. The host kept out a sharp eye and as soon as a child had finished his first plate of mush, would say, 'Oh, you have finished your mush; you want some more.' Then, before the child could object, the plate was filled with mush again. By the time he had finished that second plate, he had little appetite for the chicken and ham.

"That's the way it worked years ago in Georgia."

Yes, B. G., mush was a delicious dish that appeared frequently on the tables of Sweet Union 45 years ago. That was the day of five-cent cotton, with cotton the only money crop.

And on most of the tables there was no ham and no chicken when mush was served. You fried some white meat and made gravy to season the mush with. If you were finicky about your food, you made gravy with a little flour. In most instances, however, you added the white meat grease straight to the mush.

And left-over mush would be cut into slices and fried. That was for breakfast. Fried a golden brown, it made good eating.

Mush, maybe we had better explain, is made from cornmeal. You get the pot to boiling and then add the meal a little at the time, stirring vigorously. I don't know how long it takes to cook it, but stand back when the thick broth boils and pops, else you may have a burned hand where a plop of mush has jumped.

Cooked thinner — that is, with more water added — mush is called gruel. In Sweet Union, 45 years ago, meal gruel was often an important diet for patients convalescing after a long illness.

Mush was the original cereal in Sweet Union.

Was it a favorite in Wayne years ago?

On March 4, Henry caught a whiff of spring.

The hint of spring is in the air in Goldsboro now. One ventures from the house in a soft sun and under a baby-blue sky. You think how soft, how warm, how like a baby's smile.

But you haven't been out 15 minutes before a cold, biting, penetrating wind blows in. You shiver and wrap your overcoat about you, and know that winter is still around. Presently you are forced back inside.

But nature knows the hint of spring even more than we do. The lawns have taken on a tender new green. Buds are swelling. Pear trees have sprayed their white blooms for more than a week. Peaches have put on their delightful pink.

Mrs. Dewey Hunt brings us some of the largest and most beautiful pansies ever seen. You think they must have been grown under glass. but she says no, she grew them right by the walk to her Mulberry Street home.

Here Henry tells about the arrival of spring in his neighborhood.

Mrs. Hicks' yard is a scene to watch. The bulbs she planted some time back are breaking through. The 'Ed' camellia bush is 15 feet tall and loaded with blooms. It's the 'Ed' bush because the late Ed Pedigo wore home on his coat lapel from Beaufort the bloom which Mrs. Hicks planted and made a wonderful tree.

Mrs. M. B. Andrews was away from her yard ten days, but her flowers and shrubs smiled and bloomed and sent forth their beauty.

Mrs. Frank Jones is working, the warm spells, in her yard, Little Connie helps her.

Dan Taylor is getting everything spic and span before the annual battle against the grass on his large lawn. He has put out a new pecan tree to give shade and fruit in a few years. All around his 200-foot back yard is a border of white spirea in full bloom.

We barely missed a damaging ice storm on Monday and Tuesday. But before the week is out, the touch of spring will be back.

On March 24, Henry reported on a weekend he had spent in Sea Level.

"I must go down to the sea again, to the lonely sea and the sky."

Do you occasionally get a hankering for the sea and the waves and the winds? Does a strange restlessness stir within you that can be quieted only by the waves against the lonely shore?

It does to me. Some days ago I confessed this urge to Julian Gaskill. So when he, Mrs. Gaskill, little Thad, and Thad's dog planned a weekend at the Gaskill old home at Sea Level, they invited me along.

It was a lovely trip, just a little bit cool because of a wind that apparently came out of the north. But no rains came and we watched the changing colors of Nelson Bay under the changing sky, walked the shore, ate and slept. It was a wonderfully relaxing weekend.

Biggest attraction for the Sea Level populace and the visitor now is the Memorial Hospital which the Taylor brothers are building. The modern, air-conditioned building is rising from a site that was low and swampy until the Taylor brothers sent heavy machinery to build it up. Dredges pumped sand out of the bay and poured it on the site. Julian Gaskill is hoping that the deep holes left by the dredging will prove attractive to the fish and that schools of big ones will find their way to the spot.

"Croakers, especially, like a deep hole," says Julian, who is never happier than when he is puttering with his boat or greeting old friends in the Sea Level community.

The four Taylor brothers are building the hospital to serve Carteret County. It is a memorial to their parents. They say that the boys determined to build the hospital years ago, when their mother needed a doctor and hospital care and it was many hours before a doctor could be secured in Beaufort.

Modern roads have freed Sea Level, Stacy, Atlantic and other villages of Eastern Carteret from isolation. When Julian Gaskill left home to enter Wake Forest College 30 years ago, he had to go by boat to Beaufort. Now paved roads run to the very end of Carteret's land.

I met Maultsby Taylor, father of the famous Taylor boys. Three of the sons had no more than a high school education. They got their start in the salt and sugar business in Norfolk. When a fourth brother came of college age, they sent him to State College in Raleigh. The brothers own several large freight ships and own and operate one of the swank hotels in Palm Beach, Florida. But the brothers never forgot Sea Level and their friends and relatives here. They came back often and some months ago began to make good on their promise of a hospital for the section.

Spring passed. On June 20, Henry had a piece on 'Redbug Time'. Five days later he was back in Duke Hospital.

It is redbug time now. Go walking in the woods, sit down on a log while out fishing or picnicking, and the next day a terrible burn will tell you that the chiggers landed on you.

All natives of these parts have recollections of treatments that mothers prescribed for their children when they came down with redbugs. Favorite in Sweet Union was to rub the bite night and morning with a piece of raw salt meat. Maybe the grease in the meat covers the hole the six-legged critter has buried himself in and smothers him to death. Or maybe the salt sets up a counter irritant and one forgets the bite and sting, with the sting of the salt.

Readers were not informed of Henry's rehospitalization until August 18.

Will you please pardon a personal reference. On June 25, I had to drop everything and return to Duke Hospital for another operation for a detached retina in the left eye. Today I resume writing and editing this column.

To my scores of friends among the readers of this paper who remembered me while I was in the hospital, I am deeply grateful. Your prayers, your letters, your cards, messages and sympathetic regard made my stay in the hospital the more easily borne.

Many of you have asked about my condition. I return to the paper after a successful operation July 15. With proper precaution against over-exertion, and barring the unforeseen, I should be able to serve you as well as I have in the past. It is to this purpose that I dedicate myself. So many of you have been so wonderfully thoughtful of us and we shall always remember with humble thanks.

Mrs. Belk was with me for all of the six weeks that I was in the hospital and she joins me in this expression.

Henry's optimism was short-lived. On October 20, came the first installment of 'Hospital Notes'.

Here we are back at Duke Hospital again. I was getting along fine until about mid-morning of last week, when a dark shadow began to develop in the lower part of the left eye. It spread from then on, until we reached Duke Hospital. Friday the eye was practically covered by the shadow.

One meets such interesting people in a hospital. One of my roommates was a Mr. Fulton of Stuart, Va., a quaint mountain village I had visited while working for the Greensboro News some years ago. He recalled the fairy stones found in the secluded coves of the mountains. The tiny stones are shaped like crosses. Jewelers polish them and sell them for good luck pieces. The legend among the people of the mountains is that the angels wept during the hours when Jesus was being crucified. Wherever their tears fell, they formed little crosses, the ancient story goes. I find it a sweet and interesting legend.

At noon Dr. Anderson came by and took another look at my eye. He said he would decide Monday whether or not to operate on it again.

October 24   Hospital Notes (cont.)

You have heard people say it would be wonderful if they would go to bed for a couple of weeks. It isn't if you are bedded down with a detached retina of one eye. One can't see, when the retina is detached.

The doctor requires that you lie flat on your back. You are cautioned not to turn left or right. You are told emphatically that you must not raise your head or sit up. Generally the hospital folks put sandbags on each side of the head. If you move ever so slightly, you touch the sandbags and are reminded you aren't supposed to do that. You must not move about in the bed. Your eyes are fully bandaged to keep out even a glimmer of light. You must not sneeze. You must not cough.

The days pass tediously. Every hour is a day long and a day stretches out seemingly into a week. You concentrate on trying to be still and it becomes a great task.

Meal time requires actual expenditure of muscular energy. Every mouthful must be fed to you. All liquids and soups are taken through a tube in such a cramped position and minus light, which would add eye appeal to your food.

Your appetite wanes. You force yourself to eat to keep your strength up. Even then, you will lose around ten pounds a week.

You are accustomed to sleeping on your right or left side, turning over every hour or so, and you lie on your back taut as a bowstring hour after hour. Finally you drop off into a disturbed sleep from sheer exhaustion.

About the end of the first 24 hours, your back begins to hurt, slightly at first, and then more and more. You feel that you have been strung up on a rack and that the vertebrae are being slowly pulled apart. You would give a couple of your fingers to turn over and rest that poor back, but if you do, it may cost you an eye. This agony goes on increasingly for the first five to seven days, then it slowly diminishes as the spinal cord accustoms itself to the body's lying prone day after day.

When you get over that hump, you think you have won, but there is something else coming. The end of the spinal column begins to act like a giant tooth, or it seems as if some fiendish devil is beating delightedly away at the end of the spinal cord. You are lucky this time; the torture lasts only a day or two.

This lying prone and immobile regime, 30 years ago, was the only known treatment for reattaching a retina that had been separated. Many Goldsboro people will recall how the late Leslie Weil used this treatment with success some years ago when he suffered a retinal detachment.

The first time I ever heard of a detached retina was in 1921, when I was a cataract patient at the New York Eye and Ear Infirmary in New York City. In the adjoining room was a man, slightly beyond middle years, who had engaged in sugar cane farming in Cuba. He had bumped his head hard against a beam in the hold of a ship, where he was helping to load sugar. The blow caused retinal separation in both eyes. He came to New York seeking help and the doctors put him to bed at the Eye and Ear Infirmary on the third floor. Weeks went by and the retinas did not grow back. One night he jumped from a window to his death.

This is written on my fourth day in Duke Hospital on this trip. On the third day, the detached retina of my left eye seemingly had fallen partially back in place. The doctor said he would examine it further before deciding if there will be a new operation.

October 26   Hospital Notes (cont.)

For the fourth time this year I have undergone an operation for reattachment of the retina of the left eye. I had two other operations in

January, a decompression and one for a ruptured membrane, making six times I have undergone surgery in 1953. I should know between Nov. 4 and 7 whether the latest operation was successful. Right now everything seems to point in that direction.

Concerning the operation, suffice it to say at this time that I was on the operating table a little more than three hours, and that can get rather tedious, particularly if your frame is a little longer than the operating table.

Mrs. James Street of Chapel Hill likes to say that she "wifes" for a living.

During my three stays at Duke Hospital this year, Mrs. Belk has not only "wifed" for a living, she has been my nurse, "graduate" and practical, my constant companion and cheerer-upper, my researcher and secretary.

Her day at the hospital starts about 8 in the morning. My eyes still are completely bandaged and I am not allowed to raise my head. One of the first things she does for my comfort when she arrives in the morning is to wash my hands and the fourth of my face which shows outside the bandages. Then she hands me a wet gauze for cleaning my teeth. Next she gives me ice water and generally a glass of prune juice. That juice can become very flat to the taste after a couple of weeks. It remains, nevertheless, a necessity.

Breakfast is served between 8:30 and 9 and Mrs. Belk feeds me each mouthful. Breakfast generally consists of scrambled eggs, bacon, cereal, coffee, toast, jelly, and occasionally fresh fruit. Mrs. Belk is at pains to see that the tray reaches me while the food is still warm.

Follows my bed-making, which is kept at a minimum for retinal cases. There is no change of bed linen except for the top sheet and bedspread, which Mrs. Belk manages to see that I get each day.

We take time out from our conversation to listen to the 8 and 9 o'clock morning news broadcasts on the radio. In this way I am able to keep informed about what is going on in the state, the nation and the world.

When Mrs. Belk arrives for the day, she brings at least one morning paper and sometimes two. She finds time to give me a digest of the news in these papers before she reads me the real paper, the News-Argus, which arrives about 10 o'clock. The News-Argus gets a very careful going over.

After mail arrives at 10, we give the next hour or so to that, deciding which letters Mrs. Belk will answer in the afternoon. Then comes lunch and again she feeds me mouthful by mouthful. Then she goes away for a rest, often at the home of Harry Hollingsworth, formerly of Goldsboro, who is night editor of the Durham Herald. He comes and takes her to lunch at his house and brings her back.

When she comes back, Mrs. Belk takes dictation for the News-Argus. She uses a typewriter which Miss Henrietta Fagan, assistant to the hospital chaplain, lends her. Sometimes she types the dictation at night on our typewriter she brought with her and has in her room.

Then comes dinner around 6 p. m. and she feeds me again. At 8:45, she bids me good night.

Mrs. Belk scans the admission lists in Miss Fagan's office about twice a week to see if anyone from Goldsboro or Wayne County is a patient. Hardly a day goes by that one doesn't come in.

Both my wife and I graduated from Trinity College of Duke University. Many friends of our college years have called.

A hospital stay for a retina replacement operation is trying under the best of conditions. I could not have faced the situation calmly without the daily love and ministration of my wife.

Mrs. Belk was on the bus coming to the hospital yesterday morning. A woman she had noticed in the halls smiled and said, "Good morning. Do you work at the hospital?"

She does.

On November 18, Henry announced that he was 'Back Home Again'.

Here I am, back home again. It was some two weeks ago when I rudely walked out on you. You will remember I had been writing some notes from my bed at Duke Hospital. I was back there for the third time and the fourth operation for a detached retina of the left eye this year.

I had intended continuing the notes from Duke, but the last week I was in the hospital I simply could not. I was nauseated almost every waking hour and slept not too much. We were in Smithfield to pick up Topsy last week before the nausea completely left me. Maybe it was the joy of nearing home again that made me more comfortable.

I was completely exhausted when I reached home and went straight to bed. The combination of the operation and three weeks in a hospital bed had left me drained of all strength. During the week that I have been at home, however, I have eaten like a horse and slept twelve hours a day. My strength is returning and if I can be patient yet a little while longer, I should be as good as new.

The operation was a success and miraculously I can see again. Dr. Anderson used a different technique in the operation this time. He told me before the operation that he was going to put a "bow" in the eye when he reattached the retina. I did not press for details. Certainly he had time to put a "bow" in the eye, since I was on the operating table for more than three hours. The operation was done under local anesthetic.

As we started to leave, Dr. Anderson remarked that this time he had done a very drastic operation. He cautioned that I must be quiet, and by that he meant practically inactive for a while. Lucile asked him what I should do to prevent the retina pulling loose again, but he did not answer her question. Apparently there are no do's and don't for retina cases that will hold good in every instance. Every case seems to be different.

When am I going back to the office? Friends have asked me that one and I have asked it of myself. This morning I received a letter from Dr. Bluma in New York. She is a general practitioner but should have some knowledge of such things as detached retinas. She advises me that I should stay in bed three months.

Publisher Hal Tanner (who had taken over October 1) has been more than understanding. He insists that I shall in no way overtax myself or do other than my surgeon instructs.

So it may be another two weeks before I am back in the office. I simply must not risk doing anything that will cause the retina to pull loose again. I am hoping the "bow" technique will do the trick this time.

To the scores of you who have shown your friendly, sympathetic interest, I express deep thanks. Your friendship has made the ordeal a little easier to bear.

12

In 1953, between trips to the hospital, Henry found occasion to mount one of his infrequent stands on controversial issues. This time it was the proposed fluoridation of Goldsboro's water supply.

Water-fluoridation had become a hot issue all over the country as the result of claims by medical authorities that it would reduce the rate of dental decay, with counterclaims that it was a menace to one's health. Based on observed resistance to caries in Colorado, which had natural fluorine in its water, controlled water-fluoridation programs had been set up in 1944 in the cities of Grand Rapids, Mich., Newburgh, N.Y., and Brantford, Ontario, all of which had an essentially fluoride-free water supply. Results were still inconclusive, but many cities had adopted similar programs.

With the local health department favoring fluoridation, the Goldsboro Woman's Club named a committee, headed by Mrs. W. A. Shepherd, Jr., to work for its adoption.

On March 26, Rotarian Henry Belk reported on her discussion of the matter before the Goldsboro Rotary Club.

Mrs. W. A. Shepherd, in a talk before Rotary this week, made a suggestion. She said Rotary should join the Woman's Club and other civic organizations in pushing for improvement of our city water. She had reference to adding a chemical to the water, a chemical that would insure better teeth for our children.

Somehow we thought that adding fluorides to Goldsboro water was an assured fact, when the new water plant, now under construction, is completed. We checked and found we were wrong.

The new water plant is so constructed that equipment for adding the chemical can be installed. But this equipment has not been ordered yet. The city has made no decision. The equipment would not cost much in relation to the total cost of the water facility. The cost of adding the chemical in minute parts is small.

Scores of cities over the nation have proved, by careful records, that fluorides added to drinking water do make for healthier teeth for children. These cities have had this good thing for their children for several years. They have proved that there is no threat in any way to health from the tiny part of the chemical added to the water. Their findings have been reported by the U.S. Health Service.

Mrs. Shepherd has made a suggestion that should be followed by action.

Several Wayne dentists and the county health director have been urging the city to adopt this plan for better teeth. Now is the time to act. The equipment should be installed while the new plant is building. It probably can be done cheaper then.

The decision is one for the Goldsboro aldermen. Civic groups should make their wishes known to the Board through resolution or letter.

To implement its stand, the News-Argus began a series of articles by health authorities on the benefits of fluoridation. To give opponents a chance to be heard, Editor Belk announced that the newspaper's columns were open for debate in the matter.

A friend whose views we highly regard called to ask about the series of articles the News-Argus is running on fluorides in water for better teeth, particularly better teeth for children.

This friend, be it known, seems to be opposed to the idea of adding the chemical to Goldsboro's new water system. He wanted to know if those who think the use of fluorides is unwise would be given space in the paper to state their views.

Of course, and by all means.

The News-Argus would in no case deny publication rights to those whose view differs from the paper's. The News-Argus is a local, home town daily. Every man has a right to use the columns of the paper to express views on subjects of general interest and concern. Of course the material must not be longer than we can print. As a rule, Open Forum letters are limited to 300 words. But we consider the fluorides question of such great importance that we will use letters on it up to the length of the articles the paper is printing. But don't get personal or heated in your discussions.

And of course we will print letters favoring fluorides as they are offered.

Our position is this. The U.S. Public Health Service and the North Carolina Board of Public Health offer concrete evidence that fluorides do make for better teeth when added in minute quantity to public drinking water. Many cities over the nation have proved this fact. Health of their people has suffered in no general way from adding the chemical in the water system.

However, we realize that there continues to be discussion and opposition in some quarters to the use of fluorides. There have been claims that the fluorides may bring health changes not to be desired. The question has raged with great controversy in some cities.

Usually any new and great advance in medical techniques has caused controversy, and resentment and unfounded suspicions. Some people even to this day refuse to allow vaccination for smallpox. The vaccination was regarded as dangerous and a crazy idea when it was first advanced.

We think time and the number of cities using the system have tested fluorides as of value and harmless. But we shall open the columns to the other side of the question if any reader desires to submit material in a manner in which it can be handled.

No one took advantage of the opportunity, possibly because most readers did not have an educated opinion on the subject.

On April 20, Henry reiterated his opinion that 'Alderman Should Act'.

On Saturday yours News-Argus printed the last of a series of articles on how towns and cities can reduce decay in the teeth of their children. This is possible by adding a trace of fluorine to the city water supply. More than 340 towns and villages of the nation have adopted this plan.

Your News-Argus printed 17 articles on the subject. Sixteen of the articles showed how leading scientists and health associations endorse this new way of reducing tooth decay. One of the articles was prepared in opposition to the plan.

It is our considered and careful opinion that the preponderance of evidence shows that this new advance in health techniques offers great hope for bettering the future of our children.

Many of our readers have followed the series of articles carefully. A number of you have expressed your thanks to the News-Argus for presenting them.

Your opinion as expressed directly to us is that Goldsboro should no longer delay providing this great service to its people. Now is the logical time. We are building a new water system and plant. Arrangements are made in the new plant for the equipment for adding fluorides to the water in proper proportions. But the equipment has not been ordered. It will not cost a prohibitive sum. Goldsboro should join the hundreds of other cities which have taken advantage of this new discovery.

The Board of Aldermen will have to act if Goldsboro's children are to be protected with this new discovery. If you want this for your children, you should tell the members of the Board of Aldermen, or better still write a letter. We hope that before this school year ends, the Goldsboro Parent-Teachers Association will have passed resolutions asking the aldermen to move for the purchase of equipment needed to put this great servant to work for us and our children.

In conclusion, may we cite the opinion of Dr. Walter C. Alvarez on fluoridation of water. Dr. Alvarez is emeritus consultant in medicine for the nationally known Mayo Clinic and emeritus professor of medicine for the Mayo Foundation. He says:

"Several persons have written to chide me for approving the addition of one part in a million of fluorine to 1,000,000 parts of city water. As I said, there is no question that the procedure greatly lowers the incidence of decay in children's teeth.

"The only question then is, will the addition of the fluorine do any harm to anyone? So far as I can learn from scientific and unprejudiced sources, there is no evidence to prove that it does any harm.

"The drinking water of some cities has always contained fluorine, just as it contains traces of other elements, and so far as I can learn, the citizens of those cities have no more ill health than is found in the other cities with the same age distribution of populace.

"One writer, an educated man who should have known better, amused me by saying that fluoridation of water had proved harmful by a vote of two-thirds of the population of a big city. He might as well have said that two-thirds of the population of San Francisco had proved that the engineering design of the new Bay Bridge was technically faulty."

Regardless of scientific opinion, many people wre prejudiced against tampering with their drinking water, for one reason or another. In Goldsboro the opposition was led by a number of prominent citizens.

Dr. H. M. Stenhouse, ophthalmologist, considered fluorine, in any quantity, a hazard to health. He still does. He thinks it could be a contributing factor in the high incidence of cancer. A former commander in the U.S. Navy, he was impressed by the potency of a powder containing sodium fluoride in killing roaches aboard ship.

Banker Don Humphrey thought fluoridation would cause heart disease. Medical authorities now say it benefits the heart by helping check hardening of the arteries.

Goldsboro Attorney, Col. John D. Langston, subscribed to the theory, advanced by some, that water-fluoridation was Communist-inspired. What prompted the theory is not recalled.

W. Frank Taylor, Langston's law partner, took the view that results of fluoridation had not been sufficiently documented.

Dr. C. F. Strosnider, Goldsboro physician, said fluorine would discolor the teeth, a view shared by Dr. S. D. Poole, one of several dentists who questioned the program.

"There were two sections in the county where the wells had an excess of fluorine in the water," Dr. Poole recalled. "I observed that children drinking the water had mottled teeth."

Poole was responsible for turning businessman J. Eustace Bizzell against the proposition.

"Eustace was sold on the idea after attending a dental clinic in Philadelphia, the biggest in the country. He had them to send me some of their literature. Later he came by my office to see if I had read it. I told him no, that I had read the same kind of stuff before. When I got through exposing it, Eustace said, 'Throw the damn stuff in the trash can.' "

Poole argued that too many sweets were responsible for tooth decay in children.

"I was at a meeting of the Board of Aldermen at which Dr. S. B. McPheeters, the county health officer, presented the case for fluoridation. On the way out, he said, 'Don't you think you can put something in the water to keep children's teeth from decaying?' I replied, 'Why don't you make the schools top selling candy to them and sell fruit, instead?' "

Poole said two Greensboro dentists were almost run out of the State Dental Society for opposing fluoridation.

Editor Belk kept his word about giving opponents a chance to say their piece. He published a cartoon that newsstand operator Bill Edgerton had gotten artist Zeno Spence to draw, showing a fluoride user stretched out in his coffin with his mouth open. "Ain't he got pretty teeth?" the caption said.

While the argument was raging, the Woman's Club circulated a petition asking aldermen to adopt the fluoridation program.

"We got a lot of people to sign it when they went to vote," Mrs. Shepherd recalled.

Editor Belk suggested that the issue be voted on in the city election, but aldermen turned down the suggestion.

On August 4, the News-Argus reported that the petition had been turned over to the board.

The Board of Aldermen last night received a petition from the Goldsboro Women's Club favoring the addition of fluorides to the city's drinking water. The resolution was signed by 750 people.

The Aldermen took the resolution under advisement, but delayed any action on the issue. They are making a thorough study of the question and are attempting to hear all arguments, pro and con, before making a decision.

On August 14, the News-Argus published an editorial by city editor Gene Price, substituting for Editor Belk, who was in the hospital. It was titled 'Crackpots on Fluoridation'.

The Goldsboro Board of Aldermen has taken under study a petition asking that they adopt a program of fluoridation of the public water supply in Goldsboro. The petition was circulated by the Woman's Club and carried some 750 names.

It is only right that the Board of Aldermen study the recommendations of the Women's Club carefully before making a decision.

The Aldermen undoubtedly are not suffering any shortage of research material. What has been written on fluoridation would probably fill a small library.

But the Aldermen should be careful in evaluating what has been written. To quote the Journal of the American Dental Society: "It is to be recognized that a subject of such public health significance as the fluoridation of drinking water furnishes a peg on which free lance writers may hang a paying article, and that scores of editorials have appeared in virtually every popular magazine in the country in the past three years.

"Many of the articles are based on the observations of self-styled experts who are the same type individuals who opposed chlorination and pasteurization."

110

J. Roy Doty, paid secretary of the Council of Dental Therapeutics of the
American Dental Society, writes:

"Since scientific fact has a way of penetrating the barriers of confusion and
misinformation, there need be no concern for the ultimate acceptance of
fluoridation. It is unfortunate, however, that thousands or even millions of the
younger children of today should be denied the dental benefits of fluoridation
because of the lies and half-truths being disseminated by a relatively small but
vocal group which apparently is dedicated to the perpetuation of
misinformation."

The Aldermen should consider carefully the "authorities" quoted in each
of the articles they study. They must be careful to determine what has been
written by those who really know and that which has been written by the
crackpots.

If their final analysis is correct, and we feel certain it will be, the Board of
Aldermen will not hesitate to adopt the recommendations of the Woman's
Club.

All of the News-Argus's efforts went for nothing. On October
27, after alderment had debated the issue for over two months,
their decision was reached, and reported without editorial
comment by the News-Argus.

The Goldsboro Board of Aldermen voted unanimously last night not to add
fluoride to the city's water supply.

Action came when Alderman Bill Dees worded a resolution directing City
Manager Ralph Jones to answer all correspondence in fluoridation, informing
interested persons that board members "do not think it wise to add fluorides
at this time."

The resolution turned thumbs down on a petition signed by 765 citizens
urging that fluorides be added to the city's water. It also scotched suggestions
that the issue be put to a vote of the people.

The petition calling for a fluoridation program was submitted to the Board
in August by Mrs. W. A. Shepherd, Jr., chairman of the Goldsboro Woman's
Club committee on fluoridation. Mrs. Shepherd told the board that no canvass
had been made to secure a large number of signatures, but that it was to show
that the public was interested in fluoridation.

Among other correspondence submitted to the Board on the matter was a
letter from William A. Bland, 605 Rudolph Street, requesting that the
question be submitted to a vote of the people.

Such a suggestion was also made editorially by the News-Argus when Editor Henry Belk asked that the issue be included in one of the regular elections so that a special referendum would not be necessary.

The News-Argus ran a series of articles citing the benefits of fluorides and pointing out the lack of foundation of charges of harmful side effects of a fluoridation program.

The Aldermen said last night that they had considered a lot of material and indicated that they were still willing to give the issue further study.

"There was such a difference of opinion that we felt it best not to take any action," Aldermen Dees recalled.

Agitation continuing, aldermen in late 1954 sent a questionnaire to local dentists and physicians asking if they favored fluoridation. The majority did, but there were some notable exceptions.

Dr. Donnell B. Cobb, a prominent surgeon, said: "I do not feel that there is yet enough evidence of its value to justify its use."

Dr. Henry B. Dorr, a medical doctor, said: "Neither a yes or a no answer is possible until sufficient studies as to the harmful effects have been completed."

Dr. William Trachtenberg, a medical doctor: "I cannot say at this time, because I believe the matter is still in the experimental stage."

Dr. M. E. Bizzell, an eye, ear and nose doctor: "Have people vote on the issue."

Opposition had faded when a new board of aldermen approved fluoridation in 1960. The safety and effectiveness of fluoridation had been confirmed in 1957 by the World Health Organization based on results of controlled programs in 17 countries. In 1954, ten years after test programs had been inaugurated in Grand Rapids and two other cities, results showed that the expected dental decay in children was reduced by 65 percent. A 10-year program in Charlotte had shown similar results.

Only two persons spoke out against fluoridation when aldermen adopted it on June 20, 1960. One said it should not "be forced on anybody." The other wondered "Who can be trusted to administer such a small amount of the fluoride?" The aldermen's resolution stipulated that the percent was "not to exceed one part per million parts of water."

The board's action, the News-Argus said, "came after a Wayne Dental Society resolution asking for fluoridation was presented to aldermen two weeks ago."

Editor Belk had nothing to say about the board's decision. He had done his part, seven years earlier, in laying the foundation of public opinion.

City Manager Page Benton was instructed to initiate the program as soon as equipment could be purchased and installed. It was estimated that the equipment would cost the city around $5,000.

When fluoridation became a fact on March 6, 1961, the public had not been notified in advance of the effective date. If the water tasted any different, people quickly got used to it.

Goldsboro dentists generally agree that they treat far fewer cavities than before fluoridation was put into effect.

Now the children of rural Wayne are receiving the benefits of fluoride. In 1970, Wayne was one of several counties in the state selected for a three-year program to test the addition of fluoride to a child's diet. Seventeen county schools are participating in the experiment. Their student bodies are divided into three groups. One takes two fluoride tablets a day, another one tablet a day, and the third group none. The experiment has concluded, but results have not been made known.

13

Henry went back to work, but it was not for long. In March, 1954, he suffered a heart attack and was admitted to Wayne Memorial Hospital. Before the week was out, he had a coronary thrombosis. While still in the hospital he had a final detachment of the retina of the left eye.

The public was not told of the new eye trouble until two months later, after he had recovered from the heart attacks.

On May 15, while convalescing at Wrightsville Beach, Henry had an editorial on the passing of Senator Clyde R. Hoey.

We came in from a late lunch and automatically turned on the radio in our room. The news report was well underway and our ears pricked up. With a shock we realized the indestructible Clyde R. Hoey was dead at 76.

The syrupy voice of the broadcaster droned on. Sen. Hoey had been under the care of a doctor for the past month. Dr. George R. Culver said he was very tired, but refused to rest, insisting that he see personally every delegation which came from his home state, and there had been many delegations.

It was a good way to die. At lunchtime he had gone to his office and sat down in an easy chair for a little nap. While he slept, death from a stroke took a man the like of whom North Carolina not soon, if ever, shall see again.

Everywhere in the Tar Heel state, men, high and low, will miss his striking figure, his craggy face, and his always turned-on charm; his greeting of everyone as if the person were a close friend.

Clyde Hoey came close to the "born in a log cabin" tradition which America for generations prized so much, a tradition that now is disappearing, more is the pity. His formal schooling went only through the fourth grade.

He bought himself a Cleveland County weekly newspaper while still in his teens, using his good name as guarantee for the credit extended in the paper's purchase. He was ambitious, quick to learn, quick to sense an opportunity, and quick to prepare himself for wider service. He was one of the youngest men ever to be elected to the North Carolina General Assembly.

His days as a printer's devil in a country newspaper plant, his short period as a country editor, these were good preparation for the reading of law. The experiences had provided him with a fund of general knowledge and a quick and steadfast grasp of what he read.

Shelby, where he hung out his shingle, was beginning to grow lustily. It had some famous families dedicated to that town and to the state. The Gardners, Federal Judge Webb, Odus Mull and others. It occupied a spot in the burgeoning textile industry and in the legal profession.

Into this time of opportunity stepped young Clyde Hoey, a man of great capacity for work. The leaders of growing Shelby liked the serious, purposeful young man and they found his talents of great help. Clyde Hoey was on his way.

Whenever Hoey found himself confronted with high responsibilities, he always acquitted himself with distinction. Steady and conservative, he was marked for high service. Hoey's race against young fire-eating, liberal Ralph McDonald for the governorship of North Carolina generated more heat and fury than often is seen in the state. He barely squeaked through in a second primary. When he became governor, he worked assiduously at his job, and he went to and fro in North Carolina teaching Sunday School lessons, talking at hundreds of local occasions, and getting a personal acquaintanceship with thousands of his fellow Tar Heels.

They came to love him dearly. His stately tall figure, with its long-tailed coat and red flower in his lapel, was known from Murphy to Manteo. In the U.S. Senate, he never lost touch with the folks back home. His fellow Senators came to honor and respect him for his devotion to old-fashioned ideals and for his strength of character.

Sen. Hoey was a member of that fading genus, the silver-tongued orator, once as familiar in the South as magnolias and moonlight. And he was an artist at this. We remember what probably was his last public appearance in Goldsboro. Bill Algary, now of Asheville, brought him to town to talk before the Men's Club of the Presbyterian Church.

The same thing happened as it always did. We had gone to that meeting determined not to find ourselves thrilling at the supreme artistry of his spoken word, determined not to be hypnotized by the beautiful smoothness with which he presented his talk.

But it happened again. Before the man was half through, we found ourselves, sitting there, bathed in a delightful glow of appreciation of his art.

Always he used that art for goals and purposes which he knew to be true and laudable.

Clyde Hoey's name and fame are assured a lasting place in the history of North Carolina.

On June 2, Henry asked his readers to 'Pardon a Personal Preference'.

I'm low in my mind.

It's natural, I suppose, but I will pull out of it and when you see me, I will be as cheerful and happy as anyone.

I should have been prepared for it, and I was, but you know how, when the final pronouncement comes, sometimes you are knocked into a tailspin by something you had known all the time.

What caused it was that Dr. A at Duke told me I could not hope for sight anymore in my left eye.

He didn't say it that blunt and direct. Doctors don't. But that is what he meant. What he said was, "Come back in July."

This final ringing down of the curtain of sight in my left eye came about six weeks ago.

I was at Wayne Memorial Hospital recovering from a heart attack when I noticed an ominous shadow begin to fall across the eye. Well I might, for I had felt its baleful start before.

It was December 21, 1952. I noticed the strange shadow falling across the eye for the first time. Dr. Bizzell took a look and tried to be cheerful. He sent me to see Dr. A at Duke. Dr. A. was away on a lecture tour, or something. Dr. C. took a look.

"What do you see?" I asked.

"A detached retina," he replied matter-of-factly.

"What do you do for it?" I asked.

"Since Dr. Anderson is not here, you go home and have Dr. Bizzell blind your eyes for the next ten days. Lie flat on your back and don't raise up or turn over. Then, on January 1, you come back to us."

I did.

And it got to be almost a habit.

To begin with, Dr. A. took one look. Congenital cataracts had been removed 30 years ago. There was only a semblance of a pupil in the eye.

The first operation was to make a new pupil for the eye. After that, the eye was inflamed for some days and Dr. A. decided it protruded too far to allow a successful reattachment of the retina. A neurosurgeon was called in. He did what is called a decompression operation. It sounds mild, but far from it. I was on the operating table three hours. They cut into my left temple in two places and then pushed the eye back in its socket. I was one sick man about three days.

But I'm an impatient guy. I wanted them to get on with the job I came there for, reattaching the retina.

On the eighth day after the decompression operation, they did a retina attachment operation. But they had to do it in the dark, so to speak. The eye was filled with opacities, which prevented anyone seeing exactly where the retina had pulled loose or exactly where it should be reattached. The work was done largely from a "field of vision" test. This graph showed the spots where the eye was blind and where it could see.

Cautioned against turning over or sitting up or disturbing my head in any way, I lay flat of my back for two weeks. Lying in bed and not allowed to move can be a torture.

Finally, the bandages are taken off. Miraculously I can see. The eye apparently is as good as it ever was. Two days later, weak, tottering, hardly able to put one foot before the other, because of the long inactivity, I go home. But happy. I can see again.

There are five beautiful months. Then the retina pulls out again. I go back for another operation. I have it. After two more weeks of bed inactivity, the bandages are removed. The operation has failed this time. I go back to bed. In four days I have the operation again. It succeeds this time. I can see again and I rejoice.

I go back home, learn to walk again. Go back to work. Then, on October 6, the retina pulls loose again. It shows itself first with that shadow which forms on the lower part of the eye near the nose and gradually pulls a blackout curtain over all the eye.

I go back to Duke. There is another operation. This time the surgeons give me the works. At the end of my two weeks of bed, I develop a terrible nausea that shakes me for four days. Finally, I am ready to go home again. Seeing again, I am hopeful that this is it, that the reluctant retina has been brought under control at last.

I come home November 8. I'm happy in my work. Then on the morning of March 15, I'm awakened from a deep sleep by the shock of a heart attack. I go to the hospital. For a week I am recovering. Then two more shocks hit me. I'm put under an oxygen tent for a week.

I'm barely out of the tent when I notice that ominous shadow closing in on the left eye. It moves just a little further over the eye every day. In three days the blackout curtain is rung down and I can see no more.

I'm forced to tell the beloved wife and Dr. B., who comes by to pass a greeting, and the family doctor, Dr. D.

In my heart I know that this is it. Every retina operation, no matter how successful — and 60 percent of such operations are successful — takes just a little bit of vision. Four times that has happened to me. By now the vision is so restricted I am having to use a special reading glass to read the papers.

I know in my heart that it is useless to seek another operation for the trouble. The longest the retina has remained attached in any of the previous operations was five months and 18 days. Even if it was successfully attached again, my vision would be still further restricted.

I know all this.

Dr. A. says to delay coming to see him until I have recovered from the heart attacks.

Friday I am well enough to go back. A new medicine apparently is controlling the thyroid gland excess which may have caused all the trouble, the eye and the heart. I'm gaining weight without trying, after having lost 60 pounds. Most of my clothing begins to be too tight.

This new thyroid control medicine has changed me from a sullen, sober, dispirited, cheerless, crabbed individual to one of buoyant optimism.

Even though logic tells me how foolish I am, I'm still hoping, when I go back Friday to see Dr. A.

He peers at the eye with his piercing little electric candle.

"I'm glad you are taking this realistically," he says.

He knows how to choose his words. They mean there's no hope in trying that operation again.

But foolishly, as Ray McDonald drives me home, the spirit of depression grows stronger and stronger.

The remaining right eye has only a fifth of vision. I'll get along, even though stumblingly. With the aid of the special glass I have, I can read with the right eye typewritten letters when the ribbon is black. I can stumble through ordinary newspaper type. As I grow accustomed to using the right eye — it never worked with the left eye — I may do better.

You will please pardon this personal reference. It is a sort of therapy. It will help me to get hold of myself better and resume normal attitudes. So thank you, dear hearts and gentle people.

P. S. I expect to go to New York to consult an optometrist about a new telephoto lens for the right eye.

Henry ran a 'Letter from New York' two weeks later.

May we just call this a letter to you, dear hearts and gentle people. A simple little letter, that's all.

Here I am in New York with eight million other people, and I am just a poor country boy, dazed, confused, even bewildered.

You would have thought that it was Goldsboro Day on the Pullman coming into New York. There was the largest crowd at the station in Goldsboro I've seen in a long time except when there was some special occasion.

A number of friends and members of the family had come down to see Ed Borden and Sarah Cobb start the first lap of a journey that is carrying them to Europe with a party of friends.

And on that day and train the Barker Damerons and the Byron Donaldsons were starting to Quebec to attend the annual convention of the top producers of Jefferson Standard Life Insurance Company. Lucile and I felt flattered to know these travelers.

I had wondered if I was going to sleep on the Pullman. The noise, the jerking of the train, strange surroundings, and particularly the length of the berth. You know I am six feet and six inches tall, and the Pullman berths are only six feet, two inches long. But I slept like a log. I found I could get several inches of length in the berth by lying diagonally, my head in one corner, my feet in the other. I could vary that position by assuming a sort of S-shape occasionally.

Wonderful to behold, our son, Dr. Lipton, was at the station when we got off the train the next morning. He had gotten leave from his duties as a psychiatrist with the Child Study Center of Yale University and had come down to be with us. We had two fine days with him and he went with us for the preliminary examination at the office of Dr. F. You know it was to consult him about glasses which might give me reading vision that we came to New York.

Henry's next letter was on 'Old Haunts Revisited'.

"Remembering speechlessly, we all seek the long-forgotten language."
That line was by Thomas Wolfe.

Speechlessly, the one to the other, Lucile and I sought, the other afternoon, to recapture the long-gone days of our early years of marriage. We wandered again, for a little while, to the scenes we knew so well, when we lived here 28 years ago.

Young, ambitious, confident, we came up from Wake Forest and found quarters in an apartment at 3100 Broadway. That is at 123rd Street, five blocks from Columbia University, where I was a student.

We decided to go back to the old scenes this wise. We had been lying around the hotel on Sunday afternoon, too listless, in New York's debilitating heat, to have energy enough to plan a sightseeing trip or anything.

Then Lucile spoke the words that had been in my mind.

"Let's take a bus up Fifth Avenue to Grant's Tomb and International House," she said.

We did. Out of the forest of buildings, to the west of Central Park and along Riverside Drive, we rode. The cold waters of the Hudson River, to our left, and the trees and soft green of Riverside, were a balm to our spirits.

Ed, our son, was with us, just a little over the age we were, when we lived here.

At first we mistook the lofty Soldiers and Sailors Monument for the tomb of General Grant, but Ed set us right.

Now here is Grant's Tomb, just a little farther out than Riverside Baptist Church. We get off the bus. High and lifted up before us is International House of Columbia University. A green carpet of well-kept grass stretches before it.

We take a seat on a cement bench and rest. We talk. Somebody asks how did it happen that Grant was buried in New York.

We talk, but I know Lucile is thinking the same thoughts I am thinking.

Here, and farther down close to the river it was that we came to freshen our spirits when we were young and homesick. Here we played with our infant daughter, like that young couple there on the grass is playing with their baby.

Suppose we go to International House, somebody says. Ed recalls that this is one of five such houses which the Rockefellers have given to great institutions of learning, where students from foreign lands may live with American students and thus get the feel of democracy while studying away from home.

We talk, but my mind goes this way. Somewhere along here was the office of Dr. Brop, who served Columbia students. Remember that? It was a bitter December Sunday afternoon. The wind blew fiercely across the Hudson. In our room at 3100 Broadway, Lucile and I suddenly got the terrifying impression. The baby is sick. She is parching with fever. Her breath is coming in short, labored gasps. We grab her from the crib, spread a blanket on the bed, wrap her securely in it. I take her in my arms, hurry to the elevator, and down to Broadway.

We know nothing to do but seek the office of the one doctor we have met. That is over about five blocks. Fear oils our steps, as with long strides we hurry to his Riverside apartment office. Part of the way is up a steep hill, but that slows us none at all. A week or so later, it seemed, but actually it was less than 15 minutes, we were admitted to the doctor's office. Marie is unwrapped. The doctor examines her and looks at us a puzzled sort of way.

"There's nothing wrong with this fine baby," he says gently. "Her temperature is normal, respiration normal. She is in good shape."

Our hearts come up out of our boots. We feel a little sheepish, but the burden is rolled away. We go slowly back to our room, walking in close security and hugging our baby.

These are the thoughts as we sit a few minutes in International House. A beautiful young woman goes by, wrapped in the robe-like garments of India. Young people from a half dozen nations are walking through the lobby or seated, chatting and reading. And outside at the steps are two boys and a girl with a portable radio blaring a popular song.

We go slowly out of International House, taking a long flight of stone steps to the street. We walk slowly. We come to Broadway at 124th Street. Every step is taking us closer to our old New York home. We go uphill on the west side of Broadway. The subway divides the street. Finally we stand and look across the corner of 123rd Street. The subway comes out of the ground at this point and we have an unobstructed view. There is the apartment house where we were when we were so young.

Lucile talks. "You see that front apartment on the second floor, there on the corner above the street? We had the back room in it. It got a blaze of sun all afternoon, when there was a sun. The block on which you see the Jewish Theological Seminary, just next door, was vacant then."

We have just passed four little girls, about six, on the sidewalk. They are playing that they are learning to dance and they sing a sweet and low song, "You glide and slide, and glide and slide," accompanying the words with the motion of a waltz.

We stand and look across at our old home. Maybe it be best not to go up there and make inquiry. We did that some 15 years ago and the names we called and asked about were strange names to the ears of the building superintendent.

In New York, people come and go, in an apartment house they move in and out. And who is there to bid a farewell or a good-bye or a called greeting of "Keep in touch with me."

We stare across the street and memories come flooding in. Of Mrs. Florence, our landlady, a devout Catholic. Of her old uncle near death in the darkness of a winter night and of her rousing me to go hastily for the priest, that he may receive extreme unction and his soul be saved. Of how old Uncle fooled them and lived on and on. How it always seemed to happen that just as Lucile went in the kitchen, which we shared, the gas sputtered out in the quarter meter and we had to pay. A food budget of $5 a week. How our idea of celebrating was to go to a little dining room on Amsterdam Avenue twice a week and get a dinner for 60 cents. How that budget had to be stretched with pork and beans almost every weekend . . . How I got impatient with Marie, reaching for the salt and moving it with her baby grasp, and allowed to teach her a lesson by letting her eat some. How it made her sick, and how ashamed I was. Of Marie's being the youngest baby ever to enroll at Columbia's nursery school.

I am tired from walking. Ed calls a cab and we are whisked in a minute out of the area of old memories.

The most uplifting and stimulating experience we have had in New York was attending the movie, "The Unconquered." It is a documentary film, you might call it, showing the life of that great woman, Helen Keller, with Katherine Cornell doing the narration.

We noticed that the world premiere of the film was set for the Guild Theatre at 48th Street. We made a point to check by and ask the cost of the tickets for the premiere. We hope we didn't look too astonished when the manager said that the price would be $15. So we passed up the opening and went to the first public showing the next morning. This time the price was only one-fifteenth of what the premiere had been.

Everybody knows about Helen Keller. This native of Alabama was only 19 months old when an illness left her blind, deaf and mute. Anne Sullivan became her companion and teacher. Helen learned to read braille, the dot alphabet of the blind, and to talk. She confounded the skeptics, who said it would be impossible for one so handicapped to get a college education, by graduating from Vassar at the age of 24.

After her graduation, Miss Keller began a career as a lecturer, author and crusader for the handicapped. With Miss Sullivan serving as her eyes and mouthpiece, she toured the nation and the world. Today she is known and honored all over the world.

The film is natural, simple. In its closing scenes you are brought for a visit to Miss Keller's home in Connecticut. You see what a natural life she leads, walking in the garden, washing the dishes, putting up and taking down her clothing, chatting with friends, attending to the mail, and in the morning and at bedtime reading from her Bible in braille.

"The Unconquered" is a lift to the soul. You go away from it humble and proud that the soul of man is able to rise to such sublime heights. You hear the monotone words that come from Miss Keller: "Man does not see with his eyes alone, but with his heart, his mind and soul. He who uses these eyes truly sees."

On Sunday afternoon, Ed, Lucile and I wandered into the lobby of the great Waldorf Astoria Hotel. No reason at all. Just getting close to a famous place and hoping maybe somebody like General MacArthur, who lives there, might come by. He didn't.

Ed and Lucile got to trying to identify an evergreen plant which grew in a container at one side of the lobby. Ed said it was a philodendron plant. Lucile said she didn't think so.

As we came by the Western Union counters, Ed asked the girls there. They knew not. They said ask the bell captain, that he knew everything about the place. We did. He couldn't identify the plant.

We were by now at a corridor off the main lobby and were taking the elevator. We asked the girl operator.

She said: "I have worked here for six years, but I have never been to the main lobby yet."

The lobby was right around the corner from the elevator, not more than 100 feet.

Her remark pointed up the life of the average New Yorker. He savors little of the city's great treasures of amusement, music, stage, educational opportunities. He is chained to his existence by a job. He goes rushing to that job by subway. He comes rushing home the same way. Maybe he goes to a movie in his own neighborhood. New York is certainly a fabulous place, but to its millions it is a place of low existence. One is born, goes to school, gets married, begets children, dies and is buried without rising above the animal state of merely eating, sleeping, working. To most New Yorkers, life is a treadmill, a terrible monster in a great and dirty roar and rush.

The Indians cheated the Dutch when they sold the Island to them. Best thing would be to remove its great centers of various kinds to the hinterlands, where people would appreciate them. Remove its art and drama and museum buildings. Then take all the people out of the city and blow it to pieces. You can have it. I don't want it. It's too big and dirty and crowded for me.

Henry's next letter was headed 'Out of Darkness'.

So many of you have asked and I wanted to be absolutely sure before I answered.

For the second time in 33 years I have again been freed from darkness. You all, dear hearts and gentle people, know how I got into that dark cave, this last time. A retina that kept detaching in the left eye, the one I had depended on entirely since first I was freed from darkness.

It was in New York in 1921 that Dr. Ben Wit Key, now gone to rest, successfully removed congenital cataracts from both my eyes. To that time, I had graduated from high school, worked as a reporter for two years, and had finished two years of college. All the sight I had was a little glimmer.

I was 23 before Dr. Key removed the cataracts. I was given about half normal vision in the left eye. They said the optic nerve had died in the right eye. That was the reason it didn't see much.

If you have been shut up in a cave with no light, or maybe you got just a bit, and then came suddenly into the beautiful world of sunshine and sky and trees and moving things, if ever this happened to you, you know something of how I felt the first time I walked on the street with my glasses on. Everything was more beautiful than ever I had imagined.

No more did I run into a tree if I got in a hurry, as I had done on the school grounds back in Sweet Union. No more did I step on a big dog and have it threaten to devour me, as had happened when I was a boy. You can't describe the relief. The gathering of knowledge, previously strained and difficult, became easy. The horizon moved out far from about me.

In the subsequent years the blindness of my youth was forgotten, practically. Life was full and beautiful, people were wondrously big, or little of mind and soul, wondrously interesting.

I have previously told you how the cave closed again, when the retina first detached on December 22, 1952. How it was reattached four times with as many operations in a year, and a couple of necessary side operations. How finally it was no longer sensible to try reattaching the retina again.

The eye which had served so well was gone, for good and for sure. The right eye, which previously had done no work, became the chief one.

Out of New York for the past two years had come reports of successes by Dr. William Feinbloom in providing glasses for people of subnormal vision. How many who had never been able to read before were doing so with glasses developed by him.

You know that two weeks ago Lucile and I went to New York to consult this man about whom we had heard so much. We found him a man of pleasing personality. He holds a degree in optometry from an Indiana college and a Doctor of Philosophy degree from Columbia University. He headed the Columbia University school of optometry for a time. Optometrists know him as long a leader in research for aids for those handicapped with subnormal vision. Several years ago he was much heard of for his work in developing contact lenses.

Dr. Feinbloom must have spent more than an hour and a half the first day examining my right eye, getting acquainted with my eye history, testing every conceivable type of lense, both for reading and distance.

My great desire was for glasses that would enable me to read. I can get about, albeit stumblingly, with the right eye, but I must be able to read. That is my life, my work, my job.

This I had not been able to do since the right eye winked out in early April, when I was in the hospital with the heart attacks.

Dr. Feinbloom kept switching lenses in the heavy frames that are used for making tests. I was trying to read the cards kept about the offices for such purposes. I was a little skeptical. Presently I was reading what was listed as magazine type. Just a bit larger and more legible than newspaper type.

That was encouraging.

"You ought to be in the magazine business," joked Dr. Feinbloom.

He kept experimenting. Before I left his office that first morning, he had fitted a lense that enabled me to read, though slowly, the smallest type on the cards.

The second day confirmed the first day's tests. The end of the third day I got the new glasses and walked out of the office. Still, I held control of my heart. I wanted to be sure, from a week of trying, that I could really read again.

More than a week is passed. Every day finds me able to read just a little more rapidly and more surely with the glasses. I feel that I will have a normal reading rapidity with them in a few months.

So, if you see me doing what you may think is smelling a paper, I'm not. I'm reading it.

The glasses are a microscopic lense type. Dr. Feinbloom says if the vision in the eye fades still more, that additional aids are available.

I can see. Happy is me.

14

Henry liked to visit New York once a year — usually in October, when the theater season was in swing — but he had no desire to live in the big city. He was content to be a "country editor".

This friend I had not met up with in a long time. I was glad to see him and he was glad to see me.

He intended to pay me a high compliment, but the application so far as I was concerned, was off the mark.

"The more I read your editorials and informal pieces," he said, "the more I think you should be in New York writing for the papers there."

Thanks for your interest, friend, but no thanks for New York. I wouldn't swap Center Street for all of Manhattan Island with Brooklyn and the Bronx thrown in for good measure.

Eppie expressed it for me when he was bringing me to work a few mornings ago. I had been on a trip to Washington and was remarking how glad I was to get back to Goldsboro.

"I want to be where I can see something grow," Eppie said. And he expressed my sentiment.

I want to be where I can smell spring flowers.

I want to be where I can hear the birds sing.

I want to be where folks have time for friendliness, even in the conduct of the day's work.

I want to be where you can pick a good set of pallbearers when you die.

I want to live where the birth of a baby, or the marriage of a cousin is a big event.

I want to live where the church and the civic club and the schools are real parts of the daily life.

I want to live where there is a hearty "Good morning" and a friendly smile as you walk — yes, I said walk, not run — on the streets.

In other words, I am a country editor and I like it.

Henry wanted no part of New York, himself, but he had admiration and respect for other Tar Heels who made good in the big city. One of them was Goldsboro native Kenneth C. Royall, who had reached Gotham via Washington, where he had served as Secretary of War and later Secretary of Defense, under President Truman.

The Royalls liked to receive friends from back home at their exclusive address on Fifth Avenue. Henry said the doorman at Hotel Picadilly hardly noticed him until one evening when Royall sent his limousine to pick up the Belks.

The Royalls were plain Tar Heels whose eating tastes ran to such things as cornbread.

One of the things displaced Tar Heels miss is the cornmeal bread they learned to love as children. That is one of the important bits of information I picked up on a recent exciting stay in New York.

No less a hostess, who ranks with Pearl Mesta, than Mrs. Kenneth Royall was sighing, over a delightful dinner, that cornmeal, water ground meal, which her brother L. P. Best, Jr., sends her from North Carolina, was running low.

Mrs. Royall and General Royall, by the way, keep in close touch with the North Carolina they love. Royall is the senior member of one of New York's oldest law firms.

The Royalls live in an exclusive Fifth Avenue apartment. Mrs. Jacqueline Kennedy has an apartment in the same building. Mrs. Royall called the widow of President Kennedy a kind and friendly neighbor.

Mrs. Royall's delight is to entertain for friends from Goldsboro. And she gives the food or refreshments she serves the artistic touch which she learned from her mother, the late Mrs. L. P. Best of Warsaw.

The night the General Manager and I had a pleasant dinner with the Royalls, Margaret herself had cooked the meal, which featured turkey with cornbread dressing.

Somebody could make money with a business shipping "down home" cornmeal to displaced Tar Heels.

The Belks liked to put up at the Piccadilly because it was convenient to the theater district, being just off Broadway. Also it was run by a New Bern native, Ed Wallnau, who had made the hotel "a sort of North Carolina informal headquarters."

During a stay at the Piccadilly in November, 1962, Henry reported on an incident that had taken place in the vicinity.

We were returning to the hotel one evening when we came upon what we at first thought was a riot or other disturbance. Hundreds of shouting, yelling, frenzied people, mostly young people, were doing an Indian war dance on Broadway, or so it appeared. To walk along the sidewalk through that mob would have been difficult, so we crossed to the other side of the street. The shouting and screaming continued.

Wy asked the Piccadilly doorman what was going on.

"Ah, that is a crowd heckling 'Broadway Rose'," he said. "She is a street preacher. This riot scene takes place night after night. She gets people, mostly teenagers, to heckle her and cause a lot of noise. That brings a curious crowd to hear her preach."

During that trip to New York, Henry called on his old friend, Dr. Frank P. Graham, United Nations mediator, who had come down with pneumonia and was in Doctors Hospital.

We found that "Dr. Frank" had become a favorite with the nurses and staff of the hospital. His room was bright with flowers from many friends and admirers. One of the displays was from the North Carolina Home Demonstration Federation. The group sent its annual delegation to the United Nations while he was a patient at the hospital. It was the first time in some 10 years that Dr. Graham had not been present to personally greet the Home Demonstration group and to give them a personally conducted tour of the United Nations.

Since his doctor has ordered Dr. Frank to take it easy for a spell, Mrs. Graham can think more about that "Southern supper" she wants to give to young Tar Heel friends living in Manhattan. She wishes to keep them reminded of good eating down home. Topping's sausage would be high on the list. And she wants some real North Carolina yams, cured out so the sugar oozes from them. And there would be coarse grits.

Henry saw "two excellent plays and a depressing movie" on the trip.

For some hours after suffering over Eugene O'Neill's 'Long Journey Into Night', the movie, we speculated we might have reversed the order of our seeing the entertainments. But now that we are farther away from the O'Neill vehicle, we feel that maybe the order in which we saw the shows was the best.

128

First we saw 'Sound of Music', then 'A Man for All Seasons', then the 'Journey'.

'The Sound of Music' has been running on Broadway for a couple of years or so and on previous trips we were unable to get tickets. It still is playing to excellent houses. It is as wholesome a piece as one comes by in today's theater. It is so wonderfully normal, natural and free of the brittle, smart-alecky, insinuating obscenity one sometimes finds. The songs are tuneful but not overly sweet. We appreciated so much that none of the several songs resorted to torrid jazz or ear-splitting cacophony now characteristic of much of that called popular music.

'A Man for All Seasons' is the artistically dramatized life of Sir Thomas More, chancellor of England under Henry VIII. All I knew about him was that he had written 'Utopia', which used to be required reading in college sophomore English. But he was a man whose profile in courage is as a modern lesson. Sir Thomas went against his own best interests, his friends, his associates, and even his family, in his refusal to sacrifice principle as he saw it. Henry VIII wanted a legal divorce from Catherine of Aragon, sister of Spain's king, who had not borne him a son. He wanted to take Anne Boleyn as his new queen. More was a figure of such lustre and respect that even tacit approval from him would have made the divorce and new marriage more acceptable to the nation.

Pressure of loss of place and prestige, prison, nothing could persuade him to join in what he considered was wrong. One sees in the play the familiar types of politicians known everywhere. A well balanced cast moves the play unerringly upward in interest. It is good red meat for today as for the time of Henry VIII. It is good drama.

If you want in your entertainment an escape from life, then you do not need to see the movie from Eugene O'Neill's 'Long Journey into Night'. It is what its title says, a journey into night. A journey which reveals the torments and fears and influences which made O'Neill the playwright he was. Katherine Hepburn as the drug addicted mother broke my heart.

Chief attraction for the Belks on their trip to New York in October, 1964, was the World's Fair.

What did we see at the New York World's Fair?

Biggest impression the General Manager and I brought away was of one man seated alone and lonely in the beautiful Garden of Meditation. The Fair builders thought of everything, even this enticing and inviting Garden of Meditation.

On this bright, crisp, invigorating morning we were at the Fair, there were 53,000 other folks on the wide-spreading grounds. We decided the best way to start was to take a bus trip around the entire layout. It took nearly an hour to get aboard one of the big buses. While we waited in line, the GM noticed two women on a bus, getting ready to pull out, waving in a most friendly manner. Looking closer, the GM identified the friends as Mrs. H. G. Maxwell, Jr., and Mrs. Buddy Crawford of Goldsboro. We had heard that the Crawfords and the Maxwells would be in New York to see some World Series games, but imagine meeting up with the ladies by chance among 7 million people.

Our bus passed, among the hundreds of features, the lovely meditation garden. It was green with grass and studded with large trees. There were comfortable seats upon which the visitor was invited to relax and cogitate on the way of the world, or the message in the religious displays from the denominations which have served millions of men for 2,000 years.

Everybody but this lone man was hurrying and scurrying, or waiting in line, or refreshing himself with food, or visiting some feature. Only one out of 53,000 had felt the compulsion to go aside in quiet search of his soul, or to sit and soak up the glories of God and His handiwork.

If we had been able to get off the bus at the spot, we would have crashed the lone man's meditation with a plea for an interview. What was his name? What was his background? What was his soul's longing? Did he draw aside to meditate because he had at the moment some particular problem of life or death or pain or sorrow or depression? Or did he draw aside to enjoy the beauties, man-made, all around, and to refresh his mind and body with thoughts of his many blessings?

More probably, though, that lone meditator was at the bench by the garden when his tired feet called so loudly for rest that he sat down in response.

Henry saw a play — "The Committee" — but . . .

It left this poor country editor cold.

For one thing, he gnashed his teeth at paying $4.80 for tickets in the rear of the second gallery. And the seats were so close together that only dwarfs could have been comfortable in them.

"The Committee" had been billed as a new kind of theater. It was represented as offering an escape from the accepted stage techniques and methods, a new departure which gave broad freedom to the actors and the vehicles they employed.

130

To my way of thinking, the production was simply a bunch of skits strung together without any connection of theme or plot or music. The format was that of the vaudeville of years back, except that smut had replaced slapstick, and the conversation and action on stage were the stiletto-type thumbing of noses at subjects the average man puts faith in.

Of more pleasure to the Belks was spending a morning at the zoo with Rosemarie, their adopted granddaughter.

Without a doubt, the high spot of our trip to New York was a sunny, brisk morning at the Children's Zoo in company of Rosemarie, age three and one-half.

For admission to that fairyland place, one must be accompanied by a child. It was a toss-up as to who had the most fun, yours truly, the General Manager or the parents of Rosemarie.

The Children's Zoo is located in Central Park. It is comparatively new in New York's great array of parks, playgrounds, attractions and centers. Governor and Mrs. Lehman made the place of animals and children's books and legends a gift to the city.

Rosemarie had been to the zoo at other times and she knew exactly what she wanted to visit. She flitted around among the hundreds of other children like a butterfly. It took four adults to keep up with her.

The Belks saw a movie version of "Taming of the Shrew".

So far as I am concerned, we wasted our time.

And that goes even though the principal parts were played by Elizabeth Taylor and Richard Burton.

"The Taming", as you know, was one of the many dramatic works written by William Shakespeare in the sixteenth century. I came away from the performance wondering why the play has survived for four centuries. I felt that Shakespeare must have been in a period of low-voltage authorship when he wrote the piece.

I must admit, however, that I have a severe handicap regarding what appeals to me in a play. I cannot see the stage. I must depend entirely upon my sense of hearing.

Maybe if I had been able to see the luscious Elizabeth Taylor, I would have had a better opinion of the play. Or if I had been able to see the world-famous actor, Richard Burton, it might have made a difference to me.

But, as it was, I felt that the version was mostly sound and fury signifying nothing. Elizabeth Taylor screamed and fumed and carried on in such a fashion as to pound your eardrums. And Burton failed for me to show sufficient force and manliness to tame a shrew.

In 1969, Henry caught up with the latest in women's fashions when he was in New York.

You probably have noticed it a long time ago, but this poor country boy did not discover it until his recent week in New York with the General Manager.

For milady this winter the long coat is coming back. The latest is that the coat will be only about 2½ inches from the floor. And it sounds queer to me for a girl to be wearing a mid-thigh skirt and a coat that all but touches the floor. My guess is that the long coat, or maxi as it is called, heralds a return to sanity as to the length of skirts before many months. Mighty few girls have legs that are pretty enough to be exposed to several inches above the knees.

And one of the most awkward sights is that of a group of women gathered for coffee or something, and busier pulling down their skirts than anything else. Younger women, some of them, can get away with mid-thigh skirts, but milady who is over 45 can't properly set off the short skirts.

The Belks spent a "pleasant evening" with the family of Gene Roberts, Jr., one of Henry's proteges, who had made good in the big city. It must have produced tantalizing reveries for the old teacher who had elected to be a country editor.

The Roberts' live in the Pavilion Apartments, largest in New York, which is on 77th Street, East, a real swank neighborhood. Several thousand residents occupy the structure. Three fountains across the face of the apartment add beauty and freshness to the scene.

As we sat before a large dining room table made of rosewood, the roar of the fountains in the yard came to our ears like the sound of the sea.

Gene, Jr., among newspapermen, is regarded as one of outstanding accomplishment and promise. He is the editor of national affairs for the New York Times. Toward the end of the evening of good food and good talk, I heard the apartment bell ring. Gene said the sound was to let him know that one of the first editions of the paper for that morning had been left at the apartment door. Gene immediately checks the paper to see that any serious typographical errors are corrected.

Roberts, who did his first reporting for the News-Argus, has come up fast in the newspaper world. For a time he was city editor of one of the Knight papers in Detroit. He later joined the Times staff and headed its southeastern states news bureau. He was then shifted to Southeast Asia, where he supervised the work of six men covering the Vietnam War. The Times was pleased with his work and offered him the place as editor for national affairs.

Attending a session of the American Society of Newspaper Editors in Montreal and a hop to Nassau while attending a press convention in Miami were Henry's only excursions out of the country.

But he had ideas, as expressed in "See Rome and Die", in 1963.

Eight or nine years ago we told you of the case of the man who had a great urge to take his General Manager on a trip to Europe. He debated with himself whether to spend the money for a trip, or whether to add a second bathroom to his house. Maybe you remember that, after great soul-searching, he decided that the bathroom was more practical. Into it went the money.

Now that man is arguing with himself again.

The old craving to see London and Paris and Rome has returned with great force. By night he hears Big Ben and sees Westminster Abbey and has trouble quite getting all words from the English cabbies — in imagination, that is. And thousand-year-old Paris lights a beacon for him and the Latin Quarter calls. And from Rome he hears a voice that goes back to Caesar and the gladiators and to Paul in his prison cell and the Christians and the Catacombs.

It will take more money now to make the trip than it would have eight or nine years ago.

But this man argues right on. Last week he had fully made up his mind to go into the savings and take the money required.

This week he is not so sure. Now he is impressed with the reasoning that in event of a long illness, he would need the money required for even a two-weeks trip to the cities which built western civilization.

15

Darkness came to Henry in 1955.

The curtain did not have to descend much; he only had one-tenth vision left in one eye. But that little was "precious".

The public was not told of Henry's new round with blindness until March 9, in an editorial titled 'Back to the Hospital'.

You readers have been through so much with me; I must take you into my confidence again.

Doing that is, oh, so personal, but it purges my soul and serves as a sort of therapy.

When you read this, I expect to be back at Duke Hospital again. That is, if they have found the seven-foot bed I need. I have waited three days on that and on a room.

It came about this way.

For some weeks there has seemed to be a cloudiness over my right eye. That's my good one. The vision has been one-tenth of normal.

About three weeks ago I consulted my eye man at Duke. Then, last Thursday, I went back for a check. He confirmed my fears that changes were occurring in the eye.

Well, what do we do? I asked.

He said I should enter the hospital.

For how long?

Maybe ten days, he replied. But doctors can't lay down absolute limits for hospital stay. So many things can happen.

He said he found a fluid was forming over the cornea. And that tension was increasing.

I was telling publisher Hal Tanner about it and he wanted to know what tension in an eye was. Best I could explain was to say that you have a certain pressure you keep your automobile tires at. Seems like there is a similar pressure inside the eye. If disease or something causes the pressure to go up, there is trouble, a loss of elasticity.

So, if they have found that seven-foot bed by now, my eyes will have been bandaged and will remain so for 24 hours. That is to determine if the tension, and a fluid on the cornea, will go away. Should that be the case, then we will know that the trouble is coming from exposure.

If it doesn't, we can expect that the trouble is within the eye.

Then what? First, we go on drugs to see if that will correct the trouble. If it does not, there may be surgery.

I happened to remark that the left eye gave me a feeling all the time that there was sight in it, but just closed out by a curtain. You may remember that a half dozen operations on it over the past two years did not permanent good.

The doctor said that since all sight in it is now lost, we could, as a last resort, try an iridectomy on it. I suppose he meant to make a bigger opening in the eye, an opening that might enable him to see where the retina is torn apart. In all the previous efforts, the surgeons had to see to repair the torn retina without actually seeing what they sought to repair.

But we will see what comes.

Meantime, I will have to dictate editorials from the hospital. My Seeing Eye wife, and the best secretary anyone ever had, is with me and helping.

News-Argus Publisher Hal Tanner is showing me every consideration and understanding. His attitude and cooperative spirit have helped. City Editor Bill Justice will direct the news department in the office. I expect to keep in close touch with developments at home by telephone and letter.

Of course I have been right low in my mind since the doctor said come back. But in a way it is a relief to get a decision made. I have been almost certain for weeks that some change in the eye was taking place. Yet I would argue that I was just too much concerned with the eye and just imagining it.

So I'm facing up to things again. In due time I'll regain my composure and spirit.

Baring my heart thus brutally to public view helps, in that direction. You will understand and pardon, I feel sure.

Henry's next report was on 'Search for a Seven Foot Bed'.

One never knows from what unexpected source help may come.

Thomas Wolfe, the great North Carolina novelist, who was six feet and seven inches tall, wrote a piece about this being a six-foot world.

The late A. H. Edgerton of Goldsboro from time to time carried on his own private campaign to interest Walnut Street merchants in seeing that store awnings complied fully with a town ordinance requiring that they should be six feet six inches above the sidewalk. On one occasion he urged the writer that he should not let the subject drop. Mr. Edgerton himself was a tall man, above six feet, and he knew from experience that being forced to duck under awnings reduces one to the feeling of bobbing apples at a school carnival.

Yours truly is six feet and six inches tall.

When we were in Tampa, back in October, and walking in front of the Elks Club, a little old lady raced to catch up with us. Tilting her head skyward, she wanted to know if I was from Texas. When I replied that I was a Tar Heel born and a Tar Heel bred, she seemed much disappointed.

"I felt you were from Texas," she said, and went her way, her manner suggesting that a North Carolinian had no business being that tall.

When Dr. Anderson recommended that I come back to Duke for treatment of my eye, he said the hospital would have a seven foot bed for me when I checked in. Of course the doctors have no responsibility in the matter of room or bed facilities. That is up to the business management and the office of admissions. But Dr. A was interested in my behalf and telephoned admissions personally to request that a seven foot bed be provided for me when I checked in, three or four days later.

Among the 600 beds at Duke Hospital, three of them are seven-foot beds. The other 597 are six-foot beds, and single beds in width. Trying to sleep a six-foot six-inch frame on a narrow six-foot bed can get tiresome.

The afternoon that Lee Coward deposited us at the front of Duke Hospital and we went in to Admissions, one of the first things we were told was: "We haven't been able to get you a seven-foot bed yet, but we will have one for you soon."

We left Admissions and the boy took our bags to the receptionist on the third floor. When we had shaken hands, she said, "The seven-foot beds are in use, but we are looking for one for you."

Next we checked in with the head nurse on the hall. She turned immediately to the elusive seven-foot bed, which by this time I had decided was a rather insubstantial quantity.

"We have located the seven-foot beds. Those using them will be going out in a few days and we will get the first one that is vacated for you."

So explained the hall nurse supervisor.

We proceeded to our room, the center cubicle in a three-cubicle facility. That space and that room, by the way, were exactly what I had occupied in two of my previous visits to Duke. I felt perfectly at home.

A nurse came in to weigh me and measure my height. That is routine in checking patients in.

We got along all right with the weighing. Then she told me to stand back on the little platform scales. You know the kind that has a height chart which is pulled from a sheath and extended above the head of the subject being measured. You have seen them in the office of your doctor.

She got me on the machine and pulled out the height measuring stick. It came all the way out and she was left, puzzled looking, with the gadget in her hand.

Still holding the height yardstick, she raced out of the room and down the hall, calling the name of the hall supervisor with every step.

In a moment the hall supervisor was back with the nurse.

"How tall are you?" she asked. "Our machine won't measure you."

I told her and she put it down on the chart.

A day passed. Another day passed. Most every person with any connection with the hospital who came to my room reported that they were looking for a seven-foot bed for me.

All the time I was getting slimmer and slimmer of hope that the bed would materialize.

On the third day, Herbert, who has been an orderly at the hospital since it was established, came in smiling bright as the sun, his snow-white teeth gleaming from his dark face.

"I've got you a seven-foot bed," he said.

I got out of the little bed for a moment. Herbert rolled it out and rolled the seven-footer back, all fresh with clean linen.

"How did you get it, Herbert?" I asked, voicing my thanks.

"It's enough to say I got it, not how," Herbert replied. "Anyway, that other fellow will be wondering."

My friend, Herbert, the veteran orderly, had accomplished for me what the administrative staff and nurses had not been able to do.

You never know from what source your strength and help will come.

Henry continued to send in letters to the paper for a while, then they stopped. Nothing more was said about the eye trouble and he had been hospitalized for three weeks.

On March 20, there was a guest editorial by Col. John D. Langston, one of the founders of the Goldsboro News and a good friend of Henry's.

Did you ever see anybody like this fellow Henry Belk? You'd think he would be wringing his hands, moaning and sqawking to high heaven about his ailments, including the near loss of his sight. But not Henry. While the doctors are analyzing, diagnosing, and going through all sorts of medical mental gymnastics to determine what kind of and how much carving to do on those organs by which we ordinarily see, Henry is seeing more and looking much further ahead than most of us with so-called perfect vision. He is catching and holding an appreciation of values that one only catches and holds who, as the Master said, carries a cross.

Faltering physically under his cross, we find Henry bringing cheerfulness and comfort to the readers of the News-Argus who occasionally got bored with some of his editorial writings in the days when the physique was stronger than the spirit.

What I think Henry has been trying to tell all the hand wringers and complaining ones is that it might be a good idea, individually and collectively, to "Count your blessings." That seems to be the kind of bookkeeping our friend has been doing for some time. It must be a good system. We haven't heard him even refer to the debit side of the ledger.

Guest editorials continued to appear, then Henry was out of the hospital and doing the writing. No mention was made of what had happened to him. Apparently his eye trouble had responded to drugs.

Then he was back at Duke. On July 13, there was an editorial, "Editor Asks for Help."

I am surprised to be writing from this place again, as you are to be reading it. At this good hour the good wife and I were supposed to be putting into St. George's Harbor, Bermuda, on the Caribbean Lines steamer "Tradewind". It was a post-convention tour of the N. C. Press Association.

George and Augusta Myrover picked us up at our house about 11 o'clock last Friday morning. It was a lovely day and we felt grand to be getting away on a vacation.

George was driving a brand-new DeSoto and we took it at an easy pace. We stopped just north of Enfield at 'The Plantation' for lunch. The place was air-conditioned, the food was good, the rest rooms were clean.

At 6 o'clock we reached Fredericksburg, Va., and put up at the George Washington Motel. Highway No. 1 was just outside our door and a continual line of trucks and cars sped north and south along this Main Street of the United States.

The air-conditioned coolness of our room was heavenly. We dressed and relaxed a bit before going out for dinner. It must have been about 9 o'clock when we came back, intending to go to bed early, to be fresh for an early start to Washington, from which we were scheduled to sail the next day.

Then the trouble started that sent me back to the hospital. For no apparent cause, that I could detect, my right eye suddenly was badly swollen and aching like a sore tooth. The pain was something terrible and it continued all night long, despite copious doses of aspirin. I couldn't think, so befuddled with pain was I. Lucile took things into her hands and went to the Myrover room to get him to put in a call to the airport about schedules and reservation by plane from Washington to Durham. Eastern Air Lines had a "Silver Falcon" flight out of the National Airport at 10:23 the next morning, but it was sold out. The only chance would be to purchase tickets and stand by, with the hope that someone cancelled a reservation at the last minute.

By now I was completely blinded by the swelling and by the pain. The man at the Eastern Air Lines stand-by desk was most sympathetic and helpful. About 45 minutes before plane time, he said he thought he was going to be able to get us on the plane. He said we should check by the desk in a few minutes, even though he did not have us paged. We did this and he told us we could have the last two seats. We will never know whether he gave us priority over some other "stand-by's" because of the personal emergency which he recognized. We thought this might have been the case.

An hour and five minutes after we boarded the plane, we were at Raleigh-Durham Airport, having covered more miles than we did in eight hours of automobile driving. Forty-five minutes after we reached the Raleigh-Durham Airport, we were at the hospital and Dr. Anderson had ordered me to bed. He looked rather sober as he examined the closed eye. He ordered applications of holocaine every two hours and compresses from ice cold water almost constantly. The next morning the eye was some better but still painful.

Ordinarily such an occurrence to normal eyes would not be considered too serious, but, as you readers know, in the series of mishaps that I have had in the past three years, I lost all sight in the left eye and was left with about 10 percent vision in the right eye. Now, 10 percent vision may not seem very much, but when it is all you have, it is precious. One can't get around very freely with 10 percent vision, but if you have that vision shut off by the swelling and pain, as I experienced over the weekend, then you know just how valuable it is to you.

Not a man given to laquaciousness, Dr. Anderson worked up to his recommendation gradually. He thought it would be better if I underwent a decompression operation of the right eye. When the swellings occur and tension increases, the cornea is pressed forward and dries out. The lid will not cover the eye and protect it. There is danger that the cornea may be destroyed. A decompression operation should give promise of preventing such an occurrence.

Now just what is a decompression operation?

The surgeons open the head slightly above the temple and toward the front, and also from the top of the forehead a little above the hairline. Then they are able to remove the eye and to fix the socket so that the eye can be placed further back in the socket.

The good healthy eye normally is well housed in the socket and protected from bumps or blows. Where an eye abnormally protrudes, a decompression operation returns it to its natural position. I had such an operation on the left eye two and a half years ago. At that time I went to the operating room about 7:30 in the morning. I stayed on the operating table about five hours and was in the recovery room until 11 o'clock that night. I still remember very vividly coming to. I seemed to be in some jungle in darkest Africa that was extremely well populated with all sorts of lions, crocodiles, hyenas and every imaginable other kind of beast. And they were all screaming and yelling and wailing at the top of their voices.

But such is the miracle of modern surgery that eight days after this experience I was able to undergo an operation to reattach a retina.

Now, the question is, shall I take the chance of losing the 10 percent vision I have and periodically undergoing intense pain?

Or shall I have the decompression operation on the right eye?

Henry had the operation, but it was weeks before his readers were told about it. As in his previous stays at the hospital, he sent home columns, and when they were interrupted, friends filled in for him.

One of his pieces was titled 'From a Midnight Train'.

The Seaboard passenger train north stopped near midnight at Henderson. It would have to spend about 15 minutes there.

A New York merchant on the train, unable to sleep, recalled that his firm had a store in Henderson, and on the street near the station. He got off, walked to the store.

The display windows were lit. An earnest young man was engrossed in setting up a new display for the coming week. He was so deeply engrossed in his work that he never noticed the New York firm head watching him from the street.

The merchant returned to his train. When he got back to his office Monday morning, he wrote a letter to the manager of the Henderson store. The letter said, Find out the name of the young man who at midnight was dressing the window. Watch him and give him every chance to get ahead with us. The letter pointed out that a young man, who on his own time, and at a time when he could have been entertaining himself, preferred rather to work at his job, showed purpose and promise.

The young man didn't know about the eyes from the midnight train, or about the letter which came in, a few days later. But the extra devotion he showed to his work that night won him rapid promotion.

His record attracted the attention of another department store chain.

The young man who dressed the window at midnight on a Saturday was Arthur L. Tyler of Rocky Mount. You know him. He is the Tyler of the Belk-Tyler department store chain, which operates in nearly a score of towns and cities in Eastern North Carolina.

Another of Henry's pieces was on 'A Call to Preach'.

For many years he went up and down in Sweet Union, fighting sin. He preached from Bethelem to New Salem, from Waxhaw to Marshville, and points in between. He was one of the best known local preachers of a preaching county.

His impassioned attack on sin made the welkin ring at brush arbor and camp meeting, and at the church in the dale. He was a familiar and well loved figure. Scores of parents named their children for him.

He has long been gathered with his fathers. But in Sweet Union they still tell as a true story of how he happened to get "the call to preach."

He was plowing his rocky field on a hillside in New Salem. A couple of neighborhood boys happened to discover that they could take the old guano horn (if you were raised on the farm 25 years ago, you will know what this is) and by using it as a sort of megaphone, throw their voices for a mile or so.

They hid in the woods near where the farmer was plowing and sent an eerie "Go preach" call floating across the hillside. It wasn't a human voice, coming as it did through the guano horn. The farmer looked startled and stopped to listen. The boys from their hiding place watched with bated breath. In a few minutes the farmer went back to his plowing. Again the boys sent the "Go preach" skimming across the hillside. The farmer slapped with the lines at the mule and quickened his pace. For an hour or so the voice from the sky came, now loud, now faint: "Go preach."

The farmer unhitched the mule from the plow.
He was through with farming. He became a preacher.
That is the story they tell in Sweet Union even to this day.

16

On September 7, Henry ended his silence about his illness with 'Fight for Sight Continued'.

When you read this, I will have been five days without sight. That will continue for several weeks. Then Dr. Anderson will remove the sutures which have sealed up the right eye and we shall know if I have regained my sight, or if I will have to spend the rest of my days in darkness.

It was two months ago, you remember, when I last mentioned the subject of this continued battle for vision. I grew ashamed to mention it, but bringint it into the open gives me better preparation for whatever may be.

I underwent a decompression operation of the right eye on July 11. This was most successful. Four weeks later I had so regained vision that I was able to read with microscopic glasses, something which I had been unable to do, most days, for several months. I looked as if I were out of the woods.

Then, the day before Hurricane Connie arrived, I awoke to find the eye slightly irritated. The left, you know, lost all vision in a series of retina detachments. I paid little attention to the sore eye, but it was so intense by the afternoon that I had to go to bed. The next morning I telephoned Dr. Anderson and he said I had better come back to Duke. The storm was raging at the time, but the following morning I returned.

Dr. Anderson took one look and decided that the eye was seriously infected. I had been able to see out of it the night before, but when I reached the hospital, sight was completely gone. Smears and lab tests showed that a "strep" infection had gained serious headway in the eye, which burned like a coal of fire in my head.

For the next week, with special nurses around the clock, I received antibiotic drops of three or four kinds in the eye every 15 minutes, day and night. In addition I received, morning and evening, hypodermic injections of penicillin and streptomycin, and three times a day I got another kind of drops.

Gradually the pain subsided and a glimmer of light began to come back in the eye, a glimmer which enabled me to distinguish where a window was in the room. There remained, however, a small area in the center of the eye which was very slow to heal. So last Friday Dr. Anderson said he had decided on an operational procedure which might give the eye a better chance of healing. On Saturday morning the procedure was carried out and the eye was completely sealed off.

One happy thing about this was that Dr. Anderson said I could go home the first of the week to remain while the necessary time passed.

As usual, Goldsboro people, or former Goldsboro people, have been dropping by my room, and many of you good friends, for which I thank you very much, have sent messages.

I especially enjoyed a visit from Norwood Middleton, former News-Argus reporter, who recently was promoted to news editor of the Roanoke, Va., Times-World.

P.S. It turns out that the issue was not settled, as we had thought. The foregoing was written Friday night, in expectation that the operation would come Saturday morning. However, during the night the strep infection again gained the upper hand. And so I was put back on the routine of eye drops every 15 minutes during the day and every 30 minutes at night. If and when the infection is controlled, then we will think of the operation.

A few days later Henry asked his readers "What Quotation Inspires You Most?"

Do you have a favorite quotation from the Bible, from poetry, or from literature that has helped you in your life? One which has given you strength for the day? That renews your courage, your faith and your determination? One which has been a lamp unto your feet and a light for your pathway?

Maybe you have never thought of it, but you probably have a favorite inspirational quotation that has served you long and well.

We would be pleased to have our readers send in their favorite quotation with their reason why.

A "ham and biscuit" given to Henry by a patient on his ward boosted his morale.

Slowly I savored the rare treat and washed it down with buttermilk. And even before it was all gone, my attitude had begun to change. My spirits were lifted, my outlook brightened, and before I knew it, my dark mood had become almost gay.

The mood continued the next morning. I realized with joy that more light was beginning to penetrate through the covering left by the large ucler, for which I had been undergoing treatment for three weeks. I recognized for a certainty a splotch of light on the head of my bed as being sunlight, and it was so beautiful.

Two hours later I had my morning's examination from Dr. Anderson.

"When can I tell them at the office that I will be coming home?" I asked.

He replied, "Tell them 30 days. We now have the second infection under control, but we don't want to push it too fast, like we did the first one."

I've got to find some more ham and biscuit, or something, as a morale builder.

The morale builder came in the form of 'A Joyous Experience'.

For the first time in three weeks and four days, I dressed as if for the street, and it was a joyous experience. If ever you have spent a month or so lying around in hospital garb, you will understand what I am talking about.

The shirt seemed such a good kind friend, as I put it on, and trousers somehow raised my morale and spirits no end. The nurse who was helping me dress asked if I wanted a coat. I replied that I certainly did, because I wanted to feel like a man back at work for one more time.

And it was a delight to get into the shoes, instead of bedroom slippers, as comfy as bedroom slippers can be, occasionally. Shoes seem to snuggle to your feet and give you better support.

With the nurse guiding me, we went from the third floor to the second floor to Minot Ward, intending to see Sam Byrd, Mt. Olive's famous son, who has been a patient at the hospital for the last 27 weeks, fighting a rare type of blood infection. I wanted to repay his visit to my room over the weekend, but we found the curtains pulled back and decided he must be sleeping.

After leaving Sam's room, we decided to go out into the little porch which opens from a door on the second floor. When I stepped onto the porch, it was a grand and glorious feeling. It was a warm day and the sun was out kindly and a gentle breeze was blowing. The nurse led me over to one side of the stone porch where benches are placed. We sat for a few minutes enjoying the glory of a fall afternoon.

The spirit of adventure was high within me and to celebrate the occasion of having donned street clothes for the first time in about a month, I decided that I would go to the soda shop. That is on the first floor of the hospital. Part of the way, as we walked, the nurse guiding me, I had the strange feeling that I was walking along a narrow parapet and lifted up with walls falling away on either side.

The soda shop, as usual, was a very busy place. The nurse guided me to a seat between two tables and we sat down for a Coca-Cola. To one side was a group of young college people. Their principal conversation was about the current tight race in the American League.

"Would you like to go outside for a minute?" the nurse asked.

"That would be wonderful," I said.

She knew her way about the place and guided me to the door which opened on the outside. One step, she said, now three steps, she said, and I took them stumblingly. My feet once more were planted on God's good, green, solid earth.

We had stepped into a small garden which is largely enclosed by walls of the hospital building. Shrubs and evergreens make up most of the planting, and there are pleasant walks. The breeze was soft and caressing and the sun smiled benignly on my back. A deep sense of peace filled my heart.

We made a circle of the little walk and came back into the building through the door by which we had left. When we got back to my room, I asked the nurse how long we had been out and she said less than half an hour. It seemed a great and pleasing adventure to me.

And now for the personal information about which many of you have written or inquired. The infection seems to have been fully brought under control in the right eye again. And I am slowly regaining some perception of light and darkness in the eye. Whether I will regain an usuable amount of sight remains to be seen.

On September 23, Henry announced that he had returned home. A week later he had a piece titled 'Doing Without Sight'.

When you were a child you probably played blindman's bluff. And you probably played pinning on the donkey's tail.

In blindman's bluff, one child binds his eyes so he cannot see. Then he is given a spin around in a circle a time or two. After that, his job is to catch one of the other children. Everybody dances around him in great glee. He cannot see and the way he may misjudge distances produces ludicrous laughter.

In pinning the donkey's tail, one is blindfolded and told to pin the tail at the appropriate place on the donkey, fastened to a wall. The tail may wind up on the ears or mouth, resulting in gales of laughter.

Well, for almost two weeks now I have been engaged in what might be called a game of blindman's bluff. At the end, I shall know whether this fight for sight is successful. I returned home from Duke Hospital completely blind, as the eye under treatment is sealed off, with the lids sewn together.

I had to get reacquainted with the place, as familiar and dear as it has been for me nigh on to 30 years. But I have been getting along all right. Fortunately we have a narrow hall in the center of the house, leading from the living room, and I can touch the sides of the wall and find my way to the den, where my typewriter is, or into a second door on the right, where the bedroom is located. Or I can follow the walls straight back to the end of the hall and know I am in the bathroom.

One gets along all right finding his way around his familiar surroundings of his own house, provided things remain where they ought to be. As I undress, I must take particular pains to place every item of clothing at a particular spot, so that I can return to it and pick it up when I wish the clothing again. I wear one of the biggest shoe sizes of anybody in Goldsboro and it might seem that there would be no difficulty in finding something as big as a couple of gunboats. But shoes have a way of being perched this way or that way, and several times I have found myself flopping all over the bedroom looking for my shoes. I learned pretty quickly that bedroom slippers must be placed at a particular spot under the bed and that I must take care to place the right shoe on the right side and the left shoe on the left side.

A walking stick which Edwin Cox made and gave me a number of years ago has been a big help in finding my way around the house. With this stick going forward, as sort of an advance guard, I keep from bumping into things, and I find out where I am more quickly. I had a little trouble at first trying to locate furniture in the living room. I have a favorite big upholstered chair and I was poking around with the Ed Cox walking stick trying to locate it, so I could sit down. With no sight, you learn not to sit down too quickly, or you might find yourself sitting on the floor.

In this connection I am thinking of what happened to the late Horace King of Goldsboro when he went to a Durham eye clinic many years ago for a cataract operation. He was given a small private room. He felt around to locate the table, chairs and bed, so he would know where things were. Late that night, being unable to sleep, he decided to get up and smoke a cigarette. He knew for a certainty there had been an easy chair in one corner of the room, but somebody, maybe the nurse, had moved the chair, and when he sat down, without feeling for it, he sat on the floor with a resounding bomp. If you knew Mr. King, whom we valued highly as a friend, you can imagine the volcanic eruption that followed.

But to get back to my upholstered chair, I was feeling around with the Ed

Cox stick and I kept bumping into a small child's rocking chair, which was supposed to be against the wall on one side of the room. I poked and poked all around the living room, but always came back to the little chair. Finally, a friend came in and explained the predicament. The reason I couldn't find my chair was that the child's chair was in front of it, fencing it off, so to speak.

Ada Moore is cooking for me and looking after me in a very good fashion. Before she leaves in the afternoon, she places my supper where I can get to it. I find I am little more helpless getting things out of the refrigerator than I was with sight. I think many of us men adopt an attitude of helplessness in trying to locate food items in the ice box, for we know that somebody in the family will take pity on us and come and do all the back-bending for us and find it and deliver it in our hands. I had no trouble locating the milk, both sweet and buttermilk, in the ice box and pouring a glass of milk for myself. Then I went out to the breakfast room in the adjoining room and placed the milk on the table near what I thought was my supper. I found the supper, all right, but I had a little trouble in relocating that milk. A small breakfast room can seem an area of great expansion if you are looking for something by feeling for it. But if you continue long enough, you generally find it and it is always just about one-quarter of an inch from where you thought it was, to begin with.

I licked that one by having Ada regularly now place milk or water in a glass directly in front of the bowl in which my fruit is placed. Then I can follow the bowl with my hands on the sides of the bowl and when I get to the rear of the bowl, there will be the milk or water.

Of course all of us know a number of splendid Goldsboro citizens, who are without sight, who keep house and get along as well keeping house and looking after their clothing and taking care of their persons as a sighted person. These people think nothing at all of preparing a meal, washing the dishes, or serving the food, or doing anything that a sighted person would do.

Clayton Barwick, who runs the stand at Wachovia Bank and Trust Co., a man who has been blind for many, many years, said this to me: "All you have to do is not to lose your nerve."

Of course one has to get away from the hesitancy of asking people for help for this or the other. Friends have repeatedly found things at the house for me.

Stitches in my eye are expected to be removed in a week or two weeks, and then we shall know if I am going to be able to retain my sight in the eye which has been severely infected with an ulcer for a good many weeks.

Henry's 'General Manager' was out of town at the time. A week later he saluted her in 'My 32nd Wedding Anniversary'.

Yesterday was the dearest day of the year to me. It marked my 32nd wedding anniversary. Upon this occasion I want to pay tribute to the great institution of marriage. Using that peg, I will be a little immodest in what I shall say.

Let me put in right here that I have been married over half of my life and they, the years of marriage, have been the best ones.

The Manager and I have similar tastes. We like the same kind of poetry, the same kind of books, and we both like people.

One thing that marriage, or rather the Manager did for me, in the course of a very few years, was to cure me of black moods. I had carried over from a troubled teen period periods of inexplicable lowness of spirit. Apparently without cause I would sink into a morose silence, which might last for a day or maybe three days. Then, as it had come, the mood would lift and the sun would shine for me again.

The Manager learned to sense these moods and at such times to give me increased reason to know that she stood with me against the world. She did not nag. She did not press with unanswerable questions or suggestions. She stood the closer by me and her actions spoke in no uncertain terms of her devotion.

I know I was a sore trial. But gradually, under the ministrations of her kindness and understanding, the moods came less and less. I could live with myself more comfortably, and I know I was more comfortable to live with. Now I have not had one of those fits of depression in years.

That is not to say that all worry has been forever banished. But if I worry now, I know why or what I am worrying about.

Years of dear companionship with the Manager have done more than that for me. Following in her trail, I have come closer to the church and my faith has developed. Aided by her tolerant and understanding example, for never has she been insistant or used pressure, I have come to know that religion gives peace and assurance.

And she has saved me from many a foolish mistake. By nature I am quick to react, and there was a time when my temper flared at the slightest suggestion of what I thought was something amiss. But one cannot rush into print with his tempers, or his resentments, or his prejudices.

But I have been tempted to do so, as I have filled this column over the years. Generally I didn't get far enough overboard to be unable to talk things out with the Manager. Her broad sympathy and her great willingness to make allowances, suggested angles which I had sometimes overlooked, and put me back on the road of sweet reasonableness.

And she could do, and does do with such finesse, making sure that I am not offended in my personality, and that I am not pushed into a position of feeling that I am being driven to a change of view by pressure. She is a finished psychologist and she has sensed always how to suggest and recommend without the broadside technique.

For every day of all these years, I have known I held her full confidence and that I could count on her to hold up my hands under every circumstance, even though everyone else should turn against me.

We have seen our troubles. During the depression we faced the close threat of losing the home we had sacrificed so much to start buying. We have had our sorrows. But if one lives, he must have his troubles and his sorrows. And they have been the lighter to bear and the easier to push aside because she has been close by me, giving me courage.

So, on this 32nd wedding anniversary, I put down the record here that all who care may read.

And in putting it down, I know that I am putting down the record, different only in name and circumstance, of thousands of good solid marriages right here in our midst. In thus confessing my own happiness, in my marriage, I do so for you others, also.

17

Henry lost the game of blindman's bluff, but his readers were not told of the outcome until months later. Following 'Doing Without Sight', nothing more was said on the subject until the following April, when doing without sight had become a way of life for him.

On April 4, 1956 he addressed 'An Open Letter', subtitled 'Hope in Darkness', to Victor Riesel, the labor columnist and radio commentator, who had been blinded when thugs threw acid in his face.

I don't know you, Victor Riesel of New York City. But in a way I do. In a way you are my soul brother. For once I could see and now I fumble my way.

You have been much on my heart since news came that fiends, seeking to stop your crusading against labor racketeering, threw a chemical into your face and burned out your eyes. I followed your fight for sight over the long weeks when the doctors worked and hoped that they might save your vision.

I had nothing of the terror of your experience, but for more than three years I fought to retain some sight. The battle apparently would be won and my spirits soared. Then a new complication would come. Now, four years and ten operations later, I accept the verdict. Only a miracle will return to me any vision. But deep inside me is a conviction that miracle may happen.

And I do have a glimmer of vision in one eye, the right. I can tell the darkness from day. I can find the arm of my Seeing Eye wife when she decks herself in colors. I give thanks for this little sight, which means so much.

Like, me, you depended on your writing for a living. Like me, you will be able to continue your work as a columnist.

As for myself, I think that the darkness which has overtaken me in a way has turned on new lights. I have today a deeper sympathy, a keener appreciation and a wider, more tolerant vision than I once had. The smallnesses of everyday affairs do not rub me the wrong way, as they once did. I have learned patience. I think I have a new and finer vision which has found expression in what I write.

Like you, I was most fortunate in that all these years I have used the touch system in typing. So that great escape, the use of the typewriter, was not lost to me when the darkness came.

So often it is such a small thing that bears up the spirit and enables one to go on, to stoop and pick up the worn-out tools and build anew again. Touch typing has been like that to me. Maybe it will be to you. Words come slowly and creakingly to me in diction. But give me the feel of the familiar typewriter keys and they fit themselves together grandly.

Now you walk alone, really and truly, but keep your head up and if you wait long enough you will come to a new sense of trust in yourself. This too will pass away. Keep that in mind and hold it close to you. It will serve you as a tried and close friend in the moments of dull despair which will capture you. These moments will come. They come, you know, even in moments of high accomplishment for the seeing person, and for one in darkness they sweep in unannounced from the hidden recesses of the soul, and maul and maim.

But they will go away. Hope does spring eternal. Time will tell you and teach you what is most useful to you in putting to rout these fits of depression or in making their visits shorter ones.

Admit your handicap. Most difficult for me, and it may be for you, will be the treating as normal and average the fact that you can no longer see.

Sometimes, if there is no one around and I have to make a telephone call and do not know the number, I have to ask information. Of course I should start by saying that I am asking for the number because I am blind. Then I would get sympathetic and cordial cooperation.

So I get my number and the bristling voice says that it is in the directory. That makes me so mad that then, and only then, can I say I have had to ask because I cannot see.

Learn to laugh. I am struggling to see always something funny in the riduculous little things that can happen to you because you can't see.

One irritant I haven't yet been able to find a way to laugh at is the person who comes to you and says, "I bet you don't know who this is." People you haven't seen in a long time seem to be the ones who ask that one. Last week I ran across a boyhood acquaintance I hadn't seen in 35 years, and he asked me that one.

My power of concentration seems to be strengthened by blindness. The eye cannot wander away to distant scenes that offer distraction. For instance, I find that now I can listen to a 15-minute newscast of many items and can reproduce it on the typewriter almost in toto.

Talking books have been a spiritual uplift to me. You don't have to stop reading or seeking out great minds because you are unable to see.

I have her jotted down hastily some observations which I hope may be of help to you, Victor Riesel.

On March 28, Henry had received the Goldsboro Rotary Club's 'Citizenship Award'. It was the second time in the history of the club that the award had been made.

Henry was presented the award by Josh Horne, publisher of the Rocky Mount Telegram, before a capacity crowd gathered at Hotel Goldsboro.

The award certificate stated it was given to Henry in recognition of his "outstanding labor on behalf of his fellowman and of his many years as the able editor of the Goldsboro News-Argus, through which his personal championship of every worthy endeavor has aided immeasurably in the spiritual, cultural and economic development of his community and state."

Henry, who had been led to think that he was attending a regular meeting of Rotary, remarked that "It looks like my wife would have told me to put on a clean shirt."

A number of out-of-town newsmen were present, headed by Leslie Thompson of Whiteville, president of the N. C. Press Association.

"Our Association and newspapers throughout the state are honored by this honor coming to Henry," Thompson said.

Lynn Nisbet, Raleigh correspondent for afternoon dailies and a 'Sweet Union' native, said: "I grew up with Henry Belk and I knew him when he was a tot. I have always had to look up to him and I am proud to do so. I have never known him to look down on any of God's creatures."

As Henry had written Riesel, admitting his handicap was difficult for him. In July, 1957, he had a piece, 'Waiting for the Train', which pointed up the difficulty.

The blind, on unfamiliar grounds and far from home, have to swallow pride and ask help from total strangers. Blindness is so new to me that I cannot yet do this without feeling a wave of self-pity.

I was in the Dearborn Station in Chicago killing time until the Sante Fe's 'Grand Canyon', northern section, allowed us to get aboard. Suddenly I received a call from nature.

Wondering what to do, I finally screwed up my courage and asked the first man I met to help me to the men's room. He graciously obliged me.

Then we sat down in the waiting room and got acquainted. He was a veteran of World War 2. His age is probably 62 to 65. His wife died eight years ago. He has one daughter who lives in a Chicago suburb, while he resides at a downtown hotel. He cannot or does not drive an auto.

He was a railway mail clerk for 25 years, but had to give up his mail run because of leg trouble resulting from an operation. I had something to do with nerve control over his legs. He doesn't walk naturally. His feet are just as apt to go to one side as to the front.

"You seemed to walk all right when you helped me to the men's room," I said.

"I had you to lean on," he replied.

And I was ashamed that I had felt self-pity.

Henry had some thoughts on 'Leading the Blind'.

One of the most difficult things a blind person has to adjust to is the simple admission of being blind. It is hard. One cringes and has a sense of shame, as if he had some obscene disease.

Among things I have difficulty in submitting to are the overly solicitous ministrations of those who wish to be helpful.

And almost without exception everyone wants to lead the blind. It must stem from the Biblical reference to the blind LEADING the blind. I get along so much better when I am allowed to take the right arm of the helper. Then I can follow every motion of his body, every step, and react to his reactions. If he takes me by the hand or arm and "leads" me, I still have the lost feeling which goes when I am guiding my steps by the arm of another. To be led is to feel groping and insecure. To walk by the arm of another is to feel free.

Sometimes Henry wondered if the 'Blind Need Three Arms'.

A third arm would be mighty handy at times for the blind. One needs one arm to link to the one walking with you. You another to guide your seeing eye stick by. When it blows hard and you release one arm to hold your hat, you lost in a noisy world. Or if you have papers, magazines, and even a small package, there is a crying need for that third arm.

Still, though, that third member would be in the way, except in these instances mentioned. That means it would probably be in the way more times than not.

On 'Talking Hands'

Since I lost my sight, I find that hands talk to me. Hands, that is, that I shake in greeting.

I came up with a start the other day to realize that instinctively I had been feeling hands to get some impression of the person to whom they belonged. A hand can tell much of a man's occupation, hobbies, interests. Some hands are long and thin, with thin fingers. Some are pudgy and thick. Some hands are dry and cool. Some are sweaty and damp. Talking hands speak also of the work one does, the aptitudes one has.

In the main, however, the blind person relies on what a voice tells him as to character, interests, attitudes of a person met for the first time. A voice that is drab, spiritless, too high or too low, uncouth or hesitant, all these can reveal the inner man. And with friends, I can tell immediately from the shades and accents and quality of a voice how a person is feeling at that particular time, whether he or she is in an optimistic or pessimistic frame of mind, whether one is mad or sad, resentful or defeated.

All of us, it seems to me, learn to tell how our friends are doing on a particular day by the timber and quality of their voice over the telephone. Some telephone voices tire you out immediately. A happy telephone salutation, bright and gay and pleasant, can make you feel so much better.

'Well of Loneliness'

Within the hearts of most blind persons there is a well of loneliness. It may be covered and submerged by a buoyant and determined spirit, but, deep down, it is there. This is a world for the sighted and the sightless are cut off, fenced in, and dwell apart.

Attend a reunion of the alumni of the State School for the Blind in Raleigh. Or attend the annual convention of the N. C. Workers for the Blind, and such joyous togetherness, such laughing and singing, you seldom see elsewhere. They come together, these handicapped ones, and if they stumble in walking, or bump into an object, it is all right. Those around you are doing the same thing.

In the spirit of oneness, of being equals and in sharing a common fate, rare good humor bubbles up and spreads all around. For good stories such as Edmund Harding could use, listen in to the talk at the conventions for the blind. Walk upon the campus of the school when the sessions are going on, and from every dormitory and gathering place there will be the sound of music, a guitar speaking of love and tenderness, a piano tinkling with nostalgia, and close harmony that pushes back the dark.

The well of loneliness is temporarily forgotten.

'Two Blind Men'

The General Manager and I were seated in the lobby of the Sir Walter Hotel in Raleigh.

As you know, I lost my sight 10 years ago.

As we talked the GM, looking toward the door, said, "There is a blind man."

I found it out quickly. In a firm, confident voice, he asked no one in particular which way it was to the elevator. The GM, accustomed to looking out for me as my eyes, got up and introduced herself and offered to help.

The man turned out to be the Rev. Alphonso Jordan, one of the two chaplains at the General Assembly. He has a room at the Sir Walter for the duration.

We talked. He had heard me in a talk before the N. C. Workers for the Blind at their annual convention.

The GM helped him to the elevator. In a few minutes he was back and asking in a voice that carried across the lobby which way it was to the door.

It was plain that Rev. Mr. Jordan has broken through the reserve and shyness, the unwillingness to admit blindness that grips so many of us folks with a sight handicap.

I would have found it next to impossible to speak into a room and ask help. I would have been in real need so far as to surrender my own personality as to tell the world I was blind.

Chaplain Jordan probably is more relaxed and free with his handicap because he is willing to accept it and to bump unabashedly into furniture, as he did in the lobby. I wonder if the time will come when I shall accept being blind. Now my great effort in unfamiliar circumstances or surroundsings is so to carry myself that I hope my blindness escapes those around me.

Being blind brought Henry a frightening experience in 1963, when he was attending a session of the American Society of Newspaper Editors in Washington.

Place — the swank Statler Hilton Hotel in Washington. Time — midnight.

I had been sleeping soundly. The click, click of the door of our room being closed brought me wide awake and tensely alert. I listened. I heard nothing more.

The General Manager occupied the adjoining twin bed. I listened but could hear no sound of breathing in sleep. I called out to her. I got no response. I put out my hand to the head of her bed. It was empty in the place for the head.

"She has gone to the bathroom," I reasoned, still sitting bolt upright and tingling.

When the Red Cap had unloaded our bags, he had told us in the manner of one ordered to carry out the routine:

"Keep your room locked. Keep it locked when you are in it and when you are out of it."

As I listened, I recalled the question which A. M. Piper of Council Bluffs, Iowa, has sent up to the press conference that President Kennedy held for the ASNE that afternoon.

The ageable editor had written:

"Mr. President, isn't is possible to make Washington, D. C., the capital of our country, as safe for citizens as were the great plains from Indians and brigands when my grandparents rode across them in a covered wagon?"

It was a sassy question. Those selecting the questions for funneling to Mr. Kennedy passed it up in favor of such questions as: How will the Russians get out of Cuba? Comment on the Laos situation.

My thoughts drew back to the click, click which had awakened me and to my failure to find the General Manager.

I got up and went around the foot of the bed to the bathroom. The GM was not there.

Well, I thought, growing more anxious, she must have slipped down to the main floor to mail some letters. I knew that the mail chute on our hall had been closed earlier that evening. The GM had sought to mail a letter. She sometimes likes to dash off cards and letters after I have gone to sleep.

I recalled the tragic story on the front pages of Washington papers the day before. Young hoodlums had fatally injured a retired Baptist minister in one section of the city while robbing him of $1.29. They had beaten in his face and ruptured his windpipe with blows and kicks.

It had been the custom of the retired minister, age 72, to buy cakes and soft drinks for the children in his neighborhood.

The Daughters of the American Revolution were holding their annual convention in Washington at the same time as the ASNE. The capital press reported how one Washington business man, in his address to the 2,000 delegates, had warned the ladies to "be careful". Just what care was to consist in, I did not hear.

The speaker had said that muggings and purse snatchings and attacks by hoodlums were common occurrences.

My mind came back to the click, click which had awakened me. I had returned to bed. I got up and went to the twin bed, two steps away. I felt out, and as far against the wall as she could get was the General Manager, sleeping soundlessly.

"What is it? What is it?" she asked, sitting up.

I told her of being roused by the sound of the door closing.

"You were dreaming," she said.

At that moment the telephone in our room rang.

The GM answered.

"This is the security guard," said a man's voice. "Your door is unlocked. Please lock it."

The click, click which some sixth sense had detected had been made by the security guard as he went about the halls trying all doors.

Henry was named the North Carolina Handicapped Person of the Year in 1961. The honor was in recognition of "outstanding achievement, notwithstanding more than the ordinary hindrances."

Henry was nominated for the state recognition after being selected as Wayne County's Outstanding Handicapped person for 1960. Presentation of the county award came at a meeting of the Goldsboro Rotary Club on February 21, 1961.

In presenting the award, Dr. S. B. McPheeters, chairman of the Goldsboro Employ the Physically Handicapped Committee, reviewed misfortunes that had come to Henry, culminating in the loss of sight.

This has been more than misfortune. This has been dire calamity. Such experiences would have crushed most men. But Henry Belk burgeoned out. He became an even better writer. He expanded his activities, enlarged his acquaintances, and developed a greater feeling for his fellowman. During and since this time of calamity, Henry has become recognized as one of the distinguished civic leaders of North Carolina.

Editor Galt Braxton of the Kinston Free Press termed the award "a fitting tribute to one of North Carolina's ablest and most loved journalists. Henry Belk is indeed an inspiring example to all who know him. His refusal to accept defeat and calamity as final, provides his fellow editors, and those visually blesses, with a stirring example of a victorious spirit."

The state award ceremonies were held April 13 in the Governor's conference room at the Capitol building in Raleigh.

In presenting the award, Governor Terry Sanford said: "I didn't know you were handicapped, Henry."

Sanford added: "Henry Belk has been one of the leading citizens of North Carolina. His determination and great spirit have overcome any physical handicaps. For service to his state and because of his spirit and determination, I present him with this award."

"I am proud and somewhat embarrassed," Henry responded.

He turned the plaque over to his 'Seeing Eye' wife, who drew a round of applause from the crowded conference room.

Later Henry had some comments about the occasion and how it felt to be the handicapped person of the year.

The General Manager and I were guests at the annual banquet of the North Carolina Disabled American Veterans in Raleigh. We were there for me to receive the D.A.V. award as the North Carolina handicapped man of the year. First such award went to the late Representative Dave Hall of Sylva.

Senior Vice Commander, Miss Polly Small of Concord, expressed the hope, as the General Manager pinned the lapel piece on, that I would wear it as a symbol of how the handicapped can lead normal lives. As soon as I had a chance, I asked the GM to describe the pin to me.

"It shows crossed crutches, a laurel wreath for victory, the insigne of the early Greeks, and other symbolic representations," she said.

Inwardly I winced. The very idea of wearing crossed crutches to say to the world that I was handicapped, was hard to get used to.

But if I can, I should make myself do this, that it may be a help in getting people to understand that handicapped persons actually can be better workers in some capacities than normal people. For one thing, the record of absences and illnesses by the handicapped on jobs is better than the average.

My reaction to those crossed crutches brings to the surface the psychological block the employer generally has to the handicapped in his work force. But that is a feeling that passes in a few days, once he is accustomed to having the handicapped worker being around. Then he will not notice any difference.

You will understand if you see me wearing a lapel pin which features crossed crutches.

I have been asked how it feels to be the North Carolina handicapped man of the year.

All mixed up, I would say. I am proud, but also I am embarrassed at being designated as "handicapped".

Mostly, though, I am gratefully humbled by the nomination of me by so many good friends. These kind ones put an amazing amount of work into collecting, writing, and binding in one book material about me. Literally many score hours of work from many people went into the brochure.

I am humbled by the fact that the material is marked by heart and kindness, and deep good wishes for me and the General Manager. We shall never be able to live up to the measurements of our friends, but we are challenged to try the harder.

One impression is that there is a definite value and possible benefit to the physically handicapped by this annual promotion conducted under direction of the Governor's Employ the Physically Handicapped Committee. Dr. Junious (June) H. Rose of Greenville is the chairman. Man lives by symbolism to a great degree. From word and letter to me, I can see that physically handicapped people throughout the state draw new courage, new determination from the project. Some who have been so shocked and stunned by an incapacitating accident or illness, hearing of the project, take heart and move into the stream of normal living again.

With so many of the handicapped, a life of thumb-twiddling, groaning, moaning, whining, of discomfort to self and all around them, accompanies a handicap, be it one from birth or one from mishap. If the spirit can be lifted, if hope can be instilled, that person can show the power of mind over matter; and how quickly, the General Manager and I know, the public comes to forget or not be conscious of a handicap in one, if that person carries on with normal living.

For the overall benefit, it seems to me of greatest importance, is the spreading of the gospel among business men and plant operators of the news that the handicapped are good workers. The statistics prove this quite definitely. But there remains in the minds of most that the handicapped are not desirable workers. Quite the contrary is true if the handicapped can be fitted to the task.

Two blind operators of stands in Goldsboro helped me to hold on and start over, when I lost the fight to keep a working vision. One is Clayton Barwick. The other is George Long. Clayton is good company. He is not downhearted, ever. He said to me, quite casually, when we talked of the fact that I should not see again: "You will get along if you don't lose your nerve."

George Long lost his sight when he was in his early teens. George today is one of my heroes. He kicks not against the pricks, or complains of his misfortunes. He is happy, genial, laughing. The example he set helped me.

So also have I been helped by the example of another blind friend, John Mozingo, also a blind stand operator. John gets so much enjoyment out of life. He laughs the deep laugh of the man who knows that life is good, and who with unfailing faith moves from day to day in the untroubled realization of man's purpose and place in life.

John, George and Clayton, though I see them all too seldom, have reached out hands and given me courage and lifted me up.

Most of all, I owe a debt I shall never be able to pay to my Seeing Eye wife. The General Manager I call her. That is the truth. She is secretary, companion, a wailing wall on the days of frustration, for frustrations must come to us all. She has pushed back the loneliness and with patience and understanding she has been ever by my side. It was in recognition of her place in my life that I passed on the certificate of award, handed me by Governor Sanford, to her.

Let me not over sentimentalize. I have a deep sensitiveness at the very thought of being handicapped. This is a sensitiveness which is so strong that, if I followed my natural inclination, it could overpower me and leave me helpless to cope with the dark world.

So how does it feel to be the North Carolina Handicapped man of the year? About like the man who watched his mother-in-law drive his new Cadillac over a thousand-foot cliff. He had mixed emotions.

Seven years later, after becoming editor emeritus, Henry summed up his feelings on being blind.

I have now been blind for 13 years and after nine operations on the eyes in a futile and desperate effort to save my sight. And a glimmer in one eye was saved. What a great help that little glimmer can be, although there is not enough sight to enable me to get about.

Sometimes the consciousness of blindness hurtles in upon me and spirits droop. This is especially true if I happen to be thrown into an unfamiliar crowd, a crowd where I cannot recognize old and friendly voices.

When the blindness depression hits, my spirits hit the bottom. I am palzied with self-consciousness and, strain as I can, I cannot throw off this terrible monster that makes me feel lower than a snake.

But gradually I recover. Courage and hope and purpose and normal feelings return to me. I am not afraid to interject my comments into a general conversation. I forget that I am blind and life is happy and normal and beautiful.

I must ask Dr. Viola Titus (blind caseworker) if this up and down feeling is common to all blind people. Do they have to fight and struggle and pretend to control the low spirits that roll in almost regularly?

18

On July 6, 1954, ten days after being "freed from darkness" by the special glasses a New York optometrist had fitted for him, Henry came out with an inspired piece, 'What is News?' Years later, Charlotte Observer columnist Kays Gary said the piece "is still preserved in yellowed clippings by newsmen and others, like Ed Rankin, public relations director of Cannon Mills."

What is news? asked the Heartless One.

And putting down his glass, he answered:

News is rape, murder, suicide, shootings, maimings, fires, blasts, tragedy, storm, tornado, cyclone, hurricane, blood-in-the-gutter, more teeth scattered around and legs and arms torn off, A-Bombs and H-Bombs and sinkings and drownings and battles and carnage, abortions, seductions, divorces, Cain, Judas, Attila, Catherine de Medici, Mussolini, Hitler.

What is news? asked the Poet.

Putting down his book, he looked afar and answered:

News is moonlight and starlight and summer dawns and gentle breezes, of the essential immortality of man, his courage, his indomitable soul, "for which I thank whatever Gods may be," youth walking hand in hand, male and female, the dove's gentle coo, the thrill of an infant — your infant — as he makes the first tentative clutch of your finger, the uplift of a little hand placed confidently in yours.

Wind and sand and surf, flat plains of good earth rolling outward to the horizon, cattle grazing in green fields, a tree lifting its arms to heaven, sleep, and friendship and fellowship and faith.

Indomitable Moses, gentle Jesus, magnificent Paul, Confucious, Lin Yutang, The Prophet, Bobbie Burns, Robert E. Lee, the great general whose soul cried out in pain because he had to make war, Abraham Lincoln, Archibald Rutledge, Elton Trueblood, Plato, Aristotle, the Psalms, and the 14th chapter of John's gospel.

What is news? asked the Philosopher.

In words hard to be understood, he answered his own question.

Of man's relation to man, of man's learning what life means, of principles of truth and beauty, of ability to determine one's own place in life, of what makes courage, of what makes weakened souls, of the nature of war and peace, of things to live by, of the comfort of religion, and the great faiths, of the essential goodness of all men, of the eternal and everlasting climb of man from his apelike beginnings to an ever higher plane.

What is news? asked the Editor.

Fumbling the copy paper in his hand, he answered.

News is all of these things and more. It is a balance, one against the other. It is the mirror of life, of the reflection of little things which man gives himself to, his bornings and his dyings, his babies, his church, his clubs, his comings and his goings, and of his great loneliness and his need always for assurance. Of such is news.

On the occasion of Carl Sandburg's 80th birthday, in 1958, Henry shoved aside the Heartless One to pay his respects to the Poet.

The North Carolina Associated Press is growing up. It distributed to Sunday paper clients a good piece of reporting on the 80th birthday of Carl Sandburg, poet, philosopher, historian and deep-visioned human spirit. The Asheville Citizen sent a reporter to talk with Sandburg at his mountain home at Flat Rock.

It is a great day for North Carolina when the Associated Press departs from the channels of crime and politics and the other stereotyped forms of news to give large space coverage to a man of national significance. The Asheville reporter caught the snap and the feeling and the humor of Sandburg. We hope that the papers quite properly will show such appreciation to the member AP for the Sandburg story that it will be encouraged to stray from the old ruts often.

There ought to be a Carl Sandburg Day in North Carolina. It should center at the University of North Carolina. Upon that day all Tar Heels who have been touched and lifted by the poetry of the prairie town boy should have a chance to show their appreciation. Or Greensboro's famous Historical Book Club or Raleigh's Literary Forum should take the lead in staging the event.

If such is to come, it should come soon. At 80, there isn't much time left for any man, even a Sandburg.

Sandburg had nine years left.

Whether because of Henry's suggestion or not, a Carl Sandburg Day was held, by proclamation of Governor Luther Hodges.

Henry knew Sandburg personally and introduced him at a meeting of the North Carolina Press Association in Asheville.

It was of "little things which man gives himself to," that Henry liked most to write.

Said the Greensboro Daily News: "He interested himself in the small vignettes of life — early morning walks, animals, the plight of tall men sleeping in short beds, good food (especially barbecue), how it feels to be blind, reports on interesting people and places. He was strong on the joys of home and hearth."

"He has written about his land with wonder and delight," said the Raleigh News and Observer. "The small things that give meaning to living have not escaped him."

Henry enjoined poet-editor Sam Ragan, one of his early proteges, to "write with wonder."

"I still try to remember the injunction," said Ragan, in a piece for the News-Argus in 1951.

'The small vignettes of life'

Ben and Betty's boy is a sturdy, vibrant two-year-old. He is an only child, so far. So he is swamped at Christmas with presents from Santa and from the grandmother and from other relatives. All manner of toys, even a velocipede, which are supposed to delight the heart of a little boy, were his at Christmas.

In great profusion they jammed the living room and scattered into the kitchen area.

Benny was most interested as the gifts were unwrapped. He played with them for 15 minutes. Then he went to his old toy box. From deep within its tangles recesses he pulled out a battered old coffee can. From a lower level he dug out a teaspoon. With delight in his eyes, he sat solidly on his rump by the old toy box and began to play happily with the can and spoon.

Old friends are best.

'Tip for Husbands'

Irene has been under the weather.

"Why don't you sleep late and let Bruce get his own breakfast?" suggested the General Manager. "He could do that easily. He used to be a Boy Scout."

"Yes, but he would make such a mess in the kitchen," Irene replied. "I would rather get up and cook his breakfast than to clean up after him."

Note well, husbands. Leave a lot of dirty dishes, pans, pots, receptacles, holders, etc., if you get breakfast.

But maybe that would start a row, rather than get you your breakfast.

'Baby-sitting Granny'

Today's grandmother has a lot more fun, and trouble, than yesterday's did.

Today's grannies, and in many instances today's grandpas, are built-in babysitters. Today's young parents call much more frequently on the grandparents for help with the children. The young folks think nothing of it in taking long weekend trips or even good-sized vacations while granny or gramps take full charge of the children.

And if there are no sacrificial grandparents about, today's young parents hire a baby sitter. They have no hesitancy in leaving the children with some reliable teenager or some friend of mature years who welcomes the chance to make a little pin money.

Baby sitting, as you know, has become a big business. It solves the problem of making it possible for the mother to get away from the baby and household duties for some refreshing relaxation.

The parents of 50 years ago would have held up their hands in holy horror at the mere thought of going away for a long evening, much less a long weekend, with a sitter left in charge of the little ones.

But maybe it is a good change. Children sometimes need some good healthy neglect, if you give them too much love and tender care.

'Sweetest Sound'

What is the sweetest sound you can hear from your home? By sweetest, let us mean the sound that falls with greatest comfort and softness on the ear. The sound that raises nostalgic thrills, that carries you back and at the same time carries you ahead into the future. The sound that soothes and sustains.

The sweetest sound I can hear is on a Sunday morning when the bell calls the faithful to church. I have in mind the bell of a Negro church on East Elm Street. It has a quality of faith and hope and joy which rings across the Sunday atmosphere with a balm that is cleansing and purifying, that quiets the spirit and lifts the heart.

'It's Good to Go Home Again'

It's good to go home again. To go home to the old church. To sit again in the old pew. To visit the old Sunday School room. To greet old friends. To feel the tug at the heart as one looks around and realizes that some familiar faces are gone on.

To loiter about the old church yard. To remember the days that are gone and the events of other years.

Sunday is homecoming day at Salem Methodist Church. It's the first homecoming for this ancient church in about 10 years.

Old friends who come back from other counties and other cities will be impressed with the changes. They will see that extensive improvements have been made. They will hear the story of how a devoted church membership cooperated along many lines with the giving of money, of gifts, of labor, of services.

It will be a big day for old Salem.

Of course there will be a big picnic dinner with piles of choice foods. Some of us will eat too much.

'Going to Egypt'

Business of saluting, of making our best bow to the solid citizens of the Rosewood Community for their annual 'Going to Egypt', which fell today.

This unusual folk custom is close to the hearts of the Fork Township natives. How it originated, is shrouded in the mist of time.

But upon a certain year, just before the close of October, some families took their vittles of meat and vegetables, their crude cooking pots and kettles, and trekked to the banks of the placid Neuse. There, on low-lying banks, they kindled some fires. The women cooked up a meal that was out of this world. The children played. The men swapped jokes and kept the fire going. Some of them insisted they should make the coffee.

The crops were in. Thanksgiving was not far away. It was a time for relaxation with neighbors and a time for good eating.

The custom stuck and each year since that time 'Going to Egypt' has been repeated. It is one of the true folk customs of our county.

'Hog Killing Time'

Our long-time friends, the Rev. and Mrs. E. A. Killette of Belfast, have staged their annual hog killing. It was a great event, as it has been on their farm for, lo, these many years.

Hog killings generally aren't what they used to be, but the Killettes still make a sort of neighborhood affair out of one. The number of workers and helpers in the various phases of the killings is considerable. Everyone has his own special task.

The big dinner that goes along with a hog killing at the Killettes is the magnet that draws. Prepared and served outdoors, it is a treat to be remembered from one year's end to another. After all have eaten to a relaxed state, there is music by true folk singers. Old and loved hymns get most attention.

The Killettes are a disappearing tribe. Hog killings now are few and far between, when compared with the number some years back. At this time of the year 25 years ago, the hog killing fires would trail curling smoke across the winter landscape. Passersby could spot the hog killings by the smoke coming from around the pots of boiling water.

'How to Fry Ham'

The sweet and tender caress of real, old-fashioned, genuine country ham lingers in my mouth after breakfast an hour ago. It was from a commercial cure which recreated the artistry of my grandfather's smokehouse. It was good ham. But it was also cooked just right by the General Manager.

Needed to give the special flavor to a ham is just a little bit of its own fat. Needed also is care to see that the slice is cooked until it is tender. Some heavy-handed cooks fry ham until it has the consistency of a shingle.

The lean ham, says the General Manager, is cooked sufficiently well before the fat is done. When that stage arrives, cut off the fat, put the lean ham steak to one side, and continue cooking the fat until it is drained of excess grease, but not done to a crisp.

'Birthday Cake'

I might have known it, even before the scales shouted the bad news. In two weeks I had put on seven pounds to squash the scales at 207. That is a full seven pounds more than my doctor allows.

Of course I could blame it on the General Manager. She baked a birthday cake for me that was wonderful. It was homemade, from jump chocolate. It had plenty of butter and everything and the General Manager placed between the layer on top of the cake a seductive chocolate icing enriched with hunks of black walnut. She knows my weakness. Why did she do this to me?

'Hat Trouble'

Here I am having more hat trouble. And it has been only three years since I faced the same situation. The General Manager decided at that time that I had to have a new hat. Now she is saying again that I must have a presentable hat. She dug out of the closet a Royal Stetson that never did feel comfortable and ordered me to wear it until she could get the feather-weight fedora cleaned and blocked.

Now, that old hat was such a delight to wear. It snuggled around my bald cranium most sympathetically. It was comfortable and didn't have a hole in it. Maybe it was a bit out of shape. Shape for appearance sake, that is, not for the kindest treatment of one's head.

I think the GM tipped off Jim Roe, our circulation manager. Whenever he sees me wearing the harsh, unyielding Stetson, he allows as how he is glad to see me with a new hat.

I'll bet the General Manager told him to say that.

Of 'interesting people'

Duke, along with other universities in the nation, has grants for special studies in the aging process.

If they want a subject which demonstrates within itself that health and vigor of body and mind can be enjoyed at a ripe age, they should see Dallie Hines of Rosewood, in Wayne County. If the researchers can determine how to give us all what Mr. Dallie has, they will have completed their job.

Two days before his 87th birthday, we met Mr. Dallie Saturday afternoon on a thronged Goldsboro street. He was a straight and youthful figure. There were no balloons around his middle, no crippled joints from arthritis or rheumatism.

"How are you getting along, Mr. Dallie?" we asked.

"Just fine," he replied. "Have a wonderful pleasure with my food and everything agrees with me."

"How about your eyesight?"

"Good. I read two daily papers every day and my Bible between times. I do not tire from reading."

"What of your hearing?"

"Well, I have to be careful now to look directly at the person who is talking to me. I don't hear as well as I did at 50, but my failing there is not too great."

"Did you drive to Goldsboro today?"

"No, they (evidently meaning his family) don't like for me to drive. Goldsboro traffic has become so thick. But I drive around in the neighborhood."

Mr. Dallie has been an A-grade farmer all his life. He has worked hard from dawn to dusk. For most of his life he has dug out the crops with his mule and hoe.

Moderation has been his watchword. He loves his church and has been a steward and teacher in his Methodist brotherhood since early manhood.

Goldsboro knows him for his service on the Wayne School Board and for his prize-winning country sausage. You had to know the right man to get an introduction, with the privilege of buying that sausage every week.

Mr. Dallie is a good subject for study by those looking for the secret of staying young.

'Big Brother to Orphans'

They buried Ed M. Davis the other day at the ripe old age of 83. And they buried the best friend the Odd Fellow Home in Goldsboro ever had.

The love and service this pioneer business man gave to the orphaned children was the great force, the fulfilling purpose of his life.

For many years Davis operated his own quality grocery store. People like to trade with him, not only because he gave value received, but because he also gave a cheerful smile that left every customer a little brighter of spirit for having been in his presence.

Davis served several terms on the Board of Aldermen. His service to the orphanage grew out of the fact that he was raised at the institution. He joined the Odd Fellows at an early age and in the fraternity found satisfying contacts and friendships.

While operating the grocery store, Davis established the practice of sending fruits and vegetables to the Orphan Home in sufficient quantitites to feed the children. He did not brag about it or tell you about it. Actually, only a few knew. After retiring, he continued to send the regular food orders and to pay for them, right up until he entered the hospital several months ago.

No child at the Home had a birthday without being given a party. Ed Davis kept those birthday dates without fail and brought presents for the honorees.

A newcomer to the Home might get acquainted with the kind man and begin calling him "Mr. Davis". But quickly the newcomer learned that the proper term for Ed Davis, and the one he preferred, was "Big Brother".

'bornings and dyings'

Death, as it must to us all, has come to Homer Brock of Mt. Olive. For 32 years he was editor and publisher of the Mt. Olive Tribune.

He had been in ill health for many years, but his illness never got him down.

Homer Brock was a good editor. He was a good editor in that he made the Tribune stand for what he believed to be best for his town and county. He was a good editor in that he was not controlled by any man or group of men. He was a good editor in that he could not be pressured into taking a stand with which he could not honestly agree. He put his paper above personal profit and personal glory.

Homer Brock made a great contribution to his town and to his section through his paper.

In Fremont the other day we noticed the unusual number of mockingbirds. During the funeral service for Lem Taylor one of the glorious songsters sang throughout the services. He was perched in a tree just across the street from the Taylor home. The sweet notes blended with the music of a quartet.

Then, when the body was removed to the cemetery for committal rites, there were two mockingbirds in nearby trees. They poured out their golden melody as the service came to an end. Their joyous song seemed to be a fitting benediction to a young man who had found living such a joyous experience.

'Front Porch Lament'

Sweet were the uses of the front porch. And we have lost something fine and sweet and friendly, and even therapeutic, in its disappearance. The modern home owner abhors the front porch. A stoop or a door that has such a small area for its approach that you have to back down the steps as you open it — these have replaced the front porch, which captured the cooling breeze and bade welcome and relaxation to all.

Make a mental note as you pass any gracious old house of 25 to 50 years ago. The older the house is, the broader and longer is the front porch. It is pleasant just to sit and comtemplate the front porch scene. Tall-back rocking chairs are placed at comfortable intervals about the porch. They in their graceful lines are an invitation to comfort. The backs go up and up and up in a leisurely fashion. No matter how tall, you can rest in ease against them, and the backs are so curved that they caress the sacroillac with sheer delight.

Old boarding houses used to make a specialty of wide piazzas, or verandas, as they were called. The heavy, hearty, starchy meals were the more easily digested after a 30-minute flop in one of the rockers. And many a casual rocking chair introduction on a front porch bloomed into romance and marriage. For courting, in a more leisurely day, there was no better place for doing Cupid's work, provided the front porch was not too close to the light on the corner.

The porch had its definite therapeutic value. If one got a case of the blues, if the four walls sometimes seemed to press in harsh and hard, if one began to feel fenced in and frustrated, he could escape to the front porch. He could "set a spell" and rock and watch the world go by, and, soothed and sustained by his rocking and watching, he soon was at peace with himself and the world again.

And porches were so neighborly. Let one appear on the porch and show himself in a conversational mood, and pretty soon folks from across the street, or next door, came in to rock and chat. The ladies brought their fancy needlework or their sewing and the men had their accustomed places near the edge of the porch, so they could chew their tobacco.

It is too bad that the front porch has fallen into disrepute. In sacrificing it, we have added to life's tensions.

'Whisper of Fall'

I heard the first whisper of fall as I walked early the other morning. There was a rustling high up in the oaks and a sighing of a playful wind in the pines. It was as one whispering from a great distance, whispering of long journeys and bright seas and changing seasons. Of grass coming to peak and beginning to die away.

Of the bright blue weather to release us from Bermuda highs and low pressure troughs and sapping humidity. Of bright colors beginning to appear on the maples and dogwoods. Of a briskness in the air and birds singing after the silence of the moulting season.

A strange unease moves in the heart. A pleasant, indefinable unease. And the horizons call and the big sky is full of mystery.

Ah, holy, holy, holy.

'Replenishing the Earth'

Great nature at this season is quietly, busily engaged in replenishing herself. What she has given away in food, fiber and crops during the growing and harvesting season, she now seeks to restore with her alchemy.

The rains and winds which have washed soil into the seas for months are now being resisted. Material to restore what has been eroded is falling on the earth. Note the crunch of acorns under your feet as you walk under oak trees. Note the falling to the earth of pods and covers.

Under a grove of tall pines there is a shower of sweet smelling pine needles as the wind stirs.

Leaves drift earthward, some of them borne on the wind and carried to a distance from the trees which bore them. At a distance where there may be no growth, or sparse growth, what has been borne or washed away must be replaced.

This miracle of restoration has as its first purpose the extension and replenishment of trees, plants, shrubs, grasses. These shed or die at the coming of winter but in dying they deposit new seed to lie dormant until the warm sun and spring rains kiss them into life.

Man ought to learn from nature. He too must go into the quiet places to replenish his energies, his faith. Man must quit his full rush and revive his spirits periodically. For man, like the earth, is eroded by the beatings of time, circumstance and existence.

19

Henry had three pet topics that he liked to write on, sometimes to the boredom of his readers: his little dog, Topsy, that "owned" him and the 'General Manager' for 17 years; the virtues of Goldsboro barbecue; the accommodation problems of a tall man in an average-size man's world.

Topsy was a fox terrier given to the Belks by Roy Parker, Goldsboro parks superintendent, when she was four months old. She quickly wagged her way into their affections and was treated as a pampered child, even to the extent of being tucked in at night.

Topsy is our dog. A short-tailed creature, she needs a light covering for comfort when she sleeps.

Her routine is to go to each member of the family mornings to wag a lovable greeting. Then back to bed for a little nap of a couple of hours.

Invariably when she gets up to give her greeting, she trails her cover some feet from the bed.

The other day she made her good morning, then hurried back to bed. But she pointed to her displaced covering, looked up at us. The implication was as plain as if it had been spoken. Cover me up again, said her entreaty.

Now tell me this.

If she can indicate that she wants to be covered up, why is it that she can't reason out that she could drag her blanket to her bed and cover herself?

Topsy got the attention any child would, when she had the mumps. Or was it mumps?

It happened about the middle of July, but to this day we don't know who was right, the vet who said our dog Topsy had the mumps, or K. A. Haney who said she was bitten by a snake.

We first noticed it when Topsy's right jaw began to swell. In a day or two the jaw stuck out like a goose egg and the dog was a woebegone sight. She carried herself with complete objection and whined piteously at the slightest touch to the swollen jaw.

We took her to the vet and he made a close examination, poking, probing, looking, as the dog whined in pain.

Looking professional, he announced his findings: inflammation of the salivary glands. In other words, mumps.

What do you do for mumps in dogs? You treat it like you would a human with mumps. Give her an aureomycin capsule once a day for three days.

Topsy had taken her second capsule when K. A. Haney came to see us. He is from Sweet Union and folks from Sweet Union have a way of getting together to pass the time.

"Topsy has the mumps," we said, pointing to the dog's swollen jaw.

"That is no mumps," Haney said, flat-like. "That dog has been bitten by a snake."

Now, Haney keeps a passel of hunting dogs all the time, and has since his beginnings in Sweet Union. When he talks about dogs, he talks from experience.

"I've seen my own dogs bitten by snakes and it always looks like that," he said. "I'll bet I can cut off the hair around that swollen place and show you two tiny punctures where the snake fangs went in."

Then he continued to talk about like this.

"Topsy probably was ranging around in the neighborhood and came upon a snake, lying and ready. Snakes at this time of the year will strike quicker than they would in the spring or early summer. They lie coiled up, not straightened out, and they hit at anything that goes by.

"I remember when we were living at Jacksonville. I had a Marine friend and we were walking with his dog one afternoon. The dog was some distance from us when we heard him give a sudden yelp.

"I said to my friend, 'Your dog has been bitten by a snake.' The man said he guessed not. So we went over to where the dog had been when he yelped, and we looked and we found a rattlesnake as long as your arm. Before we could cut a good stick and kill that snake, the dog was dead.

"There are a lot of rattlesnakes in Onslow. We don't have them in Wayne much. It was some sort of not so poisonous snake that bit Topsy, I bet."

What do you do for a dog that has been snake-bitten? Haney knew the answer to that one. He tried out a remedy.

"Why," he said, "you give them some warm milk with butter in it. The butter will drain the poison to it and in a day or so the dog will be all right."

We didn't give Topsy anything except the aureomycin, but she lost the swelling in a few days and was her energetic self.

We still don't know if she had the mumps or whether a snake bit her.

Topsy accompanied Henry on his legendary early morning walks.

Topsy and I like particularly our early Sunday morning walks in spring. The sun is just getting up in the east, the houses are still with sleepers getting their final nap, there is no traffic and there is peace as we walk by the Kemp woods.

Topsy, you know, is the loving fox terrier who has owned us for the past 15 years. She is gray about the head and face, like an old lady, but she still retains that baby face look which so touches the heart when she waves her happy tail.

Topsy knows the right way to take a walk. Nothing escapes her. Every inch of ground must be searched out with a twitching nose. If there are new smells or unusual smells about a dogwood or traffic sign, she must separate them and evaluate them. Maybe she knows from her fastidious and careful sniffing what dog passed that way and when, whether it was male or female, or whether stranger creatures of woods and fields scurried along there during the darkness.

One tuft of grass will appear exactly as another to the human eye, but there is a marked difference for Topsy's discerning nose. Some spots require extensive and intensive investigation. It can take a minute or two to properly go over, she feels, even an inch or two of interesting ground. Other tufts of grass, though the same on the surface, are dismissed with a soft outward sniff which says there is nothing worth finding out here.

Those peaceful Sunday morning walks would mean so much more to the depths of my spiritual being if I could find as much in them as Topsy.

'Topsy Finds a Bone'

How does Topsy do it?

Topsy is the 16 years and 2 months old terrier who has owned us since she was four months old.

The years have made a gray lady out of Topsy, but she seems firm of limb and body. Her age shows in her gray head and in her dimmed eyes. Her sight is so clouded by cataracts which come with age, that we hesitate to allow her a little run, lest she be confused in finding her way back.

But her sense of smell seems to be as keen as it was when she was a

vibrant puppy and raced with the joy of living on the paths of the Old Golf
Course. When the General Manager and I take her for a walk, she has
unending smelling to do. Every street sign, post, every tree, every telephone
pole, every pile of leaves, she has to go over sniff by sniff.

No dry bone, no matter how old or how dry, escapes her. She picks it up
and despite our remonstrance cracks it with as much delight and gusto as
when she was a young dog. Sometimes we are able to get her to drop a bone
and come along. The very next day, however, she can go unerringly and pick
up that old bone, guided only by her sense of place and smell. How does she
do it?

'Tagged by Topsy'
You have heard often of how some actors get tagged with a particular
character they have been called on to portray. Ever after that, they are that
character, or one like it.

A man may be capable of a top performance in a straight drama, but if he
has been tagged as a comic, he has trouble getting any chance but that of the
comic.

The editor of this column is tagged by the pieces he has done about his
good fox terrier, Topsy. The editor writes 1,000 words a day, 6,000 words a
week, 300,000 words a year. Each day he has an average of three topics.

That is 1,000 topics a year. Less than 2 percent of these topics deal with
our good dog, Topsy. They range all the way from the ravings of Khrushchev
and Castro, the North Carolina political shenanigans, approval and praise for
good deeds of public service, to collards, days in Sweet Union and so on.

But the editor is tagged with Topsy. At the Elks Club the other evening,
no less than a half dozen of the cordial brothers came to talk about Topsy
and how much they enjoyed the little bits about her. Not one mentioned the
ponderous editorial of the day before, or even that afternoon in which the
problems of the world had been solved with neat dispatch.

Topsy, be it known, to our great sorrow, grows noticeably feebler. She will
be 17 years old, come December. She has owned the General Manager and the
writer since she was four months old. In that time she has produced threy
million happy tail wags, has spoken hourly of her love and devotion to us, has
insisted that the General Manger is an angel of mercy, as she is. Now Topsy is
all but blind and three-fourths deaf. She has a good appetite and on certain
days when the aches and pains of age are mellowed by a kind sun, she will
joyfully scamper to greet us when we come back from an evening or
afternoon out.

Maybe we are lucky to be tagged by such a good dog.

The Belks had Topsy put to sleep in January, a month after her 17th birthday. They were going on a trip to Raleigh and got a veterinarian to dispose of Topsy during their absence and bury her in their back yard.

"It was a kindness; life no longer held any pleasure for her," Henry wrote later. "She had suffered paralysis of the throat and could not swallow, eat or drink."

A month later Henry was still grieving over his little dog.

Most of all, we miss Topsy when we return home after an absence of hours. During the first ten years of her life, Topsy stood, eager nose against the pane, on the couch, and watched for us to drive into the yard. Then she leaped from the couch and ran to the door to greet us. If we were a little slow opening the door, she would scold us with sharp, preremptory barks. Once we were in the house, her joy was unconfined.

Then, as she grew older, she lay stretched out on the porch so she could survey the drive. When she was old and feeble, she lay on the couch as close to the door as she could get, to catch the first sound of our feet on the porch. As late as November, though blind and deaf, she knew instinctively that the General Manager was coming home from the hospital, and her happy tail beat joyful noises. When we held her up in our arms and handed her to the GM, she snuggled close to her, saying by her movements, "It's so grand to have you home."

In August, 1957, while Topsy was still living, Henry wrote a piece about another dog that won an Honorable Mention citation from the N.C. Press Association. Titled 'The Memory Lingers On', it was a lament for Bill and Nancy Sasser's dog, Sandy, which had been run over and killed.

The piece was good. It was not as good as some of Henry's writings on Topsy.

The Barbecue War

For years, Henry carried on a running war with Vernon Sechriest, editor of the Rocky Mount Evening Telegram, on the relative merits of Goldsboro and Rocky Mount barbecue.

Goldsboro had its Adam Scott, the original 'Barbecue King', and later his son, Martel Scott, who expanded the business. There was also Lloyd Griffin, another barbecue man with a large following.

Rocky Mount had its no less renowned barbecue merchant, Bob Melton, who was patronized from miles around.

The barbecue war got hot when Sechriest presented Henry a beribboned package of Rocky Mount 'cue at a meeting of the Eastern N.C. Press Association in Goldsboro. Henry sampled it gingerly and gave his verdict: "H-m! Tastes like 'possum meat."

He pursued the matter further in one of his columns.

Poor misguided Vernon Sechriest of the Rocky Mount Telegram does flipflops over the fact that a man in California wrote the Rocky Mount Chamber of Commerce about barbecue he ate in the Nash capital in 1935. With a false logic, Sechriest takes the position that the California letter proves without doubt that Rocky Mount barbecue tops Goldsboro barbecue.

Sechriest even sought by presenting to this writer samples of his city's 'cue at a public meeting to prove his point. Those samples, Sechriest, were right fair to middlin' in sweetness of pork, but far and away less than the delights of the dish captured by the Goldsboro artists.

First, friend Sechriest, the Rocky Mount 'cue is chopped too fine. It has some resemblance to mush than to the firm, tender, comforting succulence of a properly barbecued pig. In the reduction of the meat to mush, you also relieve it of its special character and authority.

Secondly, Sechriest, those heavy-handed barbecue laborers of Rocky Mount in their product do not allow for differences of individual preference. The Goldsboro artists, tender and loving in their dedication, give the sweet young pig just enough sauce as it is cooked over blackjack oak wood to impregnate it with that distinctiveness which divides the false from the true. The Rocky Mount folks put so much pepper and vinegar in their product that the taste buds are rendered helpless by the force of the sauce. So what you get is pepper and vinegar predominantly.

In referring so enthusiastically to the letter from California, the Rocky

Mount editor falls into a common error. He takes the position that the Californian actually remembers the taste of the Rocky Mount 'cue. What he looks back to, after 27 years, is refined and romanticized. That, brother Editor and gentle reader, is one of nature's greatest qualities. It is a way that life is made to seem more beautiful and lovable than it was at the time of the actual experience.

Poor Sechriest points to one resident of California uninitiated into the goodness of Goldsboro 'cue. Goldsboro, Sechriest, points to barbecue regularly flown by jet to Hollywood to assuage the palates of party guests of Anne Jeffreys and Speed Riggs. When General Kenneth Royall was Secretary of War, he threw a big party at the Pentagon for General George C. Marshall. He had at his command all the chefs of Washington and New York, but he picked Goldsboro barbecue. Goldsboro barbecue is served at all UNC football affairs and is flown by plane to celebrations and gatherings in Virginia, West Virginia and other states.

You will have to do better in this argument, Brother Sechriest, to get any attention.

Henry suggested that the matter be left to Don Hall, the "fair, trusted and knowledgeable" editor of the Roanoke Rapids Herald, to decide.

He will carefully eat, taste and evaluate Rocky Mount barbecue for six weeks. Then he will do the same for Goldsboro 'cue and come up with a verdict. That's fair enough for us, Sechriest. What do you say?

To Henry's claims for Goldsboro barbecue, Sechriest retorted that "No self-respecting pig would wind up as a morsel of vinegar-tainted, half-burned nonsense, such as that served in Goldsboro."

As for having Hall as arbiter, Sechriest asserted that the Roanoke Rapids editor's qualifications lay in the field, of "rockfish muddle, a stew composed of fish, bones, old innertubes, pine shavings, etc."

Hall declined to make any representations as to rockfish muddle, saying only that he would be glad to act as judge in the barbecue dispute.

"After all this talk, I ought to get some good 'cue," he said.

At this point, the Danville, Va., Register got into the argument.

Editor Hall may not know the risks to which he has committed himself. He may be devoid of superstition and confident of his capacity as a trencherman. On the other hand, he may be a naive newcomer to feasting on 'cue and totally unprepared for the stresses and strains a full load of Carolina 'cue can impose upon the digestive system, the heart and the waistline.

Columnist Carl Cahill of the Norfolk, Va., Ledger-Dispatch, had something on what displaced Tar Heels thought of the barbecue war, which by now had gotten wide publicity.

John A. Tucker of Virginia Beach has thrown some fuel on the greatest controversy since the cowboys fell out over the great open spaces — North Carolina barbecue.

Tucker is anxious to determine in which Tar Heel town, Rocky Mount or Goldsboro, the best barbecue is made. In an effort to set up a fact-finding body, he sent off letters to Henry Belk, editor of the Goldsboro News-Argus, and Vernon Sechriest, editor of the Rocky Mount Telegram. The letter said:

"We have a group of North Carolina natives who meet for a barbecue, slaw and North Carolina cornbread dinner as often as any of the group makes a trip home and returns with the proper ingredients.

"Naturally, we all consider ourselves experts on good barbecue. One of the fellows swears by Greenville barbecue, another argues that just so it is from Overton's or Melton's in Rocky Mount, it is the best. Another says there is none as good as Jim Warren's in Durham, while another likes that at the Little Acorn in the same city. Still another says that Cherry's in Wilson is the best. A native of Scotland Neck says nobody makes it as good as his man down there. A Martin County native who runs an eating place here says that Williamston barbecue is tops. Personally, I think the best I ever ate was at the Murphy House in Louisburg."

Tucker suggested in his letter that each town in North Carolina send him three pounds of its barbecue and his fact-finding commission will dig in and render a decision.

We hate to add further fuel to the controversy, but Tucker is aiming too far to the east for good barbecue. The only good, genuine barbecue is made in the narrow corridor between Greensboro and Charlotte, along Route 29.

The Winston-Salem Journal voiced similar sentiment.

The current squabble between Goldsboro Editor Henry Belk and Rocky Mount Editor Vernon Sechriest over which man's city has the best barbecue can be dismissed as so much down-eastern nitpicking.

The real issue, we submit, is whether any barbecue made east of, roughly Durham, is worth eating at all, with so much good Piedmont-style barbecue so near at hand. The fact that Mr. Belk and Mr. Sechriest called in another easterner, Roanoke Rapids editor Don Hall, to mediate their dispute, is indication aplenty of their provincialism. Or perhaps they recognized that had a competent Piedmont judge been summoned, he would have had no choice but to give negative reports on both the Rocky Mount and Goldsboro varieties.

The trouble with the Eastern North Carolinians is that they don't respect the integrity of a succulent hunk of pork. They shred it. They pull it apart in the same lazy, careless way that they pick cotton. Then they usually make their barbecue too moist and mushy. The only chewiness remaining is in the tough and indigestible gristle that somehow escapes the cook's eye. The Piedmont experts, meanwhile, even when preparing chopped barbecue, still manage to retain the tender cohesiveness of the meat itself. The difference between the barbecue of the two areas is not unlike the difference between backfin crab and deviled crab, or between delicately fried chicken and, perish the thought, chicken croquettes.

Troubles of the Tall Man

Henry had a lot to say about the injustices inflicted upon the tall man. His most recurrent complaint was the difficulty of finding beds to accommodate his elongated frame. When putting up at the Carolina Inn in Chapel Hill, he got his secretary, Mrs. Virginia Bell, to reserve Room 335 for him. It had a long bed.

In 1957, Henry had a piece on 'Tall Men, Arise'.

Thomas Wolfe, who was 6 feet 7 inches tall, complained that this is a world for men of much shorter height. He wasn't joking. I am 6 feet 6 inches and I can tell you that the long-legged man is continuously subjected to discomfort.

Take the pews in our beautiful new church. They are farther apart than in many a church, but the style is that pews must be cluttered with racks for holding song books, sacrament glasses, and sometimes envelope and memo holders. The knees of the man above six feet tall bang themselves continuously against one rack or the other.

If you see a long-legged guy in church squirming first this way and then that, sitting first to one side and then the other, he is not bored by the sermon. He is resting himself from abrasive contacts because the quarters are too close for him.

Movie houses and most theaters snub their noses at the tall man. Here he has to sit sidewise to sit at all, and if the party to the right or left is a stranger, it can be embarrassing, indeed.

The average store stocks nothing the 78-incher can wear, except maybe handerchiefs. Shirts have sleeves that are four inches up the wrists, ties that when tied four-in-hand, have the look of having been snipped off by a Lion's tailtwister. If he manages to find trousers long enough, the waist is too short or they have enough girth for a circus fat man.

The distressing part about it is the tendency to ignore completely that the percentage of men six feet tall or over is increasing. Hotel beds are drawing up. The double bed of spacious proportions on which the extra tall man could sleep cater-cornered is a rare thing except in great old houses which have been converted to guest houses. Dining room chairs have been so reduced in size that the back, instead of supporting the grown man, simply pinches him implacably in the region of the kidneys.

New-model automobiles have refined ways in which to torture the tall man. I am one who bangs his knees against the circular curve from the windshield when he gets in. Or he grows wiser from being repeatedly saddened by such an experience and he backs up to the seat, sits down, and then very cautiously wheels into the car. Once in, he has a couple of new troubles. Like as not, the seat is so close to the floor, he should be extending his legs straight out, lest his knees extend above his ears, but there is not enough room for that. His head touches the top of the car. He partially solves this by taking his hat off and stuffing it to one side.

There should be a National Association for Prevention of Cruelty to Tall Men. It should have its own program and its own national secretary who would continuously campaign against such devilish devices as here recited.

Tall men, arise. Shake off the habit of accepting the attitude on the part of manufacturers and distributors that you do not exist. We have taken this thing lying down long enough. We have only our chains to lose.

Ten years later, in 1967, conditions had not improved.

The Association for Prevention of Cruelty to Tall Men, started by this column some years ago, is getting nowhere. The tall boys are as meek as lambs in the matter of speaking out and demanding justice. The world has so long ignored their comfort that they take it as a matter of course and suffer in silence.

Most chairs are built with the backs so short that the tall man can't put his head back and relax. If he lets his head go back to get a snooze, it falls over the back of the chair and his neck is snapped backward.

If an extra tall man asks at the hotel or motel for a room with an extra length bed, he is glared at with astonishment by the desk clerk. The affrontery of such a request, the gall of such a plea! These views are plainly revealed on the unbelieving face of the clerk.

And if the extra tall man asks for an extension for a regular bed, one that will enable him to sleep without curving into an S, he may get instead a horse laugh. And if the hotel or motel is a progressive one and the clerk condescends with a scowl to install a bed extension, he takes the position that he is granting an unheard of and completely outlandish request.

But you under six footers try it out, that is, trying to sleep on a bed that is too short. Just climb some night into the baby's crib and see how it is sleeping there. That is about the way it is if a six foot, six inch man is required to sleep in a regulation hotel bed. He doesn't half sleep and the next morning he gets up with a bad case of backache.

And dining rooms for the public have chairs that are measured out to exactly hit the tall folks in the kidney or sacroiliac. The suffering tall man can't listen to the program for trying to find a comfortable position. And he can't sneak a nap during boring speeches for the same reason.

Worst offenders of all in torturing the tall fellows are New York theaters. Though the admission prices have accelerated one half in the past year or so, there has been no improvement in seating facilities. Actually, conditions have worsened.

And folks say to you it must be nice to be tall.

20

Thomas Wolfe was indulging in hyperbole when he said "You Can't Go Home Again."

Henry Belk went home, again and again, in fancy and in fact.

Not many weeks went by that he didn't have something nostalgic to say about his native 'Sweet Union' County. Not a year passed that he didn't return at Christmas, or in summer, to "visit with the folks and search along Monroe streets for the lost boy that was me."

He even proposed transporting a little 'Sweet Union' soil to Wayne for "feasting their eyes on" by expatriates like himself.

Know all men by these presents.

This is a contract, agreement, understanding and pledge entered into by C. Ed Worley, party of the first part, and Henry Belk, party of the second part.

As we are natives of Monroe and desire to acknowledge our debt to that town and to Sweet Union, we do pledge ourselves.

Worley, upon his next trip to Monroe, will get a pail of Sweet Union soil and return it to Goldsboro.

The soil will be from one of the red clay banks in the Pleasant Grove section, or from the bowers and forests of Goose Creek, or the secluded stillness of the forest road to the Round hole.

This soil shall not be contaminated or lessened in nostalgic value and properties by being mixed with the soil of any other county, not even the soil of Wonderful Wayne.

Worley further binds himself to keep and display the pail of Sweet Union soil at his office on South Center Street, Goldsboro, N. C. He will protect it and handle it with the due respect and attention and honor due such a sacred relic.

The soil will be available at all times where native sons and daughters of Sweet Union may come and feast their eyes on and turn back their hearts to the rosy days of swimming au natural, of berrying, of roaming the fields and woods, of bullace gathering from the top of a swaying tree which opened a vista into the blue horizon.

All such natives as Bill Gaddy, Frank Crane and Claude Grady are made associates to this agreement. They shall have special rights and privileges of looking upon and saluting Sweet Union, with full invitation to relate the air so strangely sweet in the county.

Once a year a cupful of the soil from Sweet Union may be removed from the pail and taken tenderly to Raleigh to be spread about the grave of Lynn Nisbet that he may sleep the more soundly.

Nisbet, operator of a state news bureau in Raleigh, had died of cancer. Henry had written a piece about the 'True Son of Union' when the disease was disclosed.

Lynn Nisbet revealed with marked detachment in his Raleigh column the other day that he has cancer of the lungs. He did it with the detachment and simplicity which have marked his years of writing of North Carolina politics, politicians, government and general news.

The doctors have told Nisbet he may live a short time or, at most, for a few years.

The native of Sweet Union will carry on until the erosion from the cancer cells so saps his strength that he will be forced to remain at home. You will hear more from him, we feel certain, on the subject. It will be as casual a report as of the passing scene, free from mawkish sentimentality, yet moving in its picture of a man watching death edge closer.

Lynn probably does not realize it, but he has had a decided influence on this writer. We recall vividly even now a piece which Lynn did when he was editor of the hand-set weekly "Waxhaw Enterprise". Somewhere in his travels in Sweet Union he passed a site where a house had stood. Only the chimney remained, pointing skyward and giving testimony that once family life had moved about it. The sight of that chimney made Lynn fall into a meditation which was sheer poetry. He called back the faces and the voices of people who had lived there and clothed them with meaning for life's riddle. A stripling beginner on the Monroe Journal, I read Lynn's chimney piece and felt a thrill at the reading.

Lynn was one of our earliest heroes and in the cool control, the soul mastery he has in facing cancer, he remains on our select list.

Lynn is a man of faith and is equal to that which he must bear. Hold fast, true son of Sweet Union.

His great-uncle Sid Broom was another son of Sweet Union whom Henry admired.

Word came from Sweet Union the other day that Uncle Sid Broom had died. I was a bit surprised. I had expected that they would have to hem him up on Judgment Day and shoot him. He was 95 years old.

One of his Goldsboro Broom nephews was in Monroe two weeks ago and met him on a business street. He had come to town to attend to business. He confided in the Goldsboro nephew that he was thinking of getting married again.

Next to the last time the General Manager and I visited Uncle Sid in the rock-ribbed section of Bethlehem Church was in mid-summer. It was a hot day, the kind that burn and scorch. He was in a fence corner with a hand hoe chopping out the milk and other weeds. If you have chopped weeds in a fence corner, you know what a hot task it can be.

The last time we saw him, his companion and mate of more than 50 years had passed away. He confessed he was lonely. And how was he fighting his loneliness? He was on the front porch of the big old farm house in a Kennedy rocker, reading, without glasses, U.S. News and World Report.

The section in which Uncle Sid and Aunt Wilma raised their six sons and four daughters was as difficult farm land as can be found. Flint rocks protruded from the scant fertility of the white soil. The mules pulling the plows knocked the plow points against the flint rock and sparks flew. But Uncle Sid had given up mule farming many years ago.

We moderns probably would have classified Uncle Sid as a school drop-out. But he had a native wit and wisdom that put him out front in competition as a farmer. How he accumulated a rich place out of the poor soil, only Uncle Sid knew. His secret was hard work. And he sent his children to college and they came home or established homes far away and distinguished themselves in many fields.

First thing Uncle Sid and Aunt Wilma taught their tribe was work, hard work, and the Christian way, the way of the good neighbor. And that teaching developed teachers and scientists and professional men. Uncle Sid had his God and his faith and he passed the heritage on from that flinty farm to a splendid tribe of children, grandchildren and great-grandchildren.

Uncle Sid had a brother, 'Lespedeza' Broom, who was also worthy of mention.

Grateful Sweet Union County folks have set a memorial for the late 'Lespedeza' Broom, county farm agent.   ·

His name was T.J.W. Broom, but everybody called him 'Lespedeza'. They did so because of the evangelistic fervor with which he preached lespedeza farming. His name was known across the state.

Before he got Sweet Union to adopt his views, the county was so poor that a rabbit had to carry his own lunch. Under the lespedeza farming, Union's flinty acres bloomed and blossomed like the rose. Farmers prospered. Trim brick homes with landscaped lawns replaced the tottering, unpainted frame houses.

Lespedeza seed from Sweet Union were sold far and wide at a profitable price. Union farmers went into poultry and turkey raising, and pasture farming. They discovered that half the family could work in Lancaster, or Rock Hill, or Concord, or Charlotte, and the other half could run the farm. Or the really energetic could tend the new-style farming after putting in a 40-hour week in a factory.

Sweet Union does well in memorializing 'Lespedeza' Broom.

Henry was reminded of Sweet Union at every turn.

It is cotton seed crushing time and the few remaining oil mills scattered over the state are spraying into the atmosphere an odor that is beguiling.

"It smells like baking a cake," said a Texas native, referring to the nostril delight coming from the Goldsboro plant of Hunt Foods, once the Southern Cotton Oil Company.

"It makes me think of peanut butter," said another, trying to define the odor being wafted across the city.

When I was a boy, my evening paper route carried me by the Oil Mill in Monroe. At seed crushing time, I looked forward expectantly to reaching the five blocks around the mill. My nostrils would begin to quiver with anticipated pleasure while I was still a long way off.

On misty nights, or nights when humidity was high, the odor of the oil being squeezed from the seed came close to earth and was doubly strong. How sweet it is to remember.

Remembrance was sweet about a lot of things in Sweet Union.

One thing I intend demanding from the General Manager is some sugar pea dumplings.

Childhood memory lists that sweet pleasure of early spring as something eternal. Sugar peas we called them in Sweet Union. English peas the menus called them when they were standard for Rotary luncheons.

For dear and tender dumplings, you picked them while the dew was on the vines and while the peas were delightfully tiny. In them at that time and size was the mystery of growth and resurrection.

Mama cooked the peas with ham hock. She made cornmeal dumpling into inch and a half patties. These she dropped in, to cook with the peas. They took on their own special sweetness.

Yes, drat that diet! The General Manager will have to throw it out for a real meal and see that sugar pea dumplings are coming up.

'Night Sounds'

Listening to the crickets in the grass and the cicadas in the trees, I know that there is a song of angels.

The nights sounds bring back recollections of boyhood visits to Uncle Mack's, in Sweet Union County. He lived in the country before the days of electricity or paved roads or automobiles. So the nights, when we sat on the porch, were darker and more mysterious than they are now. The cry of the Katydid was more pronounced. I would creep, as quietly as a mouse, I thought, to a tree whence came the song of a Katydid. As gently as possible I would touch the trunk of the tree, trying to touch it so lightly that the Katydid, 25 feet in the top of the tree, would not feel the touch and cease its song. But I never succeeded. No sooner had the gentlest touch been applied to the tree trunk, than the creature cut off his song immediately.

'Going Barefoot'

At your house, when you were a child, what was the date on which your mother gave her permission for you to barefooted?

At our house we started about the time of glorious bird-singing spring to pestering Mama daily on the subject. When the sun came soft and the winds shook the tiny lacy leaves with gentleness, we would go out, pick what we thought was the hottest spot, and carefully press our hands to the earth.

"Mama, it is warm enough to let us take off our shoes," we would say.

Generally the daily taking of the earth's temperature would go on until April was out, or nearly so. Then the word was given, off came the shoes and the mother earth was thrilling to feet encased in leather for a winter's time.

Some mothers approached the problem more realistically and with less fuss. They simply told the children that they could not go barefooted until May came in, and that was that.

'Mullen Tea and Hog Foot Oil'

We were talking the other day to a Goldsboro friend, native of Sampson, about folk customs and granny remedies, as spring comes around.

We said that come spring in Sweet Union, once upon a time, it was the custom for mothers to make their children drink mullen tea for a week or so. It was good for you. It toned up the constitution after the winter rundown and it prepared you for the day when fever and chills might ride the summer rain. It made you stronger and happier, at least that is what Mama said, as she forced you to drink the evil-tasting potion. A modern mother would tell you that the tea contains a bountiful supply of vitamins and chlorophyl.

Mullen tea was made from the mullen weed. The plant grew wild in Sweet Union. Maybe it does in Wayne. You could find it in almost any back yard. The mullen grows close to the ground and spreads as a broad leaf with the face turned up to drink in the sun. It is a fuzzy leaf, tiny hair-like modules covering the leaf closely.

To make the tea, you placed a handful of the carefully plucked leaves in a bowl. Then you poured boiling hot water over the leaves, allowed it to simmer, then the children had to drink it while it was steaming hot.

The Goldsboro friend, native of Sampson, confided that come spring, she regularly drinks sassafrass tea for several weeks.

"One of the first things I begin to think of, when spring comes, is a supply of sassafrass roots," she said. "I really like the tea from sassafrass."

This lady, now several times a grandmother, recalled some of the home remedies she used in bringing up her children. One of them was "hog foot oil" for colds and sniffles.

She had a letter from one of her daughters in a big city. The letter explained that the little children had been ill with colds and sniffles, "but I got out my hog foot oil and they were well in a day or so."

The conversation ended before we could find out what hog foot oil is. We had never heard of it.

We must look up the friend again and get a recipe for hog foot oil.

What were the home remedies used by Wayne mothers 50 years ago?

'Molasses Biscuit'

This unfortunate generation which is unacquainted with good fat biscuits three times a day won't know what I am talking about. But the middle-aged or beyond, who were raised in the country or in small towns, will remember with pleasure.

When us boys got home from school, many an afternoon saw us hurry to the cupboard, get a biscuit left from dinner, make a hole in it on the side with the little finger, and fill the hole with molasses. Yum, yum!

The family molasses jug had its own place in the kitchen and was replenished as it was emptied.

Molasses, we are told, is rich in iron. All I know then was that it tasted good.

Of 'Whistling'

McCall's Magazine had a piece saying men do not whistle as much as they did. The author went on to say that the happy whistle once echoed up and down the quiet streets of the little towns of America. A wife knew when to set the table for a meal when she heard her husband coming down the street whistling.

All whistling was not for happiness. As a boy, I always whistled when I had to go into a dark, unfamiliar place. The sound of my whistle scared the dark shadows away and helped me to control my legs, which wanted to scurry back to the light.

We boys had our personal whistles, which identified us to our playmates as we passed their homes. If they were at home, they would recognize the whistle and come out.

There was also the mood whistle, which was gauged to one's spirit of the moment. If one felt like a lark, he would whistle happily. If he was in a meditative frame of mind, a whistle of just the right timber could help solve his problems.

One of my mood whistles was a tune which went along with the words of a mournful blues song: "I hate to see that evening sun go down."

I adopted the sound for my mood whistle after hearing it sung by a chaingang group building a macadam side street near the Seaboard freight station in Monroe. They slaved hard all day. I wondered why they hated to see the evening sun go down.

Grandma's Old Well'

A metal basket on a rope with a metal wheel carries copy from the news room to the composing room. For some reason, the copy lift of late has begun squeaking something terrible.

It brings back to me the squeaks of the chain and wheel of the old well at Grandma's farm. And that brings, clear and graphic, images of the farm house — the cooling box outside the kitchen, the annex from the kitchen to the dining room, the flinty rocks sticking up about the yard most stubbornly.

There was a curbing around the old well. There were two buckets for drawing the water. As one came up with its cool, cool water from 30 feet below, a bucket on the other end of the chain was on its way down. A long-armed windlass directed the power of the lift. You turned the windlass by hand power, and you had to be pretty careful. If the windlass slipped out of your hand, the weight of the upcoming bucket, filled with two gallons of water, could send the windlass flying. You could break your arm if you didn't stand back quickly.

The cooling box stood at the entrance of the kitchen L or annex. It was one of my jobs, when I visited Grandma during the summer, to draw water regularly from the well and keep the cooling box properly filled.

Holes were bored above the water line in the cooler. These holes directed a stream of air through the box to make a breeze. Grandma used the cooler, made of oak and about 10 feet long, for storing butter, milk and vegetables.

The oak box, made of heavy timber, had been there a long time.

There goes that copy lift squeaking again. Just like Grandma's old well.

'Revisiting the Old Homeplace'

We went back to Grandma's old farm home during a quick visit to our diggin's in Sweet Union.

As a boy, we spent weeks visiting Grandma in the summer. In that day, the Rape place, as it was known, was hours distant over rutted, gullied and dusty roads, if summer, muddy if winter, from Monroe. Dent drove from town to the old place in 15 minutes. With Ware and the General Manager, we picked out boyhood landmarks along the way.

As a boy we picked our first and only cotton on the farm. We put our day's pickings in opposite corners of an empty room. That night I awakened to find George moving cotton from my corner to his.

I call the place Grandma's because Grandpa had died before I knew the farm. His youngest son ran the flinty acres. Graphic in my mind is a picture of the old-fashioned home high on a hill, with rolling valleys spreading out into widening vistas. Today a one-story ranch-type house has replaced the spacious farm structure I knew as a boy.

The cedar tree which stood in the front yard is still there, green and beautiful and tall. The giant oaks with their gnarled roots of huge outcroppings must have been at the farm in the days, and even before, when Clark Rape directed wagon trains that carried food to the Confederate commissary in Charlotte 25 miles away.

The blacksmith shop of those years is now abandoned and has fallen, rotted and tottering, to its knees. It staggers out an end of a field overgrown with weeds. Across the road from the dwelling is the kitchen of the original house. It was connected to the main house by a breezeway.

Our pilgrimage ended, we stood in a little knot and looked across the fields sloping away on three sides of the house. We were silent with memories as we drove away.

21

'Sweet Union' was Henry's mother love; Wayne County and Eastern North Carolina were his adopted loves.

"For Eastern North Carolina he wanted the good life, and he has sought to give vision to the best hopes and aspirations for the region he loves," said the Raleigh News and Observer. "He foresaw and proclaimed an emerging Eastern North Carolina before the fact, recognized his region's great potential, and has never stopped working for its realization."

In 1968, the year he stepped down as editor of the Goldsboro News-Argus, Henry took note of another Goldsboro man who had had a vision for his section of the state.

The late George C. Royall, father of Gen. Kenneth C. Royall, would have been much pelased at the trend of development in Eastern North Carolina now in progress.

George Royall was an original planner and looker-ahead. He recognized the potential of Eastern North Carolina and he recognized also that despite its great resources of people and raw materials, there had to be a one-for-all and all-for-one attitude to make the most of the region and its facilities.

Royall was one of the early presidents of the Eastern North Carolina Chamber of Commerce. The organization tried year after year to get the towns and counties and hamlets to pull together for getting results, for bringing in new industry, and for making the most of our great opportunity.

But a spirit of jealousy and lack of cooperation held back the region. If a city failed in an effort to land a new industry, that city did not want Wilson or Kinston or Smithfield or any other sectional competitor to get the industry.

Opposition to some nearby city getting an industry which we had lost often became the matter of bitter resentment. Development was hamstrung by the spirit of resentment which held that our nearby communities were our actual enemies.

The people have learned by now that such a spirit was damaging all around. George Royall tried as best he could to get the towns and cities and counties of 50 years ago to work together, to try to swing an industry to a nearby city if it could not be secured for Goldsboro, or Mt. Olive or Fremont.

And the lonely voice which George Royall raised in his time had finally begun to pay dividends. Now Committees of 100 and Chambers of Commerce without exception are pulling together and working as one for industrial and business development. The Division of Industry of the Department of Conservation and Development is playing an important part in changing the narrow view which held the region back.

But the section has come only a part way to what it can do and accomplish by working together. The region is at a crossroads. We are at a point where we can go forward rapidly.

And George Royall is due credit for the start made so long ago, a start against great odds.

Henry was interested in the whole spectrum of Eastern North Carolina — its industrial opportunities, its agriculture, its educational advancement, its far-flung beaches where he went to relax and "refresh" his spirit.

He liked especially to go in October.

If you want to refresh your spirit, soothe your nerves, and gain a few pounds of flesh, try an Indian Summer vacation at a North Carolina beach. Through October the sea will sing a siren song, the waves will beat against the shore with hypnotic effect, and the sun will caress your back with soft loveliness.

The "bright blue" weather which John Charles McNeil celebrated in his 'October' shines with a special glint and a tug at the heart as the waves roll in, the gulls call, the sand pipers dart, and the horizon over the ocean calls with its siren voice.

Then, if ever, come perfect days. It is still warm enough to swim in the surf. The fish are going in great schools toward the south. Sometimes they come in so close to the shore they can almost be picked up by hand. Pier, boat and surf fishing are at their best.

When October nights come at the beach they are cool enough to give invigorating sleep, while the surf gives its rhytmic call. The stars shine brighter, and man feels for a certainty that "the heavens declare the glory of God and the firmament showeth his handiwork."

One of Henry's favorite coastal retreats was Swansboro and 'Wee Hame', the summer cottage of the A. J. Smiths at the mouth of the White Oak River. In October, 1961, he wrote about 'Wee Hame' in a piece on Swansboro's annual mullet festival.

While the good Swansboro people call it the Mullet Festival, actually it is an excuse for entertaining with a lavish hand. Those hardy people just want a lot of company. They want the politicians to come among them. They want to see old friends, to call back visitors from other days. The good fish mullet is an excuse.

And before or after the big doings we expect to slip away and revisit Wee Hame on the White Oak River. There, summer after summer, when we were young, the General Manager and Marie and I, and usually a friend or two, hid and fished and relaxed, and looked out toward Goat Island of east to the ocean. There A. J. Smith annually entertained the Goldsboro Kiwanians with a fish fry. The Good Preacher's clam boxes were close to the shore and the crabs begged to be taken.

The year before Henry had written about Pastor Smith's clam fritters in connection with a piece on 'Big Clam Mountain' that had been discovered off the Carteret coast.

The man who has never had a substantial breakfast of clam fritters hasn't lived. That was a specialty of the late A.J. Smith when he summered at 'Wee Hame' at Swansboro. He kept his clam bed handy and would dig them up, open the shells and grind the clams before breakfast. My mouth waters to recall this pleasure.

My first acquaintance with clam fritters was on the old steamship 'Elizabeth City'. It plied mornings from Manteo to the Pasquotank capital. Folks would make the trip over from Elizabeth City just to get one of those breakfasts in the brisk, cool mornings. Departure time must have been 5 or 6 o'clock. I can feel now the wind on my face, the slight tremor of the old ship, the tranquilizing chug-chug of the engine in the hold.

Col. John D. Langston or Victor Meekins can tell us who the cook was. He was an artist. The breakfast had clam fritters as the main dish. Of course there were side dishes of buttermilk biscuits, sugar-cured ham, grits, eggs any style, and boiling coffee.

It was 'Corned Fish Time in Carteret' when Henry called on his old friend, Judge Luther Hamilton.

If you meet up with one of your Carteret County friends on his native heath about now, be prepared for him to show a strange restlessness. If he is a lawyer, he may seem to drift away from you and look meditatively out through the window toward the sounds and ocean and surf. It may be that he has drifted back, mentally, to the days when he joined the clan and neighbors in corned fish celebrations.

Judge Luther Hamilton, veteran barrister, long-time Democratic leader in a county which has a big segment of Republicans, leading Methodist layman, and retired Superior Court judge, confesses that at this time of the year he has a great urge to get back to some fish corning. He still feels a compulsion to salt some mullets, spots or blues away in a keg or barrel for sharpening the appetite at breakfast when winter comes.

One of his friends had just brought him some specially selected fat, firm fish for corning, a day or so before we saw him. And he was as happy as a child over the prospect of salting the fish away exactly as they ought to be salted.

Corned mullet time among coastal natives is what hog killing time is in rural North Carolina. It's not only a time when the neighbors cooperate to store up food for the days ahead, but it is an occasion for friendship, fellowship and communing with one's friends.

Judge Hamilton, as do many artists on the topic, has his own special way for cooking the corned fish. He likes to boil his carefully selected fish after they have been allowed to remain in water overnight. This observation, most likely, will draw the fire of salt fish experts who will insist that their way of fixing the delicacy is much preferred to that favored by Judge Hamilton.

The judge has another wrinkle for his salt fish breakfast. He likes to make bacon gravy and pour it over the fish. Some who have tried this menu say the product will make you fight your grandma.

Henry's trips to the coast took him from Nags Head to Calabash.

Faint, far away, yet insistent, Calabash is calling.

We made our first visit to this lovely village named for a gourd last summer. Heat lay with a smothering hand on the earth then. But Calabash was cool, with a sea wind blowing and life moving at a snail's pace.

There, gathered snugly together under ancient trees, is the largest collection of seafood restaurants and cafes of any town in North Carolina. And to call the delightful place a town is to flatter it. The people who live there are the people of the sea, or those who love the sea, and the gulls crying and the tide lapping, and they have about them the tranquility of a place of self-content.

The Belks were often transported to the coast by Mrs. Elizabeth Mitcham Stroud, office manager of the News-Argus, and her husband, Charles H. Stroud.

Says Mrs. Stroud:

Nowhere, I think, did Mr. Belk get as close to the people as he did at the little village of Calabash. On a weekend trip to Myrtle Beach, S.C., we put up at the famous Ocean Forest Hotel. It was a nice place and we were royally entertained by the management, but Mr. Belk insisted that we leave early enough to get Sunday dinner in Calabash. He wanted to enjoy its celebrated seafood while making conversation with the patrons and villagers.

Oriental was one of Henry's favorite stopping places.

How long has it been since you paid a visit to this lovely village at the mouth of the Neuse? If it has been some time, you should deny yourself the pleasure no longer. You will find many changes, but you will appreciate the special charm of the place which has been maintained.

Discriminating people who seek cool breezes, good fishing, and a relaxed pace, have found their heart's desire here. Ask Hugh and Ethel Harris. Harris came here for peace and quiet after serving as assistant N.C. Commissioner of Agriculture. He is as enthusiastic abour Oriental as he was when he entered business and began farming on the black, rich soil of the area.

You may remember that the late Lynn Nisbet let no year go by without writing a story about the Neuse, at its mouth at Oriental being the widest river in the United States. He got the information while visiting at the Harris home.

Biggest event held at Oriental during the year is the regatta, which draws entries from as far away as New York City. Gathered in the harbor, with colors of all hues, the sailboats are a beautiful sight.

Of distress to Henry was the encroachment of civilization on North Carolina's primitive Outer Banks. The inauguration of ferry service to Ocracoke in 1960 led him to lament 'Good-bye, Old Ocracoke.'

By the time summer tourists begin pouring into Ocracoke, there will be hot dog stands and hamburger joints a-plenty.

Charm and picturesqueness of Ocracoke has been that it was a place where time had stood still for two hundred years. Now that it has been opened to the world, we may expect it to become just another beach resort.

We pray that there are enough determined and far-sighted Ocracokers to organize now to keep Ocracoke as it is. The village should create a body which would be authorized to pass on types and styles of new businesses. The project deserves the energy and leadership of such a man as the island's head school man, Rondthaler.

Wherever he went, Henry found something to write about — the Texas Gulf Sulphur mining operations at Aurora; a building boom at Atlantic Beach; the 'Whittlers' Bench' at Southport.

Biggest news we found at Southport was how the women, bless their hearts, outwitted a scheme to throw overboard Southport's world-famous 'Whittlers Bench'.

Fabled in song and story, in magazine and Sunday supplement, is that 'Whittler's Bench' under old trees on the picturesque town's waterfront. There generations of old salts, home from the sea, have sat, looking lazy across the glistening waters, whittling and telling of great adventures. There the goggle-eyed urchins have stood by to absorb the sea tales and to be excited with the desire to try the life of a sailor man.

Some eager beavers in Southport came up with the idea that the bench, about whittled to bits, should be scrapped, the old trees removed and a solid stone erected to the memory of Brunswickers who have given their lives to services of the sea. The plan had gone so far as to be in the drawing stage.

Then Southport's Woman's Club got word about it. They came up with a better idea. A new cedar whittling bench would be placed to give seamen something to cut on. A giant anchor chain would be fastened around the bench in solid and attractive moorings. New trees, properly renamed for Washington and Bryan, as well as the old ones, would be dedicated.

The women saw the romance and worth of keeping the 'Whittlers' Bench' in this day of crisis and complexity. Before the modern, unimaginative planners knew what was happening, the girls had the Southport city council behind their plan 100 percent.

Never discount the power of a woman.

Henry wanted the coastal region to capitalize on its resources. He applauded a promotion program put on by the N.C. Seafood Association and efforts by the Coastal Carolina Historyland Association to attract tourists.

Through the Coastal Carolina Historyland Association, the East is seeking to get to the stream of tourists passing through the message that the region has fascinating and romantic history, and quaint villages and towns worthy of more than a glance from speeding motor vehicles.

The Historyland Association's program aims to tell the tourists the story of Virginia Dare, Ocracoke, man's first flight and Kill Devil Hill, of ancient Bath and its restoration, of Trvon's Palace, of Wilmington and Old Brunswick.

Most of all, on his trips to the coast, Henry liked to walk the beach and listen to the roar of the ocean.

There was a period of my life when I never spent a few days at the beach that I did not interest myself in trying to think out a way to harness the great power of the surf.

There is such an unaccountable amount of energy pounding against all shores. If man could find a cheap, efficient and dependable system of putting that power to work for him, he would have more energy at his fingertips than is now known.

Of course you know of certain areas of extremely high tides where projects of power generation from the sea have been carried on. But what I thought to develop was a way that could be applied to any average beating of waves with the rise and fall of the tides.

Much did I amuse myself in that direction.

22

While rhapsodizing about North Carolina beaches, Henry kept a less poetic eye on what farmers were doing in the coastal area.

Our party found farmers generally enthusiastic over prospects on a trip we made to Chocowinity, Aurora, Bayboro, Stonewall and other towns.

A traveling salesman who knows how to measure crop prospects covers the region from Robeson County east and north to Original Washington. He finds prospects bright, particularly so in the Bayboro-Oriental area.

"As you ride along the highway by thousands of acres of corn," he said, "you see the stalks so tall and level and so thick, that it is as if you were looking at a green floor upon which you could walk."

Spring was in the air when the Travel Club went to Morehead City for one of Tony's dinners. We also wanted to sniff the salt breeze, listen to the rolling sound of King Atlantic, and take the pulse of Carteret and its coming beach season.

Farmers were in their fields along the 90-mile run from Goldsboro. Just outside of Goldsboro there were two instances of men plowing with mules. You don't see that often. Generally the fields are broken with tractors.

Mechanization has come to Carteret's big Irish potato production. East of Beaufort a strange looking contraption was placing potatoes, its iron and steel snout poking into the seed container, picking up a spud, moving like an arm to the right spot for the row, where another pork-shaped arm pulled off the seed and put it at the right seed depth.

Travel Club members Langston, Hunt and Hinson said it looked like Carteret was planting an "awful lot" of early potatoes.

Counties like Carteret and Wayne, which some years back had a good early Irish potato production, failed to go mechanical with the crop and to adopt modern methods. We had only ourselves to blame when we let California, 3000 miles from the biggest consuming area, and Idaho, push us practically out of the potato market. We kept right on sending New York and other cities ungraded and unwashed potatoes. Consumers naturally preferred the graded, washed, attractively packaged products from other states.

Now we are making motions toward a comeback. The mechanical planter is an instance. Grading and washing are now accepted and more attractive packaging is catching on.

Extensive fields of cabbage, just planted, alternated with the Carteret potatoes. Cabbage is king on some Carteret back farms and when conditions are right, the grower makes a killing.

The plowring and planting spoke of spring. Coming back to Goldsboro in the late afternoon, near Kinston, we heard spring speak. A chorus of frogs from a small pond raised their voices in praise of the forces which were awakening the earth and stirring in the ditches and ponds and in the trees.

In 1963, Henry took note of the revival of truck farming, which once had flourished in the Wayne, Duplin, Sampson counties area.

There is a great increase in the number of acres of truck crops being signed from year to year to be grown under contract. The once economically important truck crop regions of Eastern North Carolina are in the front of this new trend.

Under contract growing, the guesswork is removed from truck crop production. The farmer is protected from the below cost price which often occurs on truck markets on days when the supply exceeds the demand. He is assured a stated price for his produce.

The guaranteed price is one which good farmers can make money on, and they are absolutely protected against loss if they fulfill their part of the contract.

Once contract growing has become the general practice, it will be a natural step toward the establishment of processing plants, canning, drying, freezing, juicing. Eastern North Carolina can be expected to become a vegetable processing center such as have long have operated in New Jersey and other states.

Three years later, Henry brought up food processing again.

The Extension Service, cooperating with the Department of Conservation and Development, is calling for more food processing. A seven-county study was made to evaluate interest of farmers in growing truck crops for processing. The study showed that farmers will put large acreage into vegetables and fruits if there is a good, steady, reliable market for such crops. Markets must be developed and assured before farmers will risk money and labor and time on vegetables.

The major food chains operating in North Carolina could get farmers into food crop production quicker than anything else by offering contracts for quality foods. The Extension Service should unite with C and D in persuading all food store operators to join in promoting and using truck grown locally. And farmers must be ready and willing to make good on contracts for food crops they offer.

Truck farming was one of the things Henry espoused for doing away with dependency on tobacco.

He even proposed a suspension of the growing of tobacco.

Here is a sure-fire way to put North Carolina farm income in line with farm income of livestock, grain-growing states.

Quit worshiping tobacco. Quit putting all our energies and interests and money and labor into cultivating tobacco.

In short, the best thing that could happen to North Carolina would be an absolute prohibition of growing tobacco for 10 years.

We would go through a terrible period of readjustment. Many would suffer. Business would slump for a time.

But if we could stick out our determination to quit tobacco and get more into livestock, poultry and a balanced program, we would emerge a wealthier, happier and healthier people.

Our economy depends too much on tobacco. Growing tobacco actually handicaps, limits and interferes with progress in other directions. Our business and professional men, looking around for returns for money they have to invest, too often turn to tobacco. When they get some money for investment, all they can think of is buying another tobacco farm.

It is a vicious circle. Farming does not get the operation and system that bring in so much higher family income in mid-western states. Farmers fail to develop livestock, dairying, poultry and eggs, trucks, fruits and grapes, because all they can think of is tobacco, tobacco, tobacco.

In 1958, in a talk before the LaGrange Rotary Club, Henry foresaw prosperous times for Eastern North Carolina because of increased grain storage facilities.

These grain facilities will mean that the East can expand its farming into year-around dairying, livestock, hog and poultry production. A beginning has been made.

We have frequently demonstrated that we can produce in Eastern North Carolina beef of a quality equal to that of the choicest western steaks. We can with ease and profit get into dairying on a big scale. We have so many opportunities in this field that states such as Wisconsin, a great dairying country, do not have. We do not have to fight the terrible cold of long winters, where stock has to be kept indoors. We can graze our animals nine months a year. We do not have to expend great sums in building water-tight barns.

Already our section has become one of the most important hog producing centers in the East. With adequate grain facilities, we can expand this program.

The growth of our livestock industry has brought stable, year-around meat processing operations. The money flows weekly from purchases of animals by these meat processors and rings the money bell at a merry clip.

The East has reached the big time in meat processing and poultry production. The grain-growing paradise of our East makes it a natural for the extension of the hatchery, broiler and poultry industry. We are getting in on this program somewhat late, but we are heading that way fast in a big way.

These new farm programs are freeing us from the servitude of one-crop farming.

And this change is being accompanied by industrial development. For the first time, our area is being selected for industries other than our old friends, baked-on-woods and textiles.

It was a good Rotary speech.

Five years, later, in 1963, Henry was less sanguine.

Eastern North Carolina is retreating from its opportunity in livestock by its acceptance of the feed grain program. Under this agricultural aid, growers are paid for taking feed grain out of production.

Eastern North Carolina had become a commercial corn-growing area. Near a score of counties had so qualified.

Eastern North Carolina was forging ahead with beef and swine production. We were in a position to become one of the great livestock regions of the nation.

But we have sold our birthright for a mess of pottage in reducing our feed grain, and that means mostly corn.

We were not making enough corn to feed our livestock before we sold out to the lure of cash. Now we can't go ahead with the development of livestock because we will have to buy corn from the Middle West. Our section is made more dependent on the Mid West and other grain areas for feed for livestock.

Meat producers in Eastern North Carolina must import a large percent of their needs from other states. We could raise the corn, feed it to the livestock and make a higher profit. We had made a start toward providing farm grain storage that took us out of the dependence on today's grain market.

The Grange, the Farm Bureau and the Adult Farmer classes should get over to the people the danger and threat of going out of corn production for a few dollars. We are enslaving our agriculture, and its best prospects, to other sections.

A month later, Henry took some heart from the annual swine and cattle show of the Wayne County Livestock Development Association.

Quality hog breeders like Oland Peele, John Tart, C.R. Joyner and Douglas Edgerton are making good use of the Extension Service's evaluation program. A careful set of records is kept. With this information the farmer can know whether the breed and litter are such as to promote best lean meat returns now demanded by the consumer.

Eastern North Carolina has advanced to big industry levels in meat packing. Hog raising has expanded with the packing industry, but it has not caught up. Every week thousands of hogs are shipped into Clinton, Dunn, Smithfield, Goldsboro, Wilson and other cities from distant points to supply the demands of the packers.

Wayne and other counties, through the Extension Service and groups such as the Wayne County Livestock Development Association are in the midst of a promotion to increase swine production. The purpose is to grow a bigger percentage of the meat the packers need, and to grow more meat-type animals.

Henry relied on Wayne Agricultural Agent Mark Goforth to help keep him abreast with agricultural trends.

"Every once in a while he would see or call me for information," Goforth said.

One development which Henry misjudged was a new hybrid cotton which he said held "great hopes" for the farmer.

If it hadn't been for the development of disease-resistant varieties, Eastern Carolina by now would have been practically out of tobacco production. The new types have saved the crop.

If it hadn't been for the development of hybrids, North Carolina's corn average would not have increased so remarkably in the last few years.

Now we are hearing something of a new hybrid cotton that may do for the crop that hybrids did for corn. If the first experiments are borne out by lengthy tests, we may be able to get back into cotton production on a really profitable basis.

Nothing came of the experiments, Goforth said.

Henry was a great espouser of the home vegetable garden, both for economic and health reasons.

For a family of four or five, a garden, properly cared for, and planted in good ground and properly fertilized, can reduce the food bill by several hundred dollars. But, mind you, don't pick a plot consisting mainly of old trash heap, thinking it will produce for you. If you do not have a place of good soil, you might as well not plant.

But for those who know how, a family garden can add greatly to the diet and can supply quality food for canning or freezing for the winter season.

A garden also has therapeutic value. The person who has somewhere to dig has food for body and soul. The man or woman who digs in the garden comes close to nature and God.

Turn over in your mind those of your friends who relax or exercise with daily attention to green and growing things, and you will find them people at peace with themselves and the world.

Come July, when the garden was made, it was a time for 'Perfect Eating'.

Now, if ever, come perfect foods for the delight, support and delectation of man.

The hyperbole, surely deserved, is applied to the fresh vegetable season. But there should be a more poetic and beautiful manner to describe fresh vegetable time than by such materialistic and hardy terms. For there is hardiness in the dewey fresh products from the garden, but there is more than that. There is a spiritual uplift comfort for the taste buds and a soothing caress for the soul.

Ros'near corn has been on the market for days. And what equals the delight of stewed corn seasoned lightly with white meat fat? You add the seasoning when the corn is about done, pouring it hot from the pan in which you have fried the white meat. And every stewed corn lover knows that tender biscuit crumbled into the corn makes for its crowning glory.

And tomatoes, home-grown tomatoes, perfectly ripened on the vine but pulled before they go one hour beyond maturity — how great is your name in the list of food delights.

Butterbeans, now they're a winner. This year's crop has been gently caressed by showers at the right moment, and the beans, so round, so green, so fully packed, are without blemish and most seductive.

Henry had no vegetable garden of his own, but friends kep him supplied.

My digs at Moses Rountree about his gardening have paid off handsomely. Moses delivered to the General Manager the other morning new Irish potatoes, teeny-weeny ones which combine the delightful freshness of spring rains and warm sunshine. Moses also brought along stringbeans and small yellow squash.

The potatoes Moses brought had been "grabbled", not gathered, not harvested. Grabble is a term Sweet Union County folks use. It means to stir the soft earth with the bare hands and pick out the potatoes.

The General Manager had some ham stock left over from Christmas in which she cooked those succulent beans.

Moses and Graham Hood are gardening competitors, facing each other across the street. Until Moses showed up at our house, Graham had been well ahead in good neighbor dispensations. When he reads this, I bet he will say he has had beans, squash and potatoes from his garden for weeks.

23

One of Henry's chief concerns was education.

"I think it would be fair to say that he has built more schools than any carpenter, designed more libraries than any architect, and has taught more good lessons in the cause of education than any other teacher," said then Governor Terry Sanford. "As a teacher, as an editor and as a citizen, Henry Belk has consistently championed the cause of education."

Henry jumped into the educational fight not long after coming to Goldsboro. In 1935, he was publicity chairman for a campaign to vote a supplementary school tax that would restore a 9-months term for Goldsboro schools, which had lost their accreditation as result of being cut to 8 months. The proposal failed, but was successful the next year, with Henry again managing the publicity.

In 1950, Henry supported an additional supplementary tax, which was approved by voters. In 1953, he supported a successful county school bond election which voted a then prodigious $2,236,000 for new buildings, additions and sites.

If you do not vote for issuing the bonds, we know that conditions now handicapping our children in their school work will grow increasingly serious in a year or so. A vote for the school bonds is a vote for the progress of Wayne schools and a vote for our children.

In 1954, Henry wrote an editorial that was responsible for the establishment of a college aid fund to help worthy and needy Wayne County youths through college. In the editorial, titled "What's the Matter With Wayne?", Henry cited a survey which showed that of 241 high school graduates in the county in 1953, only 57 went on to college.

Henry called for volunteers who would join him in putting up $100 each to get the fund established. Immediate response came from James S. Lewis, Jr., a Goldsboro bridge contractor, who offered to put up $500. He was followed by others and the college aid fund was on its way. During its eleven years of operation, it made loans totaling $62,000 to 133 students.

In 1957, Henry was named by Governor Luther Hodges to a Citizens Committee for Better Schools. He continued to serve on the committee under Governor Terry Sanford.

Failure of the committee to generate public support was cited by Henry in an address before the N.C. Literary and Historical Association in 1959. In his speech, made in connection with the 100th anniversary of the birth of Charles B. Aycock and the restoration of the Aycock birthplace, Henry, who had served on the Aycock Memorial Commission, called for an educational crusade that would reach the people.

To reach them, we must go among them and get to know them. Consider the North Carolina Citizens Committee for Better Schools named by Governor Hodges almost three years ago. It has campaigned through today's accepted media for better schools. But it is sad to relate that by and large it has reached only those who already were sold on education and on the need adequately, from local and state sources, to finance our schools.

The lonely tenant, working out a meager living on a small farm, matching his brawn against the machine's low-cost production, this man, whose children must remain tenants if they are not educated, this man has not been reached.

Let us not make the mistake of accepting as a fact that education is dependent mainly upon buildings and facilities and laboratories, spic and span, and gymnasiums, lunchrooms, playgrounds. Does it ever seem to you that in all our worshiping of education, our homage to it, we may miss the heart and the core?

There must be first that urge and desire, and if compulsion so much the better, to take and make our own this opportunity which Aycock so beautifully phrased as the "right to burgeon out." We must somehow plant that seed in the hearts of the parents, and they in turn will plant it in the hearts of their children. The place to start is in the home with the parents, for the parents set the pattern. The schools give to the children what the parents demand.

Any plan for any length of time, let it be emphasized, must reach the people. The people must be touched of heart and understanding and comprehension. If the people be not reached, the plan fails. Aycock's magic power with the people sprang primarily from the fact that he could reach them. He went among them with the simple words of faith and hope and challenge.

Kerr Scott knew the way when he paramounted the branchhead boys. Out there in the branchheads exist — I hardly wish to say live — the men and women on whom North Carolina's plans for the future so greatly depend. Wasn't it Jefferson who said that a wise nature has endowed the children of the poor with as much capacity as the children of the well to do? The wise government, he added, will recognize this and see that such brains are saved for the state and the future.

Any plan for our state must, if it builds well and permanently, include a way to send to college the child of superior intellect and ability who is denied that advantage by lack of money.

In that number who knows but there may be an Aycock, and Alderman, a Billy Poteat, or a Frank Graham.

Henry was an earlier supporter of East Carolina College. He was elected to its board of trustees in 1947, continuing to serve in that capacity until his death. He served a term as chairman of the board.

In 1966, Henry raised a powerful voice for giving the college university status.

Governor Moore, as one of the themes of his administration, has placed emphasis repeatedly on total development of the state. That means total development of all parts of the state.

Total development will include an institution of higher learning of university standing for the eastern part of the state. Easiest, cheapest and quickest way to attain such an institution is through East Carolina College.

You hear it said that North Carolina cannot finance another university.

North Carolina cannot afford to fail to support a university for its great, rich eastern part of the state, with more than a million people just emerging from agricultural bondage, just moving into industry, processing, mining.

Research is one of the big keys which can unlock the unexcelled treasures of assets of soil, water and forest of Eastern North Carolina.

A university is the surest and most economical machine for the total development of our assets.

The rich and populous Piedmont should support the idea of a university for the eastern part of the state, for selfish reasons if for no other. When the east has come into its own, when it has thrown off the chains of one-crop farming, it will be able to bear a greater proportion of the state's total tax load.

Aid from foundations and from special government programs is far more easily obtained if the petitions for aid come from a university than if they come from a college. Check the records and you will see that this is true. One reliable estimate shows that over 90 percent of aid for research and development that comes from foundations or federal sources goes to universities.

Applications on file from students for entry next year, plus the enrollment this year, indicate there is good prospect that the total body at East Carolina College next year will be 9,000.

Over half of the faculty of East Carolina College hold top graduate degrees. National associations of special fields of education already approve and certify the work at East Carolina.

Making East Carolina College an institution of university rank would be one of the greatest steps in the total development of North Carolina.

University status came to East Carolina College the following year, and for his work in getting it, Henry nominated Dr. Leo W. Jenkins, the president, as the 'Man of the Year in North Carolina'.

A vote by men who think would elect Dr. Leo W. Jenkins as the 'Man of the Year in North Carolina'.

Throughout Eastern North Carolina, and in many places beyond, he would be voted the distinction for the courage, energy, drive, imagination and fighting spirit he showed in getting the Legislature to vote university status to East Carolina College, the Greenville institution of which he is president. In other places in North Carolina, those who did their level best to stop the efforts of Dr. Jenkins would in all fairness still vote for him as 'Man of the Year' for the fight he put up against seemingly insurmountable odds.

You get an idea of the impact of the personality of the former Marine captain from the number of people who want him to run for Governor. In Eastern North Carolina, Dr. Jenkins in a race for Governor would outrun Bob Scott or Stickley or Broughton.

But Jenkins means more to the state right where he is now than if he were nominated for Governor — which he cannot be, since so many in the "Establishment" regard him as persona non grata.

Jenkins is working with all his amazing capacity, imagination and determination to make East Carolina University an institution of national prominence, service and effectiveness. Jenkins is no one-track-minded man. He is moving his institution into greater accomplishment and prestige at a more rapid rate than many had thought possible.

More than any other man, Dr. Jenkins has lit new fires in Eastern North Carolina and beyond. He has shaken the men of the region out of their smug complacency, their satisfaction with things as they are. He has aroused Eastern North Carolina to recognize its potential and opportunity, and he has stirred the area to full utilization of men and materials and education to advance a rich region which has been asleep too long.

Henry led in the development of dormitory facilities at East Carolina and in the expansion of the University library. He sponsored the move to add the master's degree in Library Science.

"East Carolina University was fortunate to have a man of his warm human nature, good humor and wise counsel on its board of trustees and as a member of its executive committee for many years," said Chancellor Jenkins. "His was a steadying hand during years of rapid increase in enrollment and variety of programs. He loved the institution deeply and was interested in its programs of on-going service, its growth and stature. He encouraged the young people who came to Greenville to obtain an education, and he wanted them to get the best available. Those who served with Henry on the board of trustees were constantly reminded of and inspired by his interest in higher education."

"He loved East Carolina University and was imaginative and creative in his thoughts concerning it," said Dr. J. D. Messick, predecessor of Dr. Jenkins. "He stood solidly behind the admininstration, but was always concerned that its objectives be progressive, fair and purposeful. When any new idea was presented, he analyzed it carefully before evaluating for his final judgment. If there were potential weaknesses, he pointed them out. He was never pressured into supporting anything that was not reasonably valid."

James Whitfield, Raleigh newspaperman, was vice chairman when Henry was chairman of the ECU board.

He was thrilled by ECU's growth, but wanted it to grow academically commensurate with its size. When new programs came before the board, he asked searching questions. He always had strong praise for programs of merit. Henry more or less looked upon ECU as the heart of Eastern North Carolina, realizing that through this institution rested very much the life itself of the burgeoning region it served.

His ultimate concern was the student himself. He was not merely interested in seeing a student get a degree. He wanted that degree to mean something. He wanted to see our college graduates apply themselves and contribute to the learning process of generations to come. He wanted them most of all to be good citizens, contributing their knowledge and efforts to the uplift of their communities.

Henry supported the arts efforts of the state. This was indicative of the aesthetic values he found in the finer things of life. They were meaningful to him. He believed they could be meaningful to others. He did not think of art as a necessary aspect of life, rather as one of its little bonuses.

On November 6, 1966, a ceremony was held on the campus of East Carolina University dedicating a men's dormintory to Henry.

Sam Ragan, speaker for the occasion, cited the appropriateness of the honor.

When President Leo Jenkins announced that this new $1,300,000 dormitory would be named for Henry Belk, there was unanimous applause from the state's newspapers, with public reaction matching the editorial approval of the name. It is a splendid and appropriate tribute to an outstanding leader in North Carolina. Henry has been aptly called a champion of educational opportunity for all. His beliefs are those of Aycock, who had as his goal for North Carolina a program of education that would enable every boy and girl to burgeon forth with all that was in them. With his voice and his talents as a writer, Henry had sought to bring that goal to a place of proudful achievement.

In his announcement, Jenkins had said: "Henry Belk's name will serve as a constant reminder to students who are residents of Belk Dormitory that they owe an obligation to excel as citizens of our society in return for the opportunity that has been made available to them in keeping with Henry Belk's ideas."

Henry's interest in education extended from provision for exceptionally gifted students to industrial training and the concept of community colleges. He endorsed North Carolina's School for Performing Arts as "a great cultural step forward. North Carolina is plowing new ground in this brave new venture."

In 1967, Henry came out for a 5-cent levy needed to change the status of Wayne Technical Institute to a community college by adding a two-year college program. The election carried, 4 to 1. Henry hailed the result as proof of county-wide support for giving "the fullest opportunity to all who wish to better and improve themselves. Many who never had any idea that they could go ahead with higher training will now be able to do so."

Henry was an enthusiastic supporter of Mount Olive College, an institution of the Free Will Baptist State Convention founded in 1951 "on a shoestring."

In 1968, Henry had something to say about the college's rapid rise.

What has happened at Mount Olive College is nothing short of a miracle. It seems like only yesterday that the Free Will Baptists came to Mount Olive with $6.20 and a proposal to acquire a building condemned and abandoned by the county school system. They wanted to establish a "college."

Perhaps no one took them near so seriously as they took themselves. Laboriously they began raising funds. They patched up the old building. It was the thinking of President Burkette Raper that if a quality education could be provided, the physical facilities would come.

In record time, and still in the once-condemned building, the college's academic program won full accreditation. A building program was launched. A new campus was acquired. The $6.20 beginning had developed into a multi-million dollar project.

Henry served as a vice president and director of the N. C. Literary and Historical Association. He shared its cultural aims but despaired of their appreciation by the average citizen.

Let the word "culture" crop out in talk of any group of North Carolina males and you see disdainful smirks on most of their faces. And somebody is sure to put in a caustic comment.

Look what happens when "Culture Week" comes to Raleigh. The week sees annual meetings of music, literary, historical, folklore and other organizations. There isn't a long hair or high brow in the whole memberships of hundreds which meet from day to day. But the paragraphers, the commentators and the editorial writers will aim their biggest artillery at the "Culture Vultures."

There seems to be an unholy conspiracy to make a man who has read a book, or looked at a picture, or listened to and enjoyed music, panty-waisted and excessively feminine.

The shelling of "Culture Week" is so intense and so continuous that only the hardiest of the males dare to be seen or heard. Where laymen by the thousands should be supporting by membership and by participation one or more of the cultural organizations, only a few hundreds do so. Professionals or the semi-professionals make up much of the membership.

We have a cult of the one-gallus, the branchhead, or the redneck, and this cult snickers at culture. The attitude is mainly a self-conscious pose, but it is a pose which keeps us mired to the days when we were an illiterate and uncouth people.

Henry sought to bring a little culture to Goldsboro by getting the Rotary Club to sponsor an author's luncheon during Library Week. North Carolina authors were invited to speak at the luncheon, which attracted mostly the culture cult.

A chapter of the Quill and Scroll Society at Goldsboro High School was named for Henry.

Henry would have wished no higher acclaim for his efforts in education than the closing sentence of a tribute to him in the Goldsboro Hi-News.

"For your interest and encouragement, we thank you, Mr. Belk."

24

Henry went into the quiet places of the spirit for his strength.

"He was a man of faith," said newsman James Whitfield, a close friend. "When he lost his daughter, and other tragedies befell him, his faith sustained him.

"He didn't boast of his religion; it wasn't necessary. Anyone who knew Henry Belk was able to detect the goodness mirrored in his soul. He practiced, to the best of his ability, the Ten Commandments and the teachings of Christ."

"Henry Belk was a Christian gentleman," said D.J. Whichard, editor of the Greenville Daily Reflector. "He had faith in his Creator and a great love for his fellowman."

"Henry had a magnificent capacity for compassion," said William D. Snider, editor of the Greeensboro Daily News. "Perhaps because of the personal tragedies in his life, he understood how lonely all of us are and how much we need the encouragement and strength of friends. While he was no sanctimonious goody-good, he personified a spirit of goodness and kindness which engendered the same qualities in those he encountered."

Henry detested self-righteousness. Of his beloved pastor, 'Al' Smith, he wrote: "He has none of the pontificating, holier-than-thou attitude which sometimes digs a ditch between the cloth and the man on the street."

Henry was a believer in prayer.

"When I dropped in to see him, I always had a prayer with him," said the Rev. Earl Farthing, pastor of Madison Avenue Baptist Church. "He would grasp my hand firmly and say, 'Thank you so much.'"

Henry referred to prayer frequently in his column. Once he discussed the subject in a talk before the Protestant Men of the Chapel of Seymour Johnson Air Force Base.

The General Manager and I were there at the invitation of Major Booten to "make a little noise," as Elton Warrick would say. In a sort of panel approach, we discussed great prayers which have helped man, some of them for 3,000 years. I gave comment about the prayers and their authors and the GM read them. We presented nine prayers, beginning with that beautiful statement of affirmation, the 23rd Psalm by David. Maybe some would question this being a prayer in the strictest sense of petition, but it seemed to us that it is as poetic and feeling expression of one's complete faith as we have.

In another column, Henry called for uniform interpretation of the Lord's Prayer.

We need general agreement on whether when we recite the lovely prayer in unison at public meetings, we shall pray, "Forgive us our debts as we forgive our debtors," or shall we say, "Forgive us our trespasses as we forgive those who trespass against us." Make a note to observe, the next time there is occasion for the Lord's Prayer at an inter-faith meeting involving a number of people. Part of the congregation will pray for forgiveness of "debts'. and the other part will pray for forgiveness of "trespasses". Inter-faith bodies should get together on which interpretation is preferable.

Raised as a Methodist, Henry joined Saint Paul Methodist Church after coming to Goldsboro. He changed to First Baptist, his wife's church, on the advice of his pastor, to keep the family together.

The Belks' five-year-old daughter, Marie, said, "I like Mother's church, but I like Daddy's best. It has a steeple on it."

St. Paul was famed for its towering steeple, which was a landmark for three-quarters of a century until it was toppled by Hurricane Hazel in 1954.

Henry was a deacon in First Baptist Church for a number of years.

In 1954, the Belks transferred their membership to the newly organized Madison Avenue Baptist Church, which was nearer to their home. Henry was elected one of the church's first deacons. He played an active role in the church until he lost his sight.

"He and Mrs. Belk continued to worship regularly with us," said the Rev. Mr. Farthing. "Henry was a source of encouragement to me. He would mention some of my sermons as being very helpful."

The Belks were messengers from Madison Avenue Baptist Church to the Southern Baptist Convention at Miami in 1960. Henry had a column on "Some Impressions" from the convention.

The 13,000 attending the Southern Baptist Convention here now have had 24 hours in which to evaluate Soviet Premier Khruschev's crazy man press conference in Paris.

What is the general feeling of these people from all parts of the nation to the Hitler-sounding, crude and rude nose-thumbing at the United States?

Nobody here has panicked. There was no rush to offer resolutions or to intrude the criticism of the United States into consideration at the convention.

In private conversations there have been expressions of regret in the bungled handling of the spy plane incident. But I have heard no man put such criticism above the need for closing ranks, Democrats and Republicans, behind the President.

References to K's demonstration of bad manners and ill temper crept into many of the prayers and sermons on the program. But these dominated not one speech or session.

Billy Graham was somewhat pessimistic over the world situation in the main message before the Pastors' Conference. He said that in the past five years he had held interviews with chiefs of state in 47 nations and that only five or six were optimistic that war could be avoided. But he stressed that he did not feel that war would result at this time. Graham spoke while the newsboys were still crying the extra editions over the K. outburst on the streets of Miami Beach. It was natural that a view on the situation would have been somewhat more gloomy than one after a day of deliberation.

Graham, almost casually, did make one statement which, if he had developed it, or cited authority, could have been unnerving. He said that the day had brought one of the critical days of history, indeed, one as critical as any day had brought since the crucifixion of Christ.

As a layman I have watched with growing understanding the crowds and their dedication to their work. The experience has been an eye opener for me. I have stood in the sidelines and watched, and what was a quizzical, almost nonchalant attitude has been replaced by one of open admiration. I think that I am a better man for this experience, better able to cope with life's daily grind, its trials, its joys, its sorrows.

As I have looked, listened and meditated, I feel that I have come to know why the Reds ban religion.

These dedicated Christians at their convention give a fervor, loyalty and unswerving devotion to their Jesus that is compelling. These same men and women who have prayed and laughed and talked, if they had to, could face persecution, banishment, and even torture and death for their religion.

Henry was an influential layman in the Baptist State Convention, attending most of its sessions and playing a prominent part in its deliberations. He served four years on the board of Baptist Homes for the Aging and four years on the board of directors of the Biblical Recorder, journal of the Baptist State Convention. In 1959, he was a member of a special committee that named Marse Grant as editor of the Recorder.

In 1963, Henry accused Baptists of "foot-dragging" in caring for their aged.

Best way to say it is to say it flatly. Right out in the open where the surprised state may take notice. And where the surprised Baptists themselves may quit their foot-dragging.

The million Baptists in the state have a glorious record in care for the orphans. The Baptists have a record of great service in their Bowman Gray Medical School. They have a facility second to none in their magnificently modern Baptist Hospital at Winston-Salem.

But Baptists are caring for only 160 people in their four homes for the aging.

It was not until 13 years ago that the denomination began to move at all to meet what is an increasingly great challenge and dire Christian need.

Progress had been made. There are now four homes. The fine new home for Eastern North Carolina at Hamilton, Martin County, was occupied only in the past year.

It would be logical to expect that opening of the Hamilton Home, plus expansions at Winston-Salem, site of the first home, and at Albemarle, might alert the churches to their responsibility for the aging.

Little in that direction, however, has taken place. Under the cooperative program of the churches, the Baptist Homes for the Aging receive only $7.92 of each $1,000 given. The only regular source of income for the four homes is from special collections set under the convention calendar for the third Sunday in each February. The last such special Sunday saw gifts decrease by approximately 5 percent. This came as a shock, since the need was greater, with the Hamilton Home added.

Tar Heel Baptists have not realized the need for support of the Homes. When they do, they will come forth to take care of their aging, as they have done for the orphans, the sick, and for their colleges.

Henry followed closely the progress of Baptist institutions of learning in North Carolina, in particular Wake Forest College.

In 1959, he took note of the fact that "Baptists Build".

We have hardly noticed it, but a great educational drama has been and is being enacted by North Carolina Baptists. The 870,000 Baptists in the state are quietly assuming their full responsibilities in meeting the tremendous demands for higher education that are upon us.

To their seven colleges in recent times, the Baptists have given many millions of dollars, and more are being sought. At its recent session in Greensboro, the Baptist Convention allocated $1,300,000 from its state budget for its institutions. This represents a large increase over last year.

With practically one mind, members of the convention passed a resolution which can mean great things for the youth of its 3,300 churches and for the state as a whole. The resolution creates a special committee of 21. It is charged with making a comprehensive study of the full financial needs of the colleges and bringing this information to the next convention to be held in Asheville in November.

The State Convention already has given approval for raising three of the Baptist junior colleges to full four-year status. These are Campbell, Mars Hill and Wingate.

Removal of Wake Forest from Wake County to Winston-Salem left the denomination without a four-year educational institution in Eastern North Carolina. Campbell has been under pressure ever since to add the final two years to its program, and trustees moved to meet the demand. In due time Mars Hill and Wingate are expected to move toward four-year programs.

The report of the Council on Education to the Convention showed energetic progress along all lines among the colleges, which have an enrollment in excess of 8,000.

In 1964, Henry threw his support to a plan advanced by the General Board of the Baptist State Convention.

It is good news to all of North Carolina that the General Board has given its blessing to a suggestion which would be of great help to the seven Baptist colleges in the state. The plan would authorize the Baptist colleges, subject to approval by the State Convention, to name up to one-fourth of the members of boards of trustees from other than Baptists who live in North Carolina. The Council on Christian Education of the convention has joined in the suggestion.

Baptist college boards, officers and members of the Council on Christian Education see the plan as one which could open up to the colleges new sources of aid. Foundations play a role of increasing importance in making grants to colleges. Adoption of the idea would open new doors.

Over and above the possible financial aid which might result, there is an essential fairness in the proposal. Under the present system, alumni of the colleges who move out of North Carolina are ineligible to serve on boards of the colleges. Thus the seven institutions are denied the right to the counsel and direct loyalty of many of their most outstanding and successful graduates.

Baptists would not be surrendering their colleges to outsiders if the Convention approves the expansion plan when it meets in Greensboro in November. The convention must approve nominations to the boards of trustees.

The proposal as applied only to Wake Forest fell short of a two-thirds majority by only a few votes last fall. It seems certain that a year's study, plus the six other colleges joining in the proposal, guarantees adoption of the idea at the Greensboro convention.

Henry should have known that there was no guarantee of what Baptists would do. The convention turned down not only the trustee proposal, but a resolution authorizing the colleges to participate in federal funds.

The majority of the 5,000 at the convention insisted upon retaining full, complete and firm control and to have nothing to do with what might be construed as abandoning the principle of separation of church and state.

We must have a considerable cooling off period before a new approach to the matter of support for the colleges and trustee proposal can be taken up again. The question now is how can these colleges which have served the whole state so long be assured of a program which will enable them to go forward.

The questions cannot be answered until emotions have calmed. Baptists have a way of kicking over the traces and engaging in fights among themselves. They also have a record of going ahead steadily. We expect this spirit to win in the end.

The seven old and honored colleges must not be made the redheaded stepchildren of the ‘million denominational members who make up the convention.

Baptists ended the "cooling off period" by adopting both controversial proposals in 1967. It was decided to allow one-third of the college trustees to be non-residents of North Carolina and one-sixth to be non-Baptists. And approval was given for Mars Hill College to accept some federal aid.

Henry called the latter decision a 'Great Day for Baptist Higher Education in North Carolina'.

The significance of the matter lies not so much in the actual aid involved, as it does in breaking a bottleneck which many had feared might create situations which could close or see some of the state's seven Baptist institutions of higher learning turned into other hands.

The Mars Hill break-through, however, does not solve the question. It is only a small beginning. The matter is certain to be raised at the next convention. And the men of small view who cling so tenaciously to the old ways already are organizing to force their will upon the convention a year hence. This group, or some of them, would prefer to see some of the colleges closed rather than to see them abrogate the rule of separation of church and state, as they see it.

Those who won the Mars Hill fight stand steadfast in their acceptance of the church and state theory. But they look beyond to the great need among the million Baptists of North Carolina for certified college facilities sufficient to accommodate the Baptist youth.

Henry knew his Baptists.

The strength of the Baptists is the strength of the people. How they react, what they do and how they do it, is as varied and different as men themselves. They are great because they defy tagging with one tag. They are great and growing because their never-changing tenet as a denomination is that every man is entitled to speak his own mind. And real Baptists generally do. Woe to the man or group of men who assume that they can direct, steer, insinuate, control or deeply influence Baptist actions.

Henry spoke his mind, to the accompaniment of "sweet applause", on one occasion.

It was months ago that it happened, but it still comes back as a strange, sweet, new pleasure.

At a Baptist institutions trustees conference in Winston-Salem, one man, during a discussion period, urged trustees to read all Baptist college publications with a view of censoring them, to find material with which to caution the youthful editors about their excessive realism, or their language, or their subjects.

We feel very strongly that the young idea must learn on its own how to shoot. We feel that freedom of thought and expression is necessary, that minds may develop their own directions, that they examine with care all search for truth. We feel that to censor them, to force them into conformity or patterns or grooves, is to rob them of human dignity. It is to make little men and women.

We were forced by strong feelings to argue this view in replying to the Brother who wanted boards to dominate and direct and subjugate youthful thinking.

When we had finished a round of applause rippled through the audience of some 200. It was not the courteous, polite, half-hearted applause. It was hearty, energetic and emphatic.

I felt a strange glow of pleasure. I am ashamed of it, but that pleasure stemmed, I fear, more from being approved in a position than from my satisfaction in having dared to throw an objection onto the floor.

It would be easy to become addicted to the spurious pleasure of arguing a point to feel the fattening of the ego when applause comes. The idea suggests a close and constant danger to newspapermen. It is not quite the same, but it is related. That is the danger of taking a position, or making a popular approach. Editors and reporters must keep a balance and a disinterest that enables them to see and feel fairly. If they become more interested in how their readers are patting them on the back and telling them what a wonderful job they did, if they are more interested in this than in assembling and giving information, then they have lost much for their craft and are in danger of losing the divine aloofness and coolness that must characterize good reporting and editing as concerns facts and issues.

25

Henry was a maker of newspapermen who followed his precepts in practicing their craft. Of modest pride to him was the success of numerous proteges who had sat at his feet.

"The News-Argus was a good berth for fledgling newspaper men, due to the kindly efforts of Henry Belk," said Larry McSwain, who became managing editor of the Hanford, California, Sentinel.

When Paul Barwick of LaGrange, a 1952 graduate of the University of North Carolina School of Journalism, told Dean Oscar J. "Skipper" Coffin that he was going to work for the News-Argus, Coffin remarked that he had the best job offered any of the graduates.

"Maybe not the biggest salary, but the best job, he assured me," Barwick recalled. "How right he was."

Soon after entering upon the job, Barwick did a story rewrite which Henry threw in the waste basket with the comment, "That is the worst piece of rewriting I've ever seen."

The verdict didn't discourage Barwick, who had been "goaded" by Henry before.

Barwick had gotten a taste of newspaper work in high school, when he corresponded for the News-Argus. There was a drawback, though, in his following the profession. He had been a paraplegic since his early teens.

"I didn't see how I could go to college. I thought of asking my Vocational Rehabilitation counselor to give me training in some vocation that I could follow from my wheelchair. Henry Belk told me that the only thing that stood between me and a career in journalism was lack of determination. He said I ought to follow newspaper work and that the only way I could do it was to get a college education."

Barwick took Henry's advice and went on to become editor of the LaGrange Gazette and publisher of a string of weekly newspapers. Now public relations specialist for the Eastern Region Alcoholism Program of the N.C. Department of Mental Health, he was selected as North Carolina's handicapped citizen of the year for 1972.

Working under Henry was not for the sensitive or faint of heart.

"He was a hard taskmaster," Barwick said. "Sometimes it seemed that nothing I wrote was good enough for him, and I would go home at night ready to quit. But his example was too much. I had to keep plugging, with Henry goading me."

Henry was good at goading.

"You know," said one of his friends, "Henry spends most of his time gently goading people to do things that natural human inertia keeps them from doing."

"From Henry Belk, one of North Carolina's great editors, I learned a great deal," said Sam Ragan, who was on the News-Argus in the late 1930's. "For one thing his advice on writing is as sound now as it was then. 'Write with wonder,' he said. 'Write as if you are seeing this thing for the first time. And the reader will see it that way, too.' I keep trying to remember that, to see people, to see things, to see our North Carolina with that sense of wonder."

John D. Langston, Jr., retired editor of the Durham Sun, worked under Henry on the Goldsboro News and afterwards the News-Argus. His father was principal owner of the News, but that didn't get him any favors from Henry.

"He would give me hell over what I thought were minor things. I would stay mad at him for a few days, then it would blow over. Looking back, I realize it was for my good. I received invaluable training under Henry Belk."

One of Henry's appreciative proteges was Harry Hollingsworth, veteran telegraph editor of the Durham Morning Herald.

"In looking back to the late '30's and early '40's, when I was working for Mr. Belk, the chief impression that lingers with me is that he worked me hard. Never have I come in contact with an editor who demanded so much of his reporters, or who gave so much of himself in supporting them. There was nothing he would ask you to do that he couldn't do himself, and do better — whether it was writing Sidelights, an editorial, a sports story, or any type of news story.

"I never arrived at work that I didn't find him already behind his typewriter. He had read the morning papers, probably made a few telephone calls, clipped a few stories he wanted rewritten or checked for new leads, and had measured the pulse of Goldsboro. On my typewriter I would find a list of four or five stories — never less than three — he wanted in the News-Argus that afternoon. There was never any reason accepted for not having the stories when you returned from your beat. He knew the stories were out there.

"On the job he was demanding, but never in a way that destroyed your personal sense of dignity. He was friendly, courteous, considerate, kind, and ever a gentleman. He had time for me, time to relate to me the joys and, yes, the heartbreaks, of being a good citizen and a good newspaper man; time to tell me of the importance of friendships; time to shape and mold me from the base built by my parents for a life of newspapering. One worked for his compliments. You knew he would give you hell for poor work. And you knew when you received either — or both — that he was sincere in his remarks."

When Hollingsworth left the News-Argus in 1943 to join the Parker brothers' newspapers in Ahoskie, Henry took note of his departure with regret.

All of us are going to miss Hollingsworth, but all of us are glad to see him step into a better position. He is our kind of editor. He believes in printing the news without bias or prejudice. He doesn't believe in sacred cows for newspapers. He thinks that a newspaper's job is to give the news, and that its great responsibility is to its readers and to the public. He feels as we do that a newspaper should keep abreast of trends and developments so that it may better serve the public.

Norwood C. Middleton, managing editor of The Roanoke (Va.) Times, attributed Henry's "kindly oversight" to his following newspapering as a career.

It all started while I was taking a course in journalism under Miss Ida Gardner at Goldsboro High School. That course piqued my curiosity about the professional newsman and I began making afternoon visits to the News-Argus. Mr. Belk condoned my presence and gave me the opportunity to get the feel of a newsroom by looking up a mat of some news personality occasionally. In addition, he encouraged me to send in weekly news articles from Camp Tuscarora, where I was on the staff several summers.

This sort of encouragement kept my interest alive. Then came the trial of Bruno Hauptmann for the Lindbergh kidnapping. As the trial progressed and the jury began its deliberations, Mr. Belk decided to have the News-Argus prepared for a verdict, either way it went. I recall hovering around the newsroom, entranced by the swift strokes of his pen as he dummied the stand-by pages, one for "Guilty" and one for "Not Guilty." I watched the page forms take shape on the turtles, and then began the long wait. For what now seems like weeks, I would rush to the News-Argus every afternoon, hoping to be there when the verdict came in and an "extra" would be rushed to the streets. If I am not mistaken, the verdict finally came one day about suppertime. Wherever I was, I remember telephoning Mr. Belk to ask whether there would be in fact an "extra" published, using one of the ready-to-go front pages. Oddly enough, I cannot remember his decision, but the preparedness he practiced in being ready for an eventuality has been a guidepost throughout my own career — a guidepost to plan ahead.

During my summer internship on the News-Argus I was asked to report on a speech Governor Clyde Hoey made in Mt. Olive while touring the Wayne-Duplin area. In his speech he attached great importance to the possibility that cotton would become an important ingredient in the construction of highways. In fact, some experimentation had been made in that regard and the Governor held out high hopes for its success.

When I turned in my story, Mr. Belk's experienced eye swept over my copy and immediately spotted the amateur's greatest pitfall — the unanswered question. What the reader wanted to know, he told me, was specifically how cotton could be used in highway construction and what advantages could be expected. He sent me to the telephone in quest of more information. I rounded out the story by saying that a layer of cotton, spread between the baserock and top coat, would result in a smoother ride and — more importantly, a big market for cotton.

This has been a favorite story of mine in counseling beginning reporters to spot the unanswered questions in their copy and ferret out the answers.

I am sure that my schoolboy enthusiasm for what I was doing shielded me from occasional outbursts of exasperation and sometimes wrath that Mr. Belk directed at others on the staff. I was never away from a realization that he knew news and how it should be written. He taught me much.

Henry exerted more influence than he probably was aware of on another protege, Gene Roberts, Jr., who has had a distinguished journalistic career. Roberts was city editor of the Detroit Free Press and national editor of The New York Times. Currently he is executive editor of the Philadelphia Inquirer.

Roberts was with the News-Argus for two years after finishing college and serving a stint in the Army. His first job was that of rural reporter. He did a column called 'Rambling in Rural Wayne'.

For the first few months I held the 'Ramblin' job, Mr. Belk constantly told me that I wasn't being descriptive enough in my writing, saying he couldn't really see the scenes I mentioned. He told me to end every column with the prettiest sight I had seen that day while driving about the county. At the end of each column I had to put 'Today's Prettiest Sight', and then go on to tell what I had seen that impressed me. This was to become very valuable to me. It meant that each day I had to keep myself in a posture of being constantly observant. And every day Mr. Belk sent me a note telling me whether I had been descriptive enough in my observations.

His visual memory was uncanny. I remember once describing the scene from the hilltop between Cherry Hospital and Rosewood. Although Mr. Belk had been unable to see for several years, I discovered that his memory was faultless. When I wrote about the view from the hilltop, I forgot to mention a group of pecan trees in the distance. After all those years, Mr. Belk still remembered the pecan trees and gave me hell for not including them.

He also insisted that the column be different every day and that while rambling about the county I should constantly talk to new and different people. Whenever I visited the same people during the same month, Mr. Belk would be quick to notice. He would call me in his office and suggest some remote back road that I was to drive down the next day. As a result, I came to know not only every road in the county, but almost every pig path. Being constantly challenged to go to new places and talk to new people forced me into a professional frame of mind which I hope has persisted to this day — which is to always be wary of doing the obvious and to guard against having a set group of sources.

Mr. Belk was forever trying to get me to write about the human side of the news — the miseries of people, their joys, their successes and failures. I tended to resist this kind of writing in favor of 'significant' issues. But he never let up.

I remember once covering the sheriff's office on my beat and hearing about an old farmer who had been found dead that morning in his rocking chair in a small shanty near Rosewood. Although the farmer had been dead for several days, his dog had not left his side. I remember thinking this was the kind of story Mr. Belk would like. I rushed out and talked to the neighbors and put together a tale of an old farmer who had fallen on lean times and who had outlived his family and most of his friends. All he had left was a dog that didn't desert him.

I thought Mr. Belk would like the story and he did. But one day a week later there was a shout from his cubicle. He called me in and said, "Remember the story you did a week ago about the farmer and the dog? All this time has gone by and you haven't told me what became of the dog."

So I went back and found out that, after a week, the dog was still around the house and unwanted. So I wrote another story, this time about the dog. When the story came out, the phone didn't stop ringing for hours. Almost everybody in the county, it seemed, wanted to adopt the dog.

Mr. Belk knew well that a paper that records only the 'important' can become a dull paper. He was forever interviewing me about what I had seen during the day and telling me that the things I encountered and didn't write about were usually more interesting than the ones I saw as stories. An example was Col. John D. Langston and his oak trees. One day I saw the Colonel walking along the street with a large tape measure in his hand. I stopped and offered him a lift and asked him what he was doing with the tape measure. He said he had been sitting on his back porch that day looking at his oak trees and had concluded they were probably the largest oak trees, in terms of circumference, in the entire county. To prove his point, he was walking around measuring some of the larger oak trees in town to see if his indeed weren't bigger.

When I mentioned this to Mr. Belk at the end of the day, he allowed as how I had missed an important story, that if Colonel Langston was going around looking for the biggest oak trees in the county, this was the sort of thing that readers would be interested in. I scoffed at him, but did the story. To say that people were interested in the story would be putting it mildly. We must have received a thousand calls from people who wanted us to come out and measure their trees to see if they weren't bigger than Col. Langston's. As I recall, our circulation soared while all the oak tree measuring was going on.

Ties between Roberts' family and the Belks were of long standing and close ("When I was born, the Belks loaned us Marie's little baby crib and, as far as I know, I spent my infancy in it") but that didn't make it any easier for him with Henry.

If anything, Mr. Belk was tougher on me than on the other reporters. And he insisted that if I was going to stay in the newspaper business — rather than sell tombstones — I had better learn it well.

Henry got the impression that Roberts was too money-minded for a newspaper man and suggested that he ought to go in business with his father-in-law, E. McLamb, owner of McLamb Monument Company.

The newspaper business has never been a particularly well paid profession and Mr. Belk, in particular, never made a great deal of money. Over the years he developed almost a monastical view about the business and felt — and I am dealing a little bit in hyperbole, but not much — that anyone entering the business ought to be ready to take the vows of poverty. I was prepared to make financial sacrifices to stay in newspaper work, but I was not willing to resign myself to a life of deprivation. I feel that people who believe in the newspaper business should stay in it at all costs, but keep fighting at all times for higher pay. I don't think that only the publishers should enjoy the fruits of everyone's labors. And whenever I was in a kind of militant mood about salary, Mr. Belk would conclude that I was putting a high premium on things material and that maybe my father-in-law's business was the place for me.

One thing that should be stressed about Mr. Belk was his dedication to the proposition that the public had a right to know and that no public official should stand in the way.

An incident that illustrated how tough he could be in protecting the people's rights involved a city manager named Page Benton, who came to Goldsboro about the time I joined the News-Argus. Benton was an engineer and, as I recall, an efficient organizer and administrator. But he had had little experience in dealing with the press and with the public and seemed to operate under the assumption that if too much public business were discussed in public, it would complicate the affairs of the city. After he had been in office a few months, it became apparent that news of city government had slowed down to a trickle. The city council seemed to go along with this. Most of their business, and the real debate, took place in executive sessions.

When it became apparent what was happening, Mr. Belk and Gene Price, the city editor, asked me to start covering the city manager's office and the city council meetings, and see if I couldn't figure out a way to get more news out of city hall.

I had never covered the city council before and wasn't sure where they met. When I arrived at city hall on the night of their meeting, I saw them sitting around in an office. Assuming the meeting was underway, I walked in and started taking notes. It turned out I had walked into the middle of an executive session. After considerable whispering among themselves, the council ordered me out of the room.

The next day I told Mr. Belk what had happened and he suggested that I include a paragraph, high up in my story of the meeting, saying that the News-Argus reporter had inadvertently walked into a secret session and had been kicked out. After that, the councilmen and Page Benton agreed, somewhat reluctantly that reporters could come to the executive sessions.

So I started going, but at either the first or second executive council meeting I attended, Page Benton produced a sealed envelope and told me I had to agree not to reveal its contents, when it was opened for discussion, or leave the room. I left.

The next day, at Mr. Belk's suggestion, we ran a story about the sealed envelope. As I recall, it touched off a certain amount of controversy around town, with everyone wondering what was in the sealed envelope. It became known as the mystery envelope and for several days people talked of little else.

Then Page Benton called me up one morning and demanded that I appear in his office that afternoon. I agreed. When I hung up, Mr. Belk, whose hearing was fantastic, yelled out of his cubicle, wanting to know what it was all about. When I told him, he said, "Call Page Benton and tell him I am coming with you." So I called Benton and while I was talking with him, Gene Price walked in. Learning what had transpired, he told me to call Benton back and say he was coming along, too.

So at the appointed time, we all went down to city hall. When we walked into Benton's office, he immediately made a tactical error. He started off the conversation by saying, "I called you men in today because . . . "

Whereupon, Mr. Belk picked up his aluminum cane with one hand and groped around to Benton's desk with the other hand. When he located it, he slammed the cane down on the desk and said, "Listen, you Mussolini, when you call, we don't have to come."

The upshot of the confrontation was that the executive sessions were dispensed with and "We never had any more trouble in getting news'"

A thumbnail assessment of Henry was given by Ralph Howland, longtime newspaperman, who reported for the News-Argus in the 1930's.

He was a very good editor, quick, incisive and fair. He didn't appreciate stupidity, but would go far for the man or woman who tried. Though buffeted badly by life, he retained a great sense of humor and a deep sympathy for others. I never thought he desired an abundance of material things; he knew a good life came from other things.

232

26

While teaching his craft to others, Henry carved out for himself
a unique place in North Carolina journalism.

"Few men, with a paper as small as his vehicle, have exerted so
wide an influence upon North Carolina," said Holt McPherson,
retired editor of the High Point Enterprise.

"He was a newspaperman's newspaperman," said Ashley B.
Futrell, editor of the Washington (N.C.) Daily News. "He knew
how to fight, when to fight, and what to fight with. As a
newspaperman, he was a guiding light. Informed, articulate and
dedicated, he never shot from the hip. Rather, he took dead aim.
His opinions were always filled with wisdom and right. He could
be intensely critical in the most polite terms of anyone I ever
knew. And he could offer praise in the clearest concept of anyone
I ever knew.

"As an individual, he was one of the warmest and kindliest
human beings I have known. He valued friendships highly and was
unselfish to a degree seldom seen in people."

"Among the newspaper profession in North Carolina, Henry
wielded a tremendous influence for good and set an example that
those of us left behind would do well to emulate," said D.J.
Whichard, Jr., editor of the Greenville Daily Reflector.

"He was one of newspapers' greats because he was a man of the
people," said Mrs. Elizabeth Gold Swindell, editor of the Wilson
Daily Times. "He had the interests of the people at heart and it
was all seasoned kindness and goodness. He began back in the days
of personal journalism and he never lost that personal touch. His
imprint on the newspaper profession in North Carolina will be
lasting.

"Regardless of physical handicaps, Henry enjoyed a philosophy
of life not given to many. I recall all the operations he had on his

eyes and the hope, all to no avail, which went with each one. There was never a word of complaint; but with each public speech he made, you could feel his growing in grace and acceptance."

"I knew Henry from the time he went to Goldsboro on the old Morning News," said Henry A. Dennis, editor of the Henderson Daily Dispatch. "In those days he was just about the paper, along with Lucile, who was the society editor. As editor of the News-Argus, he brought prestige both to the paper and himself. He was a qualified instructor of many young fellows on the paper who went on to higher and more responsibile positions.

"His advice was sought by leaders of the N.C. Press Association. Despite his loss of sight, he took a leading part in its varied activities. He and his 'General Manager' attended press meetings as regularly as they were held."

"Henry Belk was one of North Carolina's finest editors and citizens," said H. Galt Braxton, editor of the Kinston Free Press, shortly before his death. "He and I were close friends for many years. He was an honored guest at a party given for me on my 80th birthday in February, 1964. His greeting was one of the high spots of the occasion for me. In his remarks, he quoted Shakespeare's 'This, above all, to thine own self be true'. That is Braxton's philosophy, too,' Henry told the more than 600 people who were present."

Henry said it a little differently editorially.

Newspaper people are accustomed to being on the receiving end of tossed brickbats. They can take heart, then, when a city of 25,000 such as Kinston goes all out to show its regard for its publisher and editor. That amazing piece of news happened when Kinston, Ely Perry leading, worked up in two weeks a fabulous 80th birthday party for Mr. H. Galt Braxton.

The program ran over two hours, but there wasn't a dragging moment in it. From the singing of "Happy Birthday" to the surprised Braxton as he entered the hall, to the end, there was a warmth of good will and high regard.

Braxton, as everyone knows, is one of the most outspoken of editors. It makes no difference to him if 24,000 Kinstonians are on the other side from him, he blandly argues for his own personal view. People, all of them, respect his sincerity.

Many a time Kinstonians, to a majority, have roundly berated their editor with harsh words coming close to bitterness. Nevertheless, his courage, his unselfishness, have won him a higher place in the hearts of his people than comes to most men.

So, Brother Editor, when you feel lonely and misunderstood for something you have written, think of Editor Braxton and take heart.

"Henry Belk was impressive in stature and intellect and a great newspaperman," said W.E. (Bill) Horner, editor of the Sanford Daily Herald. "I was never quite convinced that he was handicapped in any way. He had more insight than most people with 20-20 vision."

Henry and Horner frequently quoted each other in their columns. Every spring, under the title 'Flower Census', they had an exchange on which county, Wayne or Lee, had the most early-blooming flowers and shrubs.

"Henry went to great lengths to compile the figures for his county," Horner recalled.

In 1956, the News-Argus "went on an economy spree" and dropped Horner's paper from its exchange list.

"I wrote Publisher Hal Tanner I realized there was no particular affinity of news as to Wayne and Lee counties, but that I had to have Henry's writings. The News-Argus started coming again."

"Big of frame, big of mind and big of heart, Henry Belk was a strongly catalyzing force in the life of North Carolina at a time when his spirit and counsel were much needed," said High Point editor Holt McPherson. "Few men, with a paper as small as his vehicle, have exerted so wide an influence upon North Carolina.

"For as long as I can remember, I knew and admired Henry Belk and enjoyed his friendship. In his days as president of the North Carolina Press Association, he was of tremendous encouragement to me in founding the Journalism Foundation of North Carolina. We were just begun, with only about $20,000 in hand, when he told me one day at Chapel Hill, 'You're going to get that $100,000 you want.

"We got it and have gone on to well over $500,000, but it was his faith, when the going was rough, that stimulated us to fight. He was that kind of encourager, ready to say a good word, put in a blow or a good word. The UNC School of Journalism has come to rank with the nation's best, largely because of the Foundation and Henry's faith in it."

"There was something about Henry Belk that made people and organizations claim him," said J.D. Fitz of Morganton, president of the N.C. Press Association. "The Press Association had a special, proprietary interest in him throughout his career. Henry's contributions to the Association had existed for many years before he became president in 1950, and continued as long as he lived. He continued to attend regularly the annual conventions and institutes of the Association, even when his eyesight was gone and he had to depend on his devoted 'General Manager' to guide his steps.

"Throughout his career he was a source of strength and encouragement for younger members of the newspaper fraternity. 'Mr. Henry', as many of them called him, was sought out by young newspapermen for counsel and advice, which he gave freely. He possessed a remarkable memory that served to endear him to young friends. Many a young man has been seen registering obvious pleasure when, upon approaching Mr. Belk in a convention hall or hotel lobby to pay his respects, Henry called him by name before he could identify himself. It does something to the ego of an uncertain young newspaperman when a man of Henry Belk's professional stature, deprived of sight, can recognize him by a spoken word."

Henry's interest in the younger members of the Press Association was recalled by A. Howard White, editor of the Burlington Daily Times-News.

"I started attending NCPA sessions when I was comparatively young. Mr. Henry was a veteran and had been long on the scene. He had many old friends in the Association, but took a special interest in the younger members. It seemed, in fact, that he sought us out, just as we did him. He made us feel that we belonged to the newspaper profession and were welcome in the Association. He shared thoughts on newspapering with us as we sat in the Carolina Inn lobby while attending mid-winter institutes in Chapel Hill. He gave encouragement to those of us who were much younger and greener. I knew that Henry Belk was someone to see, to talk to, to learn from, and to admire. This basic feeling for him deepened as the years passed."

White recalled a White House reception for members of the American Society of Newspaper Editors in 1964, at which he was instrumental in getting Henry introduced to President Lyndon B. Johnson.

It was a delightful occasion, with the President seeming to have the best of all, as he danced with the wives of the newsmen. All were lined up to dance with him.

Several of us from North Carolina, including Henry Belk, were in the Rose Room. My wife, Lib, suggested that we try to get the President to come from the East Room and see Mr. Henry, who couldn't get through the crowd to see him.

My wife arranged the meeting through a White House aide. It took some time for the President to get away from the ladies, but finally he and Mrs. Johnson came to the Rose Room, where he and Henry chatted away as if they had known each other for years. The President expressed his delight with several visits to North Carolina. He said he remembered well a reception given for him at Elon College. 'And I'll never forget the buttermilk served at the luncheon,' he said. 'I've never tasted such good buttermilk.'

Henry described the incident in 'L.B.J. As Host'.

Maybe you saw the picture of Yours Truly and his General Manager in the front row, as President Johnson talked to 1,000 members of the American Society of Newspaper Editors. There was this country editor and his GM as large as life.

The affair was in the Rose Garden of the White House. We had arrived early for the reception and buffet supper. Until the guests began to gather, it had not been certain the President would address the group.

If the GM's feet had not hurt from too much running around in Washington, you never would have seen us within arm's length of Mr. Johnson. By instinct, we prefer the back rows, so we won't obscure vision for those behind us. It may be, however, that the GM accentuated the aching feet because she didn't want me getting too tired. Since my thrombosis, she adroitly maneuvers for me to get as much rest as possible.

We waited 40 minutes for the President to appear, seated on the steps near the speaker's stand. When Mr. Johnson arrived, we stood up and there we were on the front row. We didn't intentionally hog the scene.

Johnson is as home-folksy as the crowd around a filling station in rural North Carolina. He is as friendly as any Branchhead boy ever was. He likes people and his 30 years in Washington have honed to a fine edge his sure touch in making friends and influencing people.

Take the speech to the editors. It was not the polished pronouncement of a Kennedy, though it had some portions of superb phrasing. But heart and compassion breathed through it as he cited the responsibility of government to do for a people what as individuals they may not be able to do for themselves.

The son of Texas has brought to the White House the cleverness of the politician. But he has also brought sincerity, conviction and purpose.

And at the climax of his talk there was no overdisplay of histrionics. Johnson ended simply by telling his guests that he and Lady Bird "want you all to come on in the house."

The buffet was set on long tables in the State Dining Room and in the large East Room, where foreign diplomats are received. Shrimp, turkey, roast beef, tongue and other meats and cheeses were spread among pickles, olives, carrots, chips and dips. Those hot Texas-style spices, the GM discovered from a pickled okra, can make hot barbecue sauce look tame. The buffet would have been complete if it had had some Goldsboro barbecue.

The band played in the East Room. There the atmosphere became intimate. President Johnson danced a few steps with one of the ladies. Then they started cutting in on him, but he was equal to the occasion, whirling them around the floor with gusto.

We had found seats on the Dolly Madison sofa in the Red Room. It was there that Howard and Lib White of Burlington found us and brought word that they would bring the President over for a chat presently. Three times they came back and said, "Don't go away." But the President kept on dancing with the ladies.

Finally, George Reedy, the new White House press secretary, came in for a talk with us. And then the President. Here again one thought he was talking to a man who was sincerely interested in people and in making new acquaintances.

William A. Shires, director of public relations at East Carolina University, developed a close relationship with Henry as manager of the N.C. Association of Afternoon Dailies.

He encouraged me, advised me, gave me a constant flow of ideas, suggestions, requests, criticism, and praise on occasion. He was a real source of inspiration and encouragement, a father-confessor and guide, but most of all a true friend for whom I had admiration, respect and deep affection.

I succeeded Lynn Nisbet as manager of the N.C. Association of Afternoon Dailies in May, 1962. Soon after taking the job, I drove to Goldsboro to see Henry, who had been one of the early guiding lights of the Association. He questioned me closely. If I was to succeed Lynn Nisbet, who had a vast store of knowledge and background information, Henry first wanted to find out what I knew about North Carolina, whether I really knew about the state or had a superficial knowledge. He questioned me about former governors, prominent people, the legislature, the Council of State, the courts, county seats and local government – the whole gamut. Apparently he was not willing to take the word of a former Belk pupil, Sam Ragan, who had recommended me for the job. I guess I passed the test on general knowledge.

Henry then wanted to know what I had in mind for the column. I told him it should be varied and interesting, dealing with a lot of subjects. I told him about places and things I wanted to write about, of people I wanted to interview, events I wanted to see and describe. We talked a long time – he let me do most of the talking. Finally he said, "I'm very pleased."

But that wasn't the end of it. His notes, his calls and suggestions began coming and he kept me on my toes in a helpful, constructive and firm way. He apparently felt that the column, with all that guaranteed space daily, was too important to let it become humdrum, boring and merely a lazy routine. I learned that he watched after it closely. He had the copy read to him every day. He would edit it as sharply as if he were wielding a blue pencil. He seldom used the column en toto, but cut it judiciously to fit the available space on the editorial page.

When I had delusions of grandeur such as becoming a North Carolina Ernie Pyle, he would bring me up short by omitting altogether a column he didn't like. I got the message. He was telling me to get back to basics.

Sometimes Henry would send me a suggestion I thought was trivial, but each time I discovered his thinking was far ahead of mine, and that he had a purpose. One was to do some background on the State Baptist Convention, looking ahead to a meeting that was some months in the future. I doubted the timeliness of such a story, but later found that some developments were shaping up that would make that session of the convention one of the most significant in its history. Henry had foreseen this. He wanted a "beat" on anything the Baptists were up to, because in North Carolina that is news in every block in town.

Once Henry suggested a story on a small town industry and the preponderance of women employed in small textile operations. In a sense, he foresaw the women's lib movement. He wanted to emphasize both the growing tendency of women to work outside the home to supplement family income and that their wages were low and their hours long, but it was work in which women were finding out they could free themselves by doing some things as well and better than men. We did a story on that in 1962 and followed it up during the succeeding years.

Although we were aware of Henry's blindness, those of us who worked with him and for him came to think little of it. We marveled more at his way of accomplishing things.

Shires had some observations on Henry's "likes".

Henry Belk
— liked to sit in a place where he would stretch his long legs.
— liked to keep his cane and his hat handy.
— said that newspapermen liked to read about themselves. He suggested for the column that we try doing a profile piece on one of our member afternoon daily editors about once a month and try to say something nice about them. He suggested an occasional story on former North Carolina newspapermen who had gone on to other fields or to places outside the state. He felt that North Carolina was a fertile field for journalists.
— liked to keep up daily with all the news published in the state's papers. He had them read to him every day by the General Manager. Even on trips he would collect all the newspapers he could and have Lucile read them, starting with the headlines and description of the size and column width of the headlines, the length of the story, where it was placed on what page, flanked by what, who wrote it, whether it was accompanied by a picture, etc., and then he would decide whether she should read all or part of it to him. He thus photographed in his mind an image of that day's papers and the details they contained. He was quick to spot anything new, or an error. Sometimes Lucile even described the ads, cartoons and comics.
— liked to take a tiny nip before dinner or at bedtime, always in the privacy of his room. While on trips he would have someone get a pint, always just a pint, usually of bourbon, at small town liquor stores. He never took more than a small drink. It was believed that this was medicinal and helped him relax when he was tired.

27

Henry knew just about everybody in public life in North Carolina — governors, congressmen; state legislators and office holders; jurists; educators; authors.

One of Henry's favorite literary men was Paul Green.

Best thing at the recent meeting of the N.C. Literary and Historical Association was the address of Paul Green. I hesitate to call any Tar Heel audience "sophisticated", but if the term could be applied in the state, it would have fitted the group who gathered to hear Green.

As he always does, the Harnett County native had as his theme his philosophy of life. And he spoke with such fervor and feeling for a better world and greater hope and broader tolerance and humanity, that those who listened were stilled and made silent. One listens to Paul Green and goes away with a greater compassion and sympathy, a new hope and faith that he can somehow lift the world higher.

In 1962, Henry complained of the dearth of published books in Eastern North Carolina.

We point with sadness and regret to a list of books issued by North Carolina in the last six months of the past year. There were scores of books issued by Tar Heels in the time covered, but so far as we could find, there was not listed one book by anyone living east of Raleigh.

Let us hasten to add that the period covered saw Ovid Pierce of East Carolina College begin work on a third novel. Again the scene will be a big river plantation timed to the days just at the end of the Civil War, but this time Pierce will be more direct and realistic. We hope in this new effort to portray a bit of the Old South, he does not sacrifice the poetic beauty and character analysis which marked "The Plantation" and "On a Lonesome Porch". None of the super-sweet, moonlight and magnolia stuff, understand, but normal people in the grip of harsh circumstance in Reconstruction days.

While the book list showed how poor we are in authorship in the East, we make a prediction. The revival, or should we say development, of a literary vocation and avocation is starting in Tobacco Land. We give Ingliss Fletcher, Bernice Kelly Harris, David Stock and others credit for that. Among the younger generation, we salute Pierce for awakening creative desires among East Carolina College students. We have met some we expect you will hear from later.

But our area, in literature, seems to be as of today as far behind the Piedmont as it is in industry.

Henry brought Pierce to Goldsboro to speak at the first annual author's luncheon sponsored by the Rotary Club, in 1958. He was followed by Ben Dixon MacNeill and Betty Smith.

MacNeill told his audience that "No enduring piece of writing can come out of an over-full belly. So few of our writers are professionals. The great bulk of writing in North Carolina is done as a sort of sideline. Writing is a hell of a way to make a living. It is also just as bad a way to make a life, that is, if you wish to be respectable, secure and composed in your old age."

Miss Smith told her hearers that "North Carolina should not sacrifice its way of life in its quest for industrialization. Governor Hodges is an attractive man. I like him. But he works so hard to get new industry. I'm against it. Pretty soon we'll look like New York and Pittsburgh and Birmingham."

Henry was for Hodges' industrialization program, especially as it related to Eastern North Carolina. In 1960, he enthused over an industrial development conference held in Goldsboro.

Nothing like it ever before happened in Eastern North Carolina. The day-long sessions were planned for 35 counties. Every county was well represented. The planners thought if they could get 200 men interested in industry, that would be excellent. Registration ran beyond 425.

Such is the new look the East is taking, on balancing its agriculture with new and varied industry, that the attendance could easily have been 1,000, had there been more promotion.

Goldsboro was pleased that its theme song of sectional selling of the East Carolina region won emphatic approval from business leaders in attendance. The theme is that when one community hasn't exactly what a new industry seeks, it will suggest some other city or county more favorably suited to its needs.

The hundreds who came to get information on community development were outspoken in declaring that Governor Hodges' hot blast at foot-dragging in the east had been a great help. The charge, given in something of red-faced anger in Raleigh some months ago, made the Easterners look at themselves more closely than they had ever done before.

Hodges' name is still magic. The reaction to his luncheon talk at the Goldsboro meeting was warm and generous.

Henry was a staunch supporter of Terry Sanford to succeed Hodges as Governor. Following Sanford's nomination in a run-off primary against I. Beverly Lake, Henry came out with an editorial titled 'People Give Sanford Mandate'.

North Carolina can point with pride to the run-off primary to pick a Democratic nominee for Governor. Tar Heels followed their usual ways. They acted true to their history and their heritage. Their rejection of racism, stand-pat-ism, their refusal to be stampeded into accepting wishes as reality, were natural for a people who think for themselves.

Sanford's overwhelming majority over Dr. Lake left no possibility of doubt that the people wanted him and his "New Day" program. The vote is a loud and clear mandate from the people to Sanford and the Legislature that North Carolina will obey the law, that North Caroina faces reality and accepts the new day and the spirit that is abroad in the world.

The Sanford majority was an order to those who govern that we shall not trifle with ways that have been tried and found wanting. The vote said North Carolina puts its public schools and the education of its children first among all things. That vote said that North Carolina will not tolerate, or even flirt with ideas and suggestions which might for even a short time jeopardize some schools. That vote said that North Carolina has watched Virginia and Little Rock and the futile floundering now going on in Georgia, and will have none of this approach.

Henry came to Sanford's defense when statistics were published showing that it had cost $20,000 more to operate the Governor's Mansion in 1962 than it had the last year of the Hodges administration.

All manners of organizations, clubs, societies and the like must be entertained in the North Carolina tradition at the Mansion. You can't stage receptions, teas and buffets without spending a lot of money. We have an idea that Governor Sanford has held more breakfasts, luncheons and dinners, to talk with people about ideas and projects, than any other governor. These affairs have been worth-while in bringing the government to the people and securing their cooperation.

There was another dining difference, besides volume, between Sanford and his predecessor.

It remained for Clifton Blue, in his Raleigh correspondence column, to note a change at the Mansion.

Guests dining with Governor Sanford are served first. He is served last. Governor Hodges followed the custom of having the first serving made to himself.

An Emily Post could probably make out a good and logical case for either form. In the old days, kings or emperors had a food taster and a wine taster. Duty of these functionaries was to partake of the meat and wine before their masters. If enemies had poisoned it in attempts on the life of the king, the taster got the dose.

Of course it is the accepted courtesy for the guest to take precedence over the host. Hence the Sanford routine of serving guests first.

At the same time, though, Governor Hodges probably put some Mansion guests at their ease by being served first. Not too many of the Branchhead boys are accustomed to a white-coated servant formally passing the food. One of these watching the Governor being served first might feel a bit more confidence when his turn came.

Henry had warm regard for 'Modest, Retiring Governor Dan Moore'.

The General Manager and I were among a group of newspapermen who had lunch at the Mansion with Governor and Mrs. Moore recently. It was a "sit down" affair and we liked what we saw and heard.

Governor Moore is working hard, mighty hard, at his assignment, one which already has produced more harsh situations and demands than many a governor has in four years.

How does Moore compare with Terry Sanford?

Moore is quieter, more inclined to shyness. He does not make conversation as easily as Sanford does. He does not show in his carriage the lift which comes to many in high office simply because of the office. Ideas do not come trippingly off his tongue. He recognizes and defers to the personality and dignity of every person who is calling on him or who is breaking bread with him.

I recalled that Weimar Jones of Franklin, an observing editor, had written that Governor Moore, in a talk before the N.C. Press Association's Midwinter Institute, seemed to suffer under the criticism which had been thrown his way. Editor Jones had the conclusion that Moore was not enough of the tough politician to shake off with no regard or consideration the sharp editorials or critical opinions thrown in his direction.

I came away from the luncheon and press conference with Governor Moore, feeling that Jones had made a trustworthy evaluation.

The very characteristic which leads Moore to listen, and even to be hurt by the slings and arrows, makes him a man whom other men, fair and willing to give justice to, presently and even quickly, find themselves liking – this strong Man of the Mountains.

Henry had a fatherly feeling for Bob Scott, stemming from his high regard for Scott's father, the 'Squire of Haw River'. They were sprung from the soil and Henry had faith in people with the soil clinging to them.

It was the 'Haw River Touch', when Scott opened his campaign for Governor.

"Now that is getting down to grass roots."

So remarked the General Manager when she read that Bob Scott opened a week of campaigning for the governorship with a chittlin' supper at Rocky Mount.

It would be accurate to say that Scott's friends opened the week with the supper. It was the old Haw River touch. It would have done credit to the late Squire of Haw River himself.

Scott can get more mileage out of the chittlin' supper than he could get out of a thousand dollars worth of advertising in all media. There is something about the mere mention of chittlings that stirs folks to smiling, or they smile because they can't have chittlings within a block of their dining room and feel absolutely superior to those who appreciate chittlings.

And a chittlin' strut is an earthy sort of occasion such as delights the hearts of Tar Heels, be they Branchhead Tar Heels or otherwise.

With this time of great affluence under Democrats, some fear that chittlings are now regarded as not fittin' eating. Some softies and snobbish ones may even insist that to stage a chittlin' strut for Bob Scott is actually to help Mel Broughton.

I can't buy the idea that North Carolina has gone so citified that its people can't enjoy chittlings as a weapon in political battle.

Henry was a fan of Scott's wife, 'Our Own Jessie Rae'.

North Carolina's First Lady, Mrs. Bob Scott, will measure up to the French high society and top government wives while on her European trip. And if you have been reading the fashion pages, you noted that Jessie Rae will be as stunningly arrayed as any of the Paris Madames.

Jessie Rae went prepared to, "When you are in Rome, do as the Romans do." She took along gowns of just above the knee length. She went prepared to don the gown of proper length to meet the style of the ladies in whose circles she was visiting.

You recall that the visit of Governor and Mrs. Scott was in repayment for the visit a half dozen leading French government officials and their wives paid to the National Governor's Conference in Colorado some months ago.

I'll bet our own Jessie Rae is as glamorous and beautiful as any of the ladies she will meet in Europe. And no couple makes a more stunning picture than Bob and Jessie Rae Scott.

Susie Sharp was another of Henry's favorite women.

Effective at the beginning of this month, North Carolina Superior Court judges, if they so desired, had the right to wear flowing black robes while presiding. Each of the 39 judges is reported to have ordered the aids to their dignity.

A High Point report says that Judge Susie Sharp, who asks no odds because of her sex in conducting a court with dignity, decorum and justice, says the idea of black robes is "perfectly absurd." That is what the report said, though the words are somewhat heated for the calm and moderate Judge Sharp. The news item said Judge Sharp felt that robes were appropriate for Supreme Court justices, but not for Superior Court judges. Nevertheless, she is wearing the robe.

Judge Sharp has a great deal of natural dignity and verve, and a lot of us would resent this charm being swaddled in black habiliments.

When a vacancy occurred on the U.S. Supreme Court due to the resignation of Justice Ramsay Clark, Henry suggested the appointment of Susie Sharp, who had been elevated to the N.C. Supreme Court.

President Johnson could pick a winner in naming Susie Sharp.

In this wise, gracious and attractive woman jurist, North Carolina has a candidate worthy and well qualified.

When Governor Kerr Scott named Miss Sharp to the Superior Court bench, some of the mere males in her profession shook their heads solemnly and insisted the feminine mind is not properly organized to dispose of judicial decisions. But the manner in which she ran her courts, the clarity with which she charged juries, the mastery of law which she consistently displayed, soon won admiration from her original critics.

Justice Sharp repeated this demonstration of superior ability and exceptional reasoning power, when she was elevated to the N.C. Supreme Court. And she would repeat her successes if President Johnson were to see fit to name her to the nation's highest court.

Henry had good friends in the state's judiciary, but that did not keep him from criticising them and their courts. On one occasion he accused Superior Court Judge J.W. Bundy of Greenville of exhibiting "the lack of control of a college freshman." Bundy had made public a "blistering" letter he had sent to Judge H.L. Riddle or Morganton who had overruled suspended prison sentences he had imposed in Wilkes County.

Henry charged, in one of his editorials, that "Courts Sacrifice Time."

North Carolina courts, from the rank of district court through that of the Supreme Court, lose time and money. And everyone who has been summoned as a witness or juror, or has had business in the courts, will agree with me.

What I am talking about is this. Entirely too many courts get off to a late start in the morning. They should have an efficiency schedule which would start them to work promptly at 9 o'clock every morning unless some unexpected emergency arises. There is no justification, as I see it, for courts to keep witnesses and others waiting unnecessarily.

And many of our courts end a day's session too early in the afternoon.

The session may be called off in mid-afternoon so court officials can drive back home to attend to personal matters or escape the late afternoon traffic.

More onerous than late starts and early quittings is the habit of adjourning court on Friday morning and reconvening about midday on Monday. When court officials decide enough work has been done for the week, they quit. That's how it looks.

Henry was sometimes critical of the General Assembly, accusing its members of playing politics. In 1963, he berated the legislators for killing a motor vehicle inspection bill.

One representative from a rural Eastern county had voted for the bill, seeing in it a good asset to highway safety. But when the voters back home heard of his vote, they kept the telephone wires hot with complaints. The county commissioners passed a resolution asking the representative to change his vote.

Sadly, reluctantly, the representative switched.

One vote killed what was a good bill.

Henry had more respect for the law-making body after attending its 1965 session.

There ought to be a law requiring every Tar Heel to spend a day, at least every five years, observing the General Assembly at work. Actually I am making a point, not suggesting a law. What I wish is that Mr. Average Tar Heel should spend enough time at the legislative sessions to understand the work that members of the House and Senate do. If one checks the routine day for a member of the Legislature, he will not be one of those who think of service in the Assembly as being soft and easy.

I made one of my infrequent trips to the Legislative Building the other day to attend a public hearing in reference to a House-passed bill to close paroles board records to the public. Our meeting was with the Senate judiciary committee, chaired by Sen. Julian Allsbrook of Halifax. Sen. Allsbrook asked permission to take up other matters calling for attention before going into the hearing. In 10 minutes his committee had disposed of the routine matters. Every man was concentrating on the subject at hand. No one talked with an associate. No one thumbed a newspaper or magazine.

The number at the hearing on the bill to seal paroles office records was so great that Chairman Allsbrook moved the meeting across the hall to the appropriations committee room. There was enough printed material piled on desks in that room to have made a half dozen "Gone With the Wind" volumes.

How different were the facilities for conducting hearings over the crowded, confused and chaotic facilities of the old Capital building when I was a witness there in 1951. Several other hearings and committee meetings were in progress in the old House halls. There was a great hubbub and the witness with the strongest voice had a better chance of making his point understood.

The late Miss Beatrice Cobb, veteran secretary of the N.C. Press Association, Mrs. Elizabeth Gold Swindell of Wilson, and others had joined me in presenting a view of the N.C. Press. I remember that Sam Ervin, Jr., then a member of the N.C. Supreme Court, had come over to join his townswoman, Miss Cobb, for the meeting.

Our appearance was before a committee which had a few House desks assigned to it at the front row and almost under what was the Speaker's big chair. To the right of our group, another committee was in session. To our left, another public hearing was pounding along. Back of our group another committee was doing the best it could to transact business.

One who worked under such conditions, or who had to go blocks away to other buildings for committee hearings, can really appreciate today's Legislative Building and its comfortable facilities. Its offices and meeting rooms, with their air-conditioned comfort, assure best attention to all business before the Legislature. Energy of members is conserved and they have not been worn to a frazzle at the end of the day.

Henry admired the new State House, but, come spring, it was a joy to revisit the old Capitol square, flop on one of the benches, and look at passers-by, and the pigeons.

The General Manager and I were ahead of time for our meeting and we sat on a stone bench in the warm sunshine. Peanut hulls littered the walkways. Pigeons were paired off, male and female, and in each pair there was one who had soft nothings to say to his or her mate. The fat birds drew near, one of them saying we were not supposed to occupy that seat unless we fed them peanuts. But, alack and alas, we had no peanuts. Four pairs of the birds drew close enough for us to have picked them up, but when they got no peanuts, they walked away.

Glorious girls passed, walking on mincing and ungraceful feet in their toothpick high heels and their narrow skirts. How can beautiful women so surrender to idiotic fashion demands as to wear short, tight skirts that reveal the form but destroy freedom of movement?

A young couple passed, their little son toddling along with them. Every 10 minutes or so, inside the Capitol, there was another crowd of sightseeing school children visiting the old House and Senate chambers, now under the direction of the Department of Archives and History.

We went back inside to the House chambers, where our meeting was to be held. Matthew Walters in blue uniform with big brass buttons, the caretaker, acted as a guide to the couple who had come to see once more the graceful, vaulted House, stately and serene. Walters is a story in himself. His closeness to history has given him a presence, set off and enhanced by his balding head with its wooly white fringe of hair.

His favorite recollection is of his nearness to President Truman, when the latter, at the time of his race for reelection, came to Raleigh to unveil the statues of the three Presidents born in North Carolina. We could talk that occasion with him, for we were a member of the North Carolina commission which directed the project, picked the sculptor, and arranged a program that drew a record crowd to Raleigh.

Walters talked on and on.

Such was the outward appearance of the peaceful scene about the old Capitol. But one could read in the faces of those passing through the corridors, and on to the new State House a block away, symptoms of the inner pessimism which has our nation hamstrung.

Why is it we are now of so little faith?

Why is it that brother looks at brother, and is suspicious of him?

Why is it that we are fearful of our youth, in its reaching and probing and questing?

Why is it we feel we must constrain and contract and bend minds to the line and pattern which we make?

Maybe you wonder what brought these questions up.

Item: The questioning of the true Americanism of a great scholar, the incident at Chapel Hill when a tennis coach is preemptorily fired for criticising things as he sees them, in a letter to the Daily Tar Heel.

Item: Unwillingness of a business leader to sanction a debate between American and English college students for fear the young men might pick a too liberal topic.

But let's go back and listen to the pigeons and watch the girls go by, and soak up spring at the old Capitol. Leave the fears to others. This wave of little faith will pass and America will again sound forth in her sure and free voice.

28

On January 10, 1966, Henry made a talk before the University of North Carolina Press Club at Chapel Hill on '100 Years of Influence of North Carolina Papers'. The talk was read by Mrs. Belk.

Henry was peculiarly fitted for the assignment. During his newspaper career, which was drawing to a close, he had known all the state's editors, most of them intimately, and was acquainted with the service they had rendered. He himself had won honors in the field.

It must have been rewarding to the blind editor to be invited to address young members of the University's School of Journalism.

***

The 100th anniversary of the News and Observer is a good occasion upon which to take a look at the place of Tar Heel Newspapers in the State in the last century.

It is a good place, a leading place, and a place the general public little knows or appreciates.

Competent and critical editors and publishers examining the North Carolina press find much to praise. The quality of the printing, the content of the product, the sense of responsibility and good citizenship, these get a good hand from the critics.

The press of today is no more the press of a century ago than the North Carolina of today is the North Carolina left in wreck and ruin, its assets used up in the Civil War.

Our State has advanced upon the backs of movements and upon the concentration of energy and determination to meet a special problem. In all these waves or movements of progress, the North Carolina press has done its part.

Charles B. Aycock had sturdy, yeoman's help from the newspapers of the day in his campaign for universal education. One man capable of passing on the subject has said that without the help of the press, Aycock could not have inspired the people with the zeal for education, the right of every child "to burgeon out all there is within him."

As usual in cases when the newspapers hit hard for an idea or a man, there were the critics and the scoffers. Some of the super-critical in the Aycock period even said that the reason the newspapers were so zealous in supporting Aycock was that they wanted to educate more people to read so they could sell more subscriptions. In the day of the Aycock campaign, the newspaper was the only means of mass communication and they held up the possibilities of a better day as preached by Aycock.

Even before Aycock's educational campaign had been launched, the press of the State were joining in pleas for more industry as a way to raise the State's economic level. The theme song of Georgia's Henry A. Grady was played over and over in our press. The development of the textile industry came as the newspapers gave much space, news columns and editorial columns, to the idea of bringing the cotton mills to the cotton fields.

Governor Cameron Morrison and the group of good roads enthusiasts he gathered around him numbered influential papers, and small papers and middle-sized papers. Paved roads and benefits thereof came more quickly to North Carolina because of the interest and efforts of the editors. The fires set by Morrison and men of that day were sparks upon which to build when Kerr Scott offered to get the State out of the mud by $200 million in bonds for farm-to-market roads. For its day, that proposal was an astonishing and staggering one. But the people caught the vision with much of the press beating the drums, and the program was approved. Now the new program for more bonds to improve highways and make them equal to the transportation load of the times looks back to the Morrison and Scott influence and the papers are again turning the faces of the people forward.

The Good Health program in which Frank Graham and Clarence Poe were great leaders got full backing from the papers. Consider how inadequate would be our hospitals for the demands of today if the State had failed to measure up in a campaign which placed a good general hospital in practically every county and saw also the development of the great medical centers at the University of North Carolina, Duke University and Bowman Gray School of Medicine of Wake Forest College.

To come closer to our own times and observations, take the role of the papers in the establishment of a system of technical education centers and of the community colleges. The report of the Carlyle Committee on the necessity for a system of community colleges to meet the population explosion which had overtaxed the capacity of our higher educational institutions, was a familiar story because their papers had given it to the people and in such language that they quickly grasped it.

In the years ahead, the establishment of the system of community colleges will be one of the most significant developments in North Carolina, and the papers can be proud they had a hand in that. Likewise the papers on their community level have carried the torch for cities and counties to move on their own, and that quickly, to carry out the program by organizing and building their own colleges.

Reference has been made to the first cries for more industry to lift us out of the poverty of one-crop farming. That cry has been intensified and better organized under Governors Hodges and Sanford; and now Governor Moore pledges to extend and broaden the effort. Editors have been so taken with the movement and its possibilities for raising wages and providing good jobs for the many thousands who do not have them that many a supercritic will tell you they have overplayed the topic, that there has been too much space devoted to the subject. What these supercritics miss is that in the drive for more industry is interwoven the drive for more culture, better education, music, the arts, drama and literature. These have not been forgotten by today's press. The arts and music and the lecture and concert are big news and played as such up and down North Carolina.

Almost every community of a few thousand, and many of less population, today has its annual art festival, and the papers in their interest support the movement.

Probably less noticed and appreciated as an influence of the press is the service of the weeklies, the semi-weeklies, the dailies and the monthly papers for taking agricultural advances to the farmer. Talk to the old timers in Extension Service ranks and they will tell you that the farmer didn't receive too cordially the efforts of the office farmers to tell them how to do better farming.

But from the word go, on Extension Service and Department of Agriculture efforts, the press joined happily and with a sense of helping in carrying the news of better ways, bigger yields, less labor, improved varieties and so on. Editors wrote about how farmers in their communities were growing more cotton or tobacco per acre, or how they were diversifying. The Extension Service and the Agricultural Service releases were published regularly. The cooperative and interested spirit among the papers opened the door to the Extension Service programs and did much to give standing and place to the work.

The towering figure in the use of the printed word to advance farming and to raise farmers was Dr. Clarence Poe, who died in October of 1964. He had joined the Progressive Farmer as a mere stripling, and became its editor and continued in this place to a ripe old age. He was editor at the time of his death. He built the Progressive Farmer to a publication with over a million subscribers. His wise counseling and his leadership and fairness which showed through the pages of his publication made him one of the most influential men of his time.

Let's not get the idea, however, that the North Carolina press devotes all its interest and space to promotional subjects.

The papers have been strong voices for good government, stable government, and fair government, from the township to the State level and to the federal level. The North Carolina press has not been for sale. The North Carolina press has not been the slave of special interests or candidates.

Good government is a habit in North Carolina. The papers

assign their best men to cover the courthouse, city hall and Capitol beat. The late Col. Joseph E. Robinson, founder of the Goldsboro Argus, along with Charles B. Aycock and J. W. Nash, flaunted as his banner this couplet.

"This Argus o'er the Peoples' rights doth an eternal vigil keep;

No soothing strain of Maia's son can lull its hundred eyes to sleep."

Today's editors would blush to use such a high-sounding term to describe the work of their papers, but most North Carolina editors still accept the responsibility of keeping a sharp eye out for the people as regards the ham politician, the demagogue, or the downright sneak who would feather his own nest from the government till.

There is no hush-hush when the grand jury finds something wrong. There may be and are varying degrees of covering the news, whether sensationally, in scare-head style, or in brief form, news of the doings of boards and committees and office holders, but the news is printed.

The advance of the North Carolina newspapers is well told in the change of editorial emphasis from that of the early years of the century to that of today.

In an earlier day the editors amused their readers with sharp and harsh criticisms of other editors, or men of public position or of different parties. Language was unrestrained, vitriolic, scathing. But the pieces often lacked sufficient facts to back up the tongue-lashing they gave out.

One editor of that period wrote that another editor was not fit to carry guts to a hog.

Most papers of the earlier day were largely political organs supporting and backing a particular party or candidates. That practice for which let us give thanks, has gone by the boards.

Today's North Carolina papers are largely Democratic, but independent Democratic. They reserve the right to criticize and object to the ideas or programs or doings of leaders of their own party if they disagree with them. Independence and good sense largely determine what the papers are saying today.

The late Joe Caldwell of the Charlotte Observer played a great part in changing the emphasis from politics to independence and news. He drew brutal criticism but his list of subscribers kept going up. Other editors, noting that the people were interested in something more than heated words and bias, turned in that direction.

Josephus Daniels was a red hot Democrat from his youth to the day of his death at an advanced age. Daniels without a doubt is the greatest editor and figure produced in North Carolina by the newspaper craft in the past 100 years.

His example of fearless courage and his great worth to the State and nation were universally cited by every editor of today who responded to a letter from me asking for comment on North Carolina editors and papers.

The purpose of The News and Observer from its founding was well summed up in the direction Josephus Daniels left to his heirs in his will:

"I advise and enjoin those who direct the paper in the tomorrows never to advocate any cause for personal profit or preferment. I would wish it always to be 'the tocsin' and devote itself to the policies of equality and justice to the underprivileged. If the paper should at any time be the voice of self-interest or become the spokesman of privilege or selfishness, it would be untrue to its history."

Jonathan Daniels, editor of the paper since the death of his father, has continued unswervingly the place of the paper as a guardian of the rights of the people and particularly as a watchdog on State government.

At a North Carolina Press Association meeting at Chapel Hill, the late Billy Carmichael (William D., Jr., formally) jestingly observed on a program that his father, resident of the Carolina Inn, where the meeting was being held, and a man who was aged and hard of hearing, had been unable to sleep the night before because of the goings-on of the editors in their talkfests.

Jonathan Daniels quipped that the legislature was in session and he had gone home early to get a good night's sleep.

"I didn't know anyone on the News and Observer ever slept while the Legislature was in session," quipped Carmichael.

Charlotte had its Joe Caldwell, Raleigh had its Josephus Daniels and Greensboro had its Earle Godbey, editor of the Greensboro Daily News, and its Gerald Johnson. The Greensboro Daily News established a great tradition of independence and sound reasoning on its editorial page. The tradition continues to this day with Dr. H.W. Kendall as contributing editor and William D. Snider as editor. Snider succeeded Kendall last July, after the latter had served as editor 35 years.

Most parts of the State have had newspapermen who have left their imprint on their local and even larger scene.

Elizabeth City had W. O. Saunders of the weekly Independent, and also the scholarly Herbert Peele of the Daily Advance. Saunders is remembered most often in conversation for the "stunt" pieces he pulled off. For instance, he made national news by wearing his pajamas down Broadway on a hot summer day. And when a man threatened to kill him, Saunders printed in his Independent that he would be at a certain address at a certain time and dared the threatener to come after him.

The American Magazine, tops in popular magazines for its day, brought the colorful Saunders to its staff in New York. But the restrictions were grating to him and he returned to "Betsy City", as Josephus Daniels always wrote it.

Yet Saunders was a man of great vision and his challenging editorials are credited with giving inception and incentive to the development of what is today one of North Carolina's great resort and tourist areas — Kitty Hawk, Wright Memorial, bridges over the sounds, the stirring outdoor drama, "The Lost Colony", and the development of the region from Elizabeth City to Hatteras as a great hunting and fishing area.

Where Saunders pricked stuffed shirts and called out for sanity in all things, Herbert Peele built his town and his section on hard work. He was of a more conservative stripe than Saunders, but he too saw the possibilities in the sun, and sand and surf of his section, in its history as the place of first settlement in North

Carolina; and what he wrote raised up supporters and organizations to bring about his dream.

Peele was greatly helped in his long career on the Advance by Mrs. Peele, a woman of education and poise.

Rocky Mount has its Josh Horne. Although he is slowing down a bit, Horne is as interested and determined as ever to show how North Carolina can go forward. Horne and Peele teamed up to help bring one of the earliest commercial airlines into northeastern North Carolina. Horne also got the State's tourism budget off to a good start by his chairmanship of the first committee of the Department of Conservation and Development in this field.

Goldsboro had its Col. Robinson, and its Col. John D. Langston, and its Julius Bonitz, a German immigrant who is often called the father of Goldsboro public schools. A grateful city presented to Bonitz, editor of the Goldsboro Messenger, a large gold watch, appropriately inscribed, for the work he did with his paper in securing a vote favorable for a special tax levy for public schools, the first such special election in the State.

Wilson had its Elder P.D. Gold and its John D. Gold and today a daughter of the latter, Mrs. Elizabeth Swindell, follows in her father's footsteps. She made history when she was selected the first woman president of the N.C. Press Association and won high praise for her work during the year 1964-65, that she served.

Kinston has its Galt Braxton, editor of the Daily Free Press, for many years. Mr. Braxton is still going strong and hitting out as hard as ever in his editorials. He probably is the oldest working newspaper editor and publisher in the State. Kinston at times has thrown brickbats at him in showers for some stand that was not popular. But Kinston always has honored him for his fearless sincerity. And Mr. Braxton doesn't mind standing out alone. And what does Editor Braxton look back on with a particular pleasure? On his paper having been a great force in the introduction of purebred hogs.

The Durham papers, the Morning Herald and the Sun, have had their "Old Hurrygraph" Robinson and W.N. Keener and John Barry.

Chapel Hill had its Louis Graves, a master craftsman and a winner in the "low key" school of journalism. His Chapel Hill Weekly won admiring comment from all into whose hands it fell. Louis Graves was a true Tar Heel. He had a secure place in New York journalism. A call came for him to come home and succeed to the place of professor of Journalism. He was a good teacher but he felt freer in writing, without shouting or sensationalizing, about Chapel Hill, its dogs, its trees, its walks, its birds, its flowers. And also about great forces in the wide, wide world.

Chapel Hill had also the color and the invigorating influence of a great newspaperman, Oscar J. Coffin. He became teacher of journalism and continued in this capacity long enough to train a generation of top-flight reporters and editors.

Coffin didn't cramp his style with dreary books and procedures. But he opened up to the students in his class a bright and challenging world where the workman was worthy of his hire, and there were ideas to be examined, sacred cows to be milked. Inspiration he gave, candles which he lit, and friendships which he shared, helped his students to give a good account of themselves in the workaday world.

Monroe had its Roland Beasley, editor of the semi-weekly Monroe Journal. With his brother, G. M. Beasley, he established the Journal and from time to time he had to go at other newspapers — the establishment of the Whiteville Reporter, a journal of government and comment in Raleigh, a weekly in Charlotte, and with his nephew, John Beasley, the Goldsboro Daily News.

Always he went back to Monroe and sat back and rocked and read the papers, from the Kennedy-like rocking chair. He never was happier than when engaged in philosophic comment on men and the times. Without doubt he was one of the best editors I ever knew. I got my start on the Journal. In his day he was a leader of thought and social progress. As a member of the General Assembly from Union County, he secured passage of the State's first child labor law, and introduced legislation that resulted in the Samarcand school for girls. He helped write North Carolina's first compulsory school attendance law, a mother's aid law, and the first corrective prison law. As the State's first Commissioner of Public Welfare (he was also the first in the U.S.), he set up a system of juvenile courts. His son, Roland, Jr., and nephew, George, Jr., now operate the Monroe Journal, which has recently merged with the Monroe Enquirer as the Enquirer-Journal.

Gastonia had its Atkins family, Concord its Sherrills, and Salisbury its Hurleys, still continuing the tradition.

Winston-Salem knew the force of Santford Martin's editorial pen. He is still remembered for his having pointed the way for his city and and section.

In Johnston County its semi-weekly, the Smithfield Herald, inherited a noble tradition from its late co-founder T.J. Lassiter, Sr. This tradition was carried on by his widow and since her death has continued under Thomas J. Lassiter, Jr.

The Brock brothers of Mt. Olive carry on for the Tribune the work of their father, the late Homer Brock.

Ahoskie had its Roy Parker, Sr., and now has the third generation of the Parker family issuing snappy papers for Hertford County and other counties in that region. It was the dream of Roy Parker, Sr., which led to the establishment of the Roy Parker School of Graphic Arts at Chowan College. This school for teaching composing room personnel has provided training for capable young people in a field where there is a great demand for such help. John McSweeney has trained many A-students.

Shelby had its Weathers family as editors and publishers. Roxboro for scores of years was served by Editor J.W. Noell. At Greenville the third generation of Whichards is going strong, and the younger generation is taking advantage of the advance in methods and printing.

Asheville's D. Hiden Ramsey, retired publisher of the Asheville Citizen and Times, also got listing on every roll of influential editors.

The newspaper publishing field is today an important part of the business scene in North Carolina. But the N.C. Press Association is no brain-washing outfit, offering its members a line or slant. It hires no paid lobbyists and indeed it does not have a paid executive secretary.

The late Miss Beatrice Cobb of Morganton, for more than 30 years unpaid secretary of the Association, gave her duties all the loyalty and devotion that any paid secretary could have given. Her example is being followed today by J.D. Fitz of Morganton, who succeeded her.

Wallace Carroll, editor and publisher of the Winston-Salem Journal and Sentinel, had this to say on an important contribution of the Tar Heel press:

"There is one field in which I think the North Carolina press has played a significant and constructive role. That is in the field of race relations.

"The North Carolina newspapers I see have dealt with the race problems in recent years with considerable frankness. They have printed the news, but they have done it responsibly and without sensationalism. They have also used their editorial columns to foster the kind of sane and reasonable atmosphere in which the people of this State have been able to adjust to new circumstances.

"If you will compare what has happened in North Carolina with what has happened in areas where the press failed to lead in this field and even tried to ignore the whole problem, you will see that the North Carolina press has something to be proud of."

29

Henry reached his 70th birthday on May 8, 1968. On August 8, three months later, he was made editor emeritus of the News-Argus. It was "a new position" the announcement said, "a position which heretofore has not been filled."

"Emeritus" sounded important, but Henry was not fooled by the high-sounding title. He was well acquainted with the definition of the word as it applied in his case: "retired from active duty because of age, but retained on the rolls."

It was announced that he would write a daily column for the paper and would "be available for editorial conferences."

Being "available" didn't mean anything, but the column became Henry's life blood.

Doubtless he was cheered by what the press said about his retirement, including the News and Observer.

It's hard to think of Henry Belk as an editor emeritus. But as far as he is concerned, the most difficult part of it, as he said the other day, is telling people how to spell and pronounce it.

Still, even with the "emeritus" title, it's good news for the readers of the Goldsboro News-Argus, and the rest of Eastern North Carolina, that he will continue writing. Readers can expect in his column a continuation of the grace and good will, as well as the good sense, that have marked his highly personal editorials over the years.

Henry Belk has been on the scene in Goldsboro for more than 40 years, and his influence has extended far beyond the bounds of Wayne County to all of North Carolina.

North Carolina is better for his presence. And it's good that his special brand of journalism will still be with us in his column.

Of special satisfaction to Henry must have been the comments of the Monroe Journal.

It is good to know that the announcement that Henry Belk has been made editor emeritus of the Goldsboro News-Argus reassured his readers that his popular editorial columns will continue to appear. He is one of the last of the folksy journalists.

We remember when Henry Belk was cutting his newspaper teeth in our office. His vision even in those early high school days was greatly impaired, but stouter determination made the necessary adjustments required to continue his education and earn a place reserved to North Carolina newspaper immortals. Our lifelong friend and contemporary has made many contributions, but none as potent as his inspiration to the handicapped and his reminder to us who are not afflicted that we have a built-in inclination to drag our feet.

On September 4, Henry took note of another editor who was approaching "emeritus" stage.

Editor Robert L. Gray of the Fayetteville Observer in a short time will join ranks with those classified as "Editor Emeritus." Come in, Bob, the water is fine.

I am gradually getting accustomed to the rarefied title. What readers note most is that the picture of myself, doctored by Artist Zeno Spence, which appears daily with my editorial page column, has a bit more hair than I am entitled to. Folks like to "guy" me about that.

Brother Gray has been editor of the ancient Fayetteville Observer enough years to be told to ease up a bit. He is of a famous newspaper family. His father before him won distinction as an editor through work in North Carolina and on Collier's magazine. His mother was the first woman ever to enroll at the University of North Carolina. A sister, Frances Gray Patton of Durham, authored the famous "Good Morning, Miss Dove" and other books and short stories of quality.

Bob worked in Raleigh and was an information officer in the Air Force for several years before he settled down to his old home of Fayetteville. In his term with the Air Force as a PIO in World War II, he was assigned to Hollywood. And he was assigned quarters to the home of one of the Hollywood actor millionaires. When he got orders for Europe, he was routed by Seymour Johnson Field at a time when there were several times more men at the base than there were accommodations. Bob found himself domiciled in a tent in redbug territory. Quite a come down from his Hollywood diggings.

Assignment to Europe for Bob specified that no alcoholic beverages were to go along. Bob, the story goes, had some Scotch sealed in cans and marked it "tomato juice". Always you could count on Bob to spice life for himself and those about him in delightful humor.

Elsewhere, Henry had something on 'Pay of Congressmen'.

Authoritative word from Washington is that Congressmen will increase their pay from $30,000 a year to $45,000 at the next session. The word is that the $15,000 increase in pay already is set up in such a manner that a direct vote will not be necessary.

A salary of $45,000 a year will put members of Congress too far out of the range and circumstance of the average American. In putting the Congressmen in such a category that they cannot feel and understand the load and life and circumstances of the average American, the nation also will be putting the Congressmen in a more difficult role to know and sympathize with the average American.

Henry continued to write about the little things of life, for which he was known.

Susan came to our house with her cute little mouth wide open. The six-year-old lady wanted us to know that she had lost two front teeth.

"And the fairies left two dimes under your pillow?" said the General Manager.

Everyone knows that the good fairies recognize nerve and good conduct from little folks who have surrendered front teeth. When our daughter was coming along, the going price of the fairies was 10 cents.

"No," said Susan. "I got two quarters."

The good fairies have met the rising price competition.

On September 23, Henry made note of an honor that had come to his old friend, Henry A. Dennis.

Here is something the likes of which you very seldom see or hear about.

The Vance County Commissioners have named the county's new office building the Henry A. Dennis County Office Building. The name honors the editor and publisher of the Henderson Daily Dispatch.

More often than not, as Josephus Daniels said in a talk when the Goldsboro Chamber of Commerce saluted the News-Argus, on its 60th anniversary, editors and papers get more rocks and kicks than they do commendation. Mr. Dennis richly deserves the honor which his neighbors have given him.

Goldsboro will be particularly interested in the recognition given the Henderson editor. He was graduated from Goldsboro High School as a student enrolled from the Odd Fellows Home. Though he has been away from Goldsboro more than 50 years, he still retains a deep regard for the city and its people. He keeps up with folks with whom he was associated as a boy and comes back at times for reunions at the Odd Fellows Home.

On September 26, Henry had a piece from High Point, where he was attending a meeting of the Governor's Committee on Employment of the Handicapped, of which he was a member.

"I cried because I had no shoes until I met a man who had no feet."

That's the way I always feel when I come away from a meeting of the Governor's Committee on Employment of the Handicapped, such as was held in High Point. Attendance numbered 225 men and women from all parts of the state. Most of those present were engaged in carrying the message to the state that the handicapped person, trained and fitted to the proper job, is a good worker. And many in attendance are persons who have found dignity and independence through training and service from such groups as the Governor's Committee. In the latter group you see men and women on crutches, or in wheel chairs, or men and women who are so crippled their noses are near the ground when they walk.

There was a diverting mix-up at the meeting help at the Furniture Mart in High Point. Governor Moore arrived at the building to deliver the awards honoring the workers for the handicapped. By error he was taken by elevator to the wrong floor. He ended up at High Point Rotary's meeting instead of that of the committee for the handicapped. And here is the pay-off. Speaker for the Rotary was the Republican candidate for governor, Jim Gardner.

Governor Moore looks as "fit as a fiddle" and as relaxed as can be. His carriage is that of a man at peace with the world.

On October 30, a testimonial dinner honoring Henry and his 'General Manager' was held at the Sir Walter Hotel in Raleigh. The testimonial was initiated by East Carolina University President Leo Jenkins in appreciation of Henry's contributions to "education and progress". Master of ceremonies was Sam Ragan, executive Sunday editor of the News and Observer.

More than 300 attended the dinner, including editors and writers from across the state. Invocation was by the Rev. W. W. Finlator, pastor of Raleigh's Pullen Memorial Baptist Church, who characterized Henry as a journalist dedicated "to speak and write not to please men, but to reveal truth."

Speakers included ex-Governor Luther Hodges, State Senator Robert Morgan, Dr. Leo Jenkins and R. Penn Moore of Goldsboro, who said, "It is in the area of usefulness to others that has distinguished these lovable people."

"This is a happy occasion," Hodges said. "It puts gladness in our hearts to say to you and your dear wife, Henry, how much we love you. Since we're the same age, Henry, I can tell you you've got a long way to go."

State Senator Lindsay Warren, Jr., of Goldsboro, read a message from Governor Moore saying, "Please express my personal appreciation to Mr. Belk for his many years of devoted service to North Carolina and for the many capabilities in which he has served so well."

Expressions were read from Lt. Gov. Bob Scott, former Governor Terry Sanford, William Friday, president of the Consolidated Unversity, Brodie Griffith, president of the N.C. Press Association, and Holt McPherson, retired editor of the High Point Enterprise.

"His character, his humor, and his unerring insight into the State and its people shall always be an inspiration to me," said Sanford.

"Dear Henry and Lucile," Scott wrote. "The State of North Carolina is very proud of both of you. And we are greatly in your debt for the editorial leadership you have given us over the past forty years."

Said Friday: "These humble and courageous people utilize the power of the press to encourage better education, to promote a sound and progressive economy, and to establish better government. Most important of all, they have taught us the

266

importance of compassion, faith, beauty and spirit as the essential elements of our lives."

Ragan read a wire from Vice President Hubert Humphrey which said: "His (Belk's) has been a strong and effective voice in promoting the best interests of North Carolina for decades. I trust that his community, his State and the nation will continue to have the benefit of his counsel as editor emeritus of the Goldsboro News-Argus."

After listening to all the tributes, Henry rose and said: "Dear Hearts and Gentle People. I've got to change the pace of this or I'll be crying all over the place. No man ever heard so many obituaries."

Next day Henry was back at his columnist's job with a piece on 'New Presidential Car'.

President Johnson has accepted delivery of a new White House automobile which is a dilly. It is 21 feet long. The giant machine was manufactured by Ford Motor Company at a cost said to run to half a million dollars. It features many devices which add to the safety of the President and his party when traveling or riding in parades. A car with the safety features the Johnson car has would have prevented the death of President Kennedy at the hands of an assassin.

Communication facilities from the vehicle are as complete as those from or to the White House. A push button platform rolls out for the benefit of Secret Service men who accompany the President.

The giant auto brings to mind the swank vehicle purchased by the late Faison Thomson, Goldsboro attorney. Attorney N.W. Outlaw, a close friend of Thomson, took a look at Faison's new car and decided he had to have one as big and imposing as that of his friend. He put in his order for one exactly like it.

When Outlaw's car was delivered, he called on the auto salesman to take off the front bumper and to extend it by two inches by adding iron washers to push the bumper forward.

"It must be at least that much longer than Faison's," said Outlaw.

On November 6, Henry got around to writing about the testimonial dinner.

Maybe by now I can write lucidly about that dinner they gave for the General Manager and me in Raleigh. But I am not completely out of the haze in which the affair plunged me.

First thing we heard about a dinner was when Dr. Leo Jenkins called from Greenville. He said he and his missus wanted me and the GM to have dinner with them in Raleigh. We accepted the invitation and learned some days later that an open invitation had been given to our friends to be present at the dinner.

Col. C. F. McKiever, head of the Seymour Johnson Air Force Base section of East Carolina University, took over details in Goldsboro. Rotarians put plans in the hands of Graves Lewis for a bus from Goldsboro to Raleigh. Penn Moore was assigned to make the formal presentation for Rotary, which I joined three months after we came to Goldsboro in 1926. That makes me the oldest Rotarian in point of continuous service in Goldsboro.

One of the men present for the dinner, with whom I had a good chat, was Dave S. Coltrane. He and Mrs. Coltrane were greeting friends in the audience from Morganton to Ahoskie. Coltrane in his long and distinguished government career probably became acquainted with more community leaders than any man now in public service.

As he milled among the more than 300 friends, Coltrane was losing no chance to urge cooperation and help for North Carolina's Good Neighbor program.

And less than 10 hours later he was dead from a heart attack. Mr. Coltrane had reached his 75th birthday, but appeared as tough as a pine knot as he greeted friends at the dinner. His sudden death shocked the entire state. It will be difficult to find a replacement for him as chief of the Good Neighbor Council. No man in my memory ever held so many top government assignments and discharged them with such modest and unassuming distinction.

On December 4, Henry had something on 'Crawfish Bisque'.

Mayor Harang of Thibodaux, La., doesn't know it, but he gave the Thanksgiving dinner of the General Manager and me a certain extra dillip.

Our young friends, Bob and Joyce Johnson, had invited us to eat turkey with them. On the night before Thanksgiving, Georgia Tanner arrived home from a visit with her grandchildren in Thibodaux. She brought with her a generous sized container of crawfish bisque, or should I say crawfish stew, or maybe it is entirely correct to say crawfish soup.

Hal Tanner, Jr., of the staff of the Thibodaux daily paper, the Daily Comet, had borrowed the already cooked bisque, stew or soup from Mayor Harang in order to give the Belks a bit of extra education in good and special foods from Louisiana. So we added this to Joyce's tender and sweet young turkey, and it makes me smack my lips to remember the feast.

The Cajun country people raise the crawfish in ponds and sell them on the gourmet market at a price about that of lobsters.

On December 19, Henry had something to say about 'Ragan's Paper'.

Already there are indications that Sam Ragan will continue and expand the qualities of the Southern Pines Pilot, which have made it a distinguished paper in its class.

The Pilot announces that Ragan's popular column, "Southern Accent", will come to Southern Pines with its author. The column has been among the best read features of the Sunday "Old Reliable", which Ragan has served so well for many years.

Ragan bought the Pilot from that splendid newswoman, Mrs. James Boyd. Mrs. Boyd assumed editorship of the Pilot upon the death of her husband, novelist James Boyd, and continued it in the tradition he had set, one of quality and responsibility.

I expect to see Ragan give the Pilot a voice for the fine arts. But he will seek first to give the news.

Ragan has been a leader in the field of fine arts and in literature. And he has been an authority to which young people wishing to break into writing or newspapering could turn. Sam's office has been something of an employment agency for would-be reporters or writers in North Carolina.

Look for the Pilot under Ragan to have its own class and color, to be more than just a good weekly newspaper.

Look for the Pilot under Ragan to become something in the newspaper field which the Independent of Elizabeth City was under the later W.O. Saunders. Saunders was a hard-hitting editor who did what Carl Sandburg remarked could be done with a weekly. Sandburg was introduced by the General Manager to Ruth Grady of Kenansville. She remarked that Ruth published a weekly.

Sandburg looked Ruth over with great deliberateness and said, "You can raise a lot of hell with a weekly."

Ragan is not likely to be the hell-raising type of editor, but he will give the news and with a flavor of good writing.

Running the column was about all that Henry was up to, any more.

"He was beginning to change mentally and physically after I had been with him about three years," said Mrs. Virginia Bell, who was Henry's secretary from April, 1965, to February, 1971. She is now in charge of the Goldsboro office of Congressman David N. Henderson.

"He had begun having dizzy spells," Mrs. Bell recalled. "He called me in his office and said for me to sort of keep an eye on him. One morning he got real dizzy and said he felt like he was going to pass out. I called his physician, Dr. G.C. Dale. He checked Mr. Belk's heart and told me to get him some black coffee. He told Mr. Belk to go home and stay a few days, which he did.

"Mr. Belk relied on me a good deal the last year and a half I was with him. He had become forgetful. We would go over his mail and sort out the letters that needed answering. He got a lot of mail. 'Virginia, you go ahead and answer that one,' he would say. He thought I was a good writer. Once he said, 'The piece you had in the paper yesterday was monumental.' I didn't know whether to feel complimented or not. I wrote short features for the paper.

"He depended on me for many things. I would get some nabs and a coke for him about 11:30. He would go home for the day about 1:30, after the paper came out. I would call a cab for him. He could sit in his office and tell when the press was rolling. Occasionally he would go downstairs to the press room. He knew his way about the building.

"I would walk him to the Rotary noon luncheons at the hotel. He'd put on his old hat, pick up his cane, and we'd set forth. One day I took him in my new car. 'What's this?' he said, feeling of the seat belt. He buckled it on and almost never got out of it when we reached the hotel.

"He had a habit of holding on to his old hats. He said they felt better on his head. One day Rabbi Fabian came in with something in a box. It was a new hat. 'I wanted to do something for you,' he told Mr. Belk. Mr. Belk said he would save the hat for Sunday and special occasions.

"We laughed a lot together. He told me we were a lot alike. For one thing, both of us had cold hands. When I interviewed him for the job, he wanted to know why my hands were so cold. I told him they stayed cold. He said, 'So do mine.'

"Two or three weeks after I went to work for him, he came in one morning and told me to get somebody on the phone. I was a little slow finding the number and he said impatiently, 'Ask Elga (Elga Nichols, the woman's editor), she knows how to find it. I told him I was perfectly capable of finding the number, myself. He never spoke crossly to me after that.

"He was very observant. He could tell from the tone of my voice what kind of mood I was in, when I came in, in the morning. 'What's wrong with you?' he would say. 'Nothing,' I would reply. 'Oh, yes, there is,' he would insist.

"He could tell when I was wearing a yellow dress. He said yellow was the only color that registered with him.

"He would talk to me about his childhood. He said he liked to help his mother cook, and hung around the kitchen when other boys were playing outside. He said when he went to church with new shoes on that squeaked, he would go down to the front, so everybody would hear the squeaks and know he was wearing new shoes. He told me he gave up teaching because he didn't feel he was getting through to the students.

"He carried a buckeye seed in his pocket, which he had had for years, for good luck. Somebody brought him a small box of them, which he passed out to his friends."

Mrs. Bell has one of the five dollar bills Henry gave her each year for a Christmas present. An accompanying note says: "Thank you, Virginia, for all the help you have been to me during the year."

Mrs. Bell was with Henry for about nine months after the News-Argus moved into its new home on Berkeley Boulevard on May 11, 1970. Henry was proud of the paper's expanded facilities, but missed his accustomed surroundings, she said.

The new location was two miles from downtown Goldsboro, where he had held forth for 44 years. Friends couldn't drop in on him, as they had in the past. The new plant had a lounge where hot coffee was available ("I got him a cup every morning," Mrs. Bell said), but it was not like taking a coffee break with friends at Central Lunch.

Nor could Henry get around, as he had in the old building. The men's rest room was some distance down the hall and there were other doors in between.

Henry could not complain about his new accommodations. He was given a cheery office near the front of the building and it was better appointed than any he had used before. At his wish, pictures of the 'General Manager' and their daughter, Marie, when she was a little girl, were hung on the walls, along with autographed pictures of Terry Sanford and other important friends. Henry had his same desk and the old L.C. Smith typewriter which he had used since starting out as an editor. The News-Argus had it cleaned for him when he was away on vacation. And there was a wash tub, painted yellow which he had used for discarding waste paper.

Henry was set up in style, but he had little to do except turn out his column, and he was lonely and frustrated.

Also, his health was deteriorating. He suffered from arteriosclerosis and hyperthyroidism.

On May 5, 1971, while attending a trustee meeting at East Carolina University, Henry blacked out and fell from his chair. He was taken to a Greenville hospital and the next day transferred by ambulance to Wayne Memorial Hospital in Goldsboro. On May 25, while still in the hospital, he underwent a prostate operation which left him confined to his home from then on, except for occasional public appearances. He continued his column about six months before his death; after that, friends filled in for him.

On August 9, 1972, his condition becoming progressively worse, Henry was admitted to Guardian Care Nursing Home. He was accompanied by his 'General Manager', who took a room at the nursing home to be near him. She is still there.

Henry died in his sleep in the early morning hours of Friday, October 20.

"I was sitting beside his bed and heard him draw his last breath," the 'General Manager' said.

30

Henry's death came as a shock to most people, the seriousness of his condition having been kept from the public. Many thought he would eventually resume his column.

Friday's News-Argus carried an editorial by Eugene Price, who had succeeded Henry as editor. It was titled, 'Death, As It Must To Us All'.

"Death, as it must to us all, has come to . . . "

So began Henry Belk on hundreds of occasions as he commented on the passing of fellow citizens of his beloved Goldsboro and North Carolina.

Now, death, as it must to us all, has come to Henry Belk.

No one was ever more aware of death and its inevitability than was Henry Belk. But his was not a mournful and fatalistic philosophy.

The inevitability of death, to Henry Belk, was a challenge to enjoy to the fullest his friends and his community and his opportunities to be of service to his fellowman.

His friends were legion. His contributions were monumental. His faults were few. His sins, if, indeed he had any, were unintentional.

Henry Belk was a frequent target of tragedy. He accepted it with courage and dignity. Perhaps it was his personal experience with and understanding of tragedy that gave him such great compassion of others in the time of their misfortunes.

In his 74 years he never indulged in self-pity to our knowledge.

Only once was there a hint of it and it surfaced then in a moment of agony over learning of the death of an especially close friend.

The last summons had come to a number of Henry Belk's companions that year.

But the death of this especially close one had been sudden and shocking and completely unexpected.

He accepted the news with characteristic silence.

He leaned far over his chair until his forehead rested on his typewriter. Then a sob shook his great frame as he whispered:

"All my friends are gone."

They were not, of course. Nor are all of Henry Belk's friends dead today. Nor will they be for many, many years. Henry Belk made friendships that will endure. And his inspiration will live on and on in children and grandchildren of those he knew.

Because he understood great losses, Henry Belk would today permit his friends some moments to sit in the shadows and weep over his passing.

But even in this sad hour we can do justice to Henry Belk only if we focus on the goodness and greatness of the life he lived, rather than on his leaving it.

Henry Belk over the years had accepted, with dignity, the inevitability of this hour. Now it is here.

Death, as it must to us all, has come to Henry Belk.

Hundreds of Henry's townsmen and fellow journalists from across the state attended the funeral at Madison Avenue Baptist Church and the committal rites at Willow Dale Cemetery.

Henry's pastor, the Rev. Earl Farthing, stressed the fact that he not only was a respected leader of North Carolina, but was equally revered at home.

Let it be known equally well that Henry was not without honor in his own community. He chose to be a part of this community and this community chose him. It had been a long and beautiful romance.

You see, here at home he was the same tall man that he was everywhere else. He could see above and beyond trivia and grasp essentials. Here, too, he was that kind, gentle, gracious human being who saw persons not as possessions but as treasures and treated them so.

Sorrow and praise were voiced by the state press and public leaders.

Said Duke University President Terry Sanford: "Henry Belk was a creative citizen and a stout defender of the value of an enterprising press. More than that, throughout his life, his devotion to public causes made him one of the most valuable North Carolinians of his generation. He was a significant force in the advancement of North Carolina in many ways. Duke University feels a special loss because of his long relationship with this institution."

"I think he was one of the greatest North Carolinians of my lifetime," said State Attorney General Robert Morgan, chairman of the board of trustees of East Carolina University. "ECU will always be indebted to him, for, long before anyone else was publicly advocating the advancement of the institution, he was writing about the contributions it would make to the boys and girls of Eastern North Carolina."

Said Dr. Leo Jenkins, chancellor of East Carolina University: "Henry Belk was a great American. He called things the way they were and as a result his word was highly respected by those who disagreed as well as those who agreed with him. He will be greatly missed on our board of directors because he was an inspiration to all of us."

"Henry Belk was one of North Carolina's finest citizens and a great newspaperman," said Sam Ragan, publisher of The Pilot in Southern Pines. "Above all, he was a man of humanity, dedicated to his community and his state."

"North Carolina has lost one of its really great citizens with the passing of Henry Belk," said the Morganton News Herald. "In recent years, Editor Belk had been virtually blind. Instead of being an overpowering handicap, his growing blindness seemed to his friends to increase his spiritual vision and his sensitivity to the needs of people. Instead of secluding himself on the sidelines of life, this remarkable man moved out into the center of the stream."

"Henry Belk was the most widely beloved of all North Carolina editors," said the Durham Morning Herald. "He wielded an influence which far transcended the limits of his own paper's circulation area and extended throughout North Carolina. His counsel was heard with the greatest respect and his word carried weight in the highest circles of state government."

"Above and beyond his professional talents as editor and educator, which were substantial, Henry Belk was a big man — in heart and physique," said the Greensboro Daily News.

For almost half a century, in the Eastern Carolina community of Goldsboro, he dedicated his life to the interesting and important profession of editor — that is, afflicting the comfortable and comforting the afflicted.

Sprung from the Union County clan of Belks — a family as distinctly Carolinian as any among us today — he was a six-foot-six lumbering and in late years gaunt figure of a man, of slow and measured speech reflecting his thoughtful demeanor but graced with ready wit and warm smile. In later years, after the onslaught of blindess, which he not only endured but triumphed over, he seemed even more self-contained and serene. His blindness, as sometimes happens with those who suffer unexpected affliction, enhanced his ability to peer deeply into the problems of others.

His devoted wife, Lucile, became his eyes, sustaining him through a long series of eye operations and reading to him newspapers, books, and magazines which kept him remarkably abreast of contemporary affairs.

The Belks became familiar figures at public functions and ceremonies around North Carolina — he seeming, in size and appearance, some character out of Shakespeare or Dickens and she dauntlessly pushing him outward into the world to greet and encourage and contribute brightness out of darkness.

Few North Carolinians had a wider circle of friends, as proven when some 300 of them gathered for a testimonial dinner at Raleigh's Sir Walter four years ago to do him homage. They admired Henry Belk's character and beauty of spirit — his compassionate outlook on life seasoned by suffering, ever joyous and unself-seeking. They felt, as we do, that here was a man who genuinely cared for others and who epitomized the best qualities of the good editor and the good citizen.

Augustus Fitch ("Gus") Carrere should be the one to "wrap up" Henry's story, as newspaper folk say.

Henry was probably closer to Gus than to anyone else, excepting the 'General Manager'.

They had been together on the News-Argus since the depression days of the 1930's, when the paper was struggling to get on its feet. Henry looked after the news end and Gus, as advertising solicitor, brought in the money that kept the paper going.

Gus came to the News-Argus in 1932 from the Kinston Free Press, where he had been employed five years. A native of Charleston, S.C., he had previously worked on the Charleston News and Courier for 20 years.

"On the Free Press, times had gotten so bad that we drew only what it took to live on. The News-Argus salary wasn't much, but I knew I could count on it. Talbot Patrick was a smart man."

Gus went with the News-Argus as circulation manager, but after two years took on the additional duties of advertising manager.

"I was practically the advertising department. I sold ads and collected for them, turning the money over to Mr. Patrick."

Henry and Gus were good friends from the start, despite a disparity of 10 years in their ages.

"We thought a lot of each other. Henry didn't mind lighting into the others, but he only cussed me out one time. I was late with my advertising copy one Saturday and he accused me of wanting him to have to come back after dinner. He talked real mean to me. I held my tongue, but after he got back in his office, I called him on the phone and said, 'Dammit, Henry, you owe me an apology.' He agreed I was right and dictated an apology to his stenographer which he sent me with instructions to read it to everybody who had overheard his remarks. He could be very abrupt with a person, then he would feel sorry for it and try to make amends."

During an ice storm several years back which knocked out electric service in Goldsboro, Gus and his wife, whose home was heated by gas, put the Belks up for the duration.

Gus retired in the fall of 1970, several months after the News-Argus had moved into its new home. He was 80 and he didn't like riding back and forth on the highway to work. In appreciation of his long service, he was retired at full pay.

Pictures of Henry and Gus hang side by side in the foyer of the News-Argus building. It would have been a toss-up as to which would have been voted "Mr. News-Argus" by the paper's staff. Both were equally revered.

Henry seldom let a week go by that he didn't pay a visit to Gus.

"We would talk about old times. Once he said, 'Gus, you and I are growing old.' Henry did more listening than talking. The ladies did most of that. If Lucile said anything uncomplimentary about a person, Henry would cut her short by saying, 'Now Lucile.' When he got ready to leave, he would say, 'Well, mama, it's time to put me to bed.' "

Henry frequently had something to say about Gus in his column. One of his pieces was titled 'Diet and Health'.

Duke University Medical Center has a multi-million dollar study on aging in progress. The scientists seek to find out what it is that makes some people old at 40 and others young and spry at 77.

Gus Carrere falls in the latter category. He still walks 20 miles or more every day as an advertising salesman after retiring as News-Argus ad manager ten years or more ago.

No one would guess, who did not know, the age of this Charleston native by looking at him or watching him in action.

And Gus has consistently violated all the recognized rules of diet for health. He is a rice eater par excellence. His delight is in well-cooked rice with tomato gravy. And he is perfectly happy with a diet that ignores greens and salads and milk. Give him rice and tomato gravy (as Charleston folks prepare them) and he is happy and ready at any moment to out-walk anybody 20 years his junior.

In all the years I have known Carrere, he hasn't varied a pound in weight. And he follows the most unusual meal routine.

"I never eat breakfast until about 2 in the afternoon," he says, casually and not boasting. "I get a cup of coffee for breakfast and that is all. That is all I want or need until the afternoon. I couldn't work on a big breakfast."

Once Gus was a patient at the hospital. He never touched the breakfast they sent him, although the dietician tried various special devices to tempt him to eat. He just let the breakfast go back to the kitchen untouched.

Noting he was not eating breakfast, the physician ordered glucose to build up his strength.

"Why are you giving me this?" Gus asked, for he was recovering rapidly from major surgery and was in no pain.

"But you aren't eating any breakfast," said the technician. "You need the glucose to keep up your strength."

"But I have never eaten any food at breakfast," Gus explained, and they took away the glucose.

If Duke can discover how and why Gus stays so young and so vigorous, despite his breaking all rules of diet, it will be a great boon to mankind.